C000068383

# INDEX
ON CENSORSHIP

**INDEX ON CENSORSHIP 4&5 1994**

# EDITORIAL

# Sweet are the uses of monopoly

'Monopoly is a terrible thing, until you have it'. Rupert Murdoch, making one of his more endearing statements, should know; and Christopher Hird, describing the rise and rise of the Murdoch empire, tells us some other things we should know about its owner. As control over the mass media is gathered into fewer and fewer hands, with corporate profits increasingly dominating decisions, *Index* looks at media moguls worldwide, and asks to what extent this concentration of ownership endangers plurality, diversity, risk taking and dissent. As Leo Bogart puts it: 'How few owners, controlling what percentage of a nation's mass communications, constitute a menace to democracy?'

Murdoch has tried to persuade us that satellite television is a force for democracy, bypassing totalitarian governments and beaming messages direct to the people. Even if these messages were quite as enriching as he claims, (in the developing world they've been heard to say 'You chase colonialism out the door and it comes back through the sky') it turns out not to be quite like that. Satellite is a costly business, and to make a profit accomodations have had to be made with national governments, totalitarian or not. Ted Turner, speaking in Hong Kong, seems to go out of his way to turn a blind eye to the issue of freedom of expression when it comes to getting CNN into China.

And what does this concentration mean for political bias and editorial control? While David Walter tells the near-incredible story of Berlusconi, who used his private television channels to win the election in Italy and went on to lay hands on the public channels, it's less well known that Roberto Marinho, rapidly developing in Brazil one of the biggest media empires in the world, uses his media hegemony without scruple to promote the candidates he favours in presidential elections. Clive Hollick, one of the UK's newest and brightest media stars, is clear that government must develop new regulatory mechanisms and a definition of monopoly that reflects the reality of the modern media.

But monopoly is not the only issue inhibiting the democratising of the airwaves. Matthew Hoffman, talking about the high hopes for the Internet, reminds us that in the sixties there was a 'vision of a benign global village', where new technologies would allow an unlimited number of people to broadcast their own messages. This hasn't happened. Access to the hardware and marketing the product demands vast resources. Freedom once again loses out to finance.

Freedom to write is losing out to fundamentalist fury in Bangladesh and Mauritius, where Taslima Nasrin and Lindsey Collen have been threatened with rape and death, one by Muslim, the other by Hindu extremists. Both women explain what made them take their stand, and we publish some of their work. How Islam sees the world continues to be fiercely debated. Abdullahi An-Na'im, writing from within the Muslim framework, argues that Western views on universal human rights can't be accepted by people from the Muslim world unless they are seen to have legitimacy from their own perspective. Over Algeria, the French have been taking the predictable oppositional position to the Islamic Salvation Front (FIS). And yet surely, as our country file shows, Algeria of all places requires a double distance — on the one hand from a corrupt, ruthless and inefficient government which refused the results of an election which would have taken power out of their hands; on the other, FIS, bringing the threat of intransigent authoritarianism that has come to characterise the Islamists, prepared to endorse killing for what it claims is its right. Algeria presents us with those difficult questions — is it legitimate to behave undemocratically if you think you're saving democracy? Is violence ever justified?

'A city cannot be murdered so long as a single urban being survives in it and carries it everywhere.' Scheherazade 2001, a theatrical initiative from Sarajevo, has used the healing power of story-telling in theatres all over Europe to keep alive the spirit of the city — indeed of former Yugoslavia. *Index* publishes some of these stories, with two powerful pieces from Zoran Filipovic and Bogdan Bogdanovic, as a reminder that even when their own story has dropped from the headlines, for those people the hell goes on.

*Ursula Owen*

# CONTENTS

Vol 23 (New Series) Nos 4&5 September/October 1994   159-160   ISSN 0306 4220

Vol 23 (New Series) Nos 4&5 September/October 1994   159-160   ISSN 0306 4220

# LETTERS

## V for viewing

From Catherine Siemann
*Acting Executive Director*
*Feminists for Free Expression*

On behalf of Feminists for Free Expression, I would like to congratulate you on the redesigned *Index on Censorship*. It is impressive in both form and content, and should prove an even more effective voice in the fight for free speech and human rights worldwide. The extent and balance of your coverage is commendable.

However, Anne Nelson's article, 'Colours of Violence,' [*Index* May/June 1994] is disappointing and inaccurate. Critically, Nelson perpetuates the myth that the connection between television violence and real-life violence has been established, while citing little actual evidence. The hypothesis that images of violence cause violence in real life is not supported by history. The two most violent periods in America this century have been the period from 1980 to 1981, and from 1929 until about 1932, when there was no television and most

people lacked regular access even to the movies. The National Research Council and any good history book show that rates of violence in nineteenth century cities were even higher.

The hypothesis is also not supported cross-culturally. Industrialised countries with high television viewing (such as Denmark, England, Japan, the Netherlands, France and Switzerland), with the exception of the United States, have low violence rates. On the other hand, many developing nations have low television viewing and very high rates of violence.

The American Psychological Association (1993) and the National Research Council of the National Science Foundation (1993) conclude that violence is caused by parental abuse, rejection and neglect, accompanied by factors such as poverty and the belief that educational or job

FIRUZ KUTAL

opportunities are closed because of racial or ethnic discrimination. Unfortunately, many of the empirical laboratory studies have such small statistical significance and small samples that, although it is popular to cite them in the rush to blame television for violence, they are unreliable as explanations for real life violence. It is likely that children who watch too much television are trying to escape, if only vicariously, homes in which there is contempt, fighting and abuse. These are the real causes of violence and the problems we need to address.

Further, Nelson cites the V-chip and such similar devices as commendable at best, and at worst 'the newest electronic toys to be purchased to gather dust on a shelf'. We fear that the implications of the V-chip could be far more significant. Such groups as the Motion Picture Association of America (the organisation responsible for movie ratings), the American Library Association, the American Booksellers Association, and the arts and literary groups have protested against the V-chip and V rating. The V-chip would block all programmes, categorically, that had a V rating, so that any parent who wanted to watch a program like *Apocalypse Now* or *The Battle of Algiers* would have to make a special call each time. Thus, the V-chip also has a significant impact on adult access to programmes. The committee which determines which programmes will be given V ratings would consequently have enormous power. An anonymous committee responsible to no electorate or government body would make decisions

about the entire range of arts and entertainment that comes across television. The alternative that we do support is a device where parents could block individual programmes, thus allowing them the discretion to make their own decisions in providing guidance for the viewing of their children.

# Václav Havel has no clothes

From Yugo Kovach
*London, UK*

A few years after the peasant Kingdom of Serbia defied Imperial Vienna, a country called Czechoslovakia was born. From the start it was cursed with the Sudetenland problem which happily resolved itself in 1945 with the expulsion of some 3.5 million Sudeten Germans. Unfortunately, a new curse emerged, namely Communism, but in due course it was deftly despatched in a velvet revolution led by a dissident playwright called Václav Havel who became the country's federal president.

He tried to preserve the federation but failed. The Czechs and Slovaks went their own ways, not even bothering with a confederal fig leaf. Václav Havel's reward was the presidency of the new Czech Republic. The country he presided over was, for all practical purposes, the ultimate nationalist dream in that it encompassed all fellow nationals in an ethnically homogeneous state.

There was only the little problem of denying citizenship to 100,000 resident gypsies. However, the essentially mono-ethnic nature of the Czech Republic more or less guaranteed that it would be amongst the first of the ex-Communist countries to achieve membership of the European Union. No wonder President Havel took to worrying about the state of the world, particularly the partitioning of a mini-Yugoslavia called Bosnia. (Historians to this day are puzzled as to why the earlier partition of Yugoslavia itself, orchestrated by the international community, evoked so little concern amongst Havel and his fellow liberals).

President Václav Havel was eventually awarded the Soros Peace Prize for political courage as exemplified by his interview in your magazine [*Index* July/August 1994]. He urged the world's statesmen to aid and abet the Confederation encompassing unitary Croatia and the Muslim-Croat Bosnian Federation in its attempts to annex centuries old Serb ethnic lands. He was among the last of the Eminent Liberals to acknowledge that the Washington-brokered Confederation was in reality a cover for the resurrection of the World War II anti-Serb tactical alliance of Croats and Muslim Slavs.

# David Holden

From Nan Levinson
Boston, Massachussetts

I was touched by the memorials for David Holden (*Index* July/August 1994), which captured his spirit and effect on all of us who worked with him. With his talent for life, David stood *Index* on its head and had us dancing in the streets — sometimes literally. There's triumph, he reminded us, in laughter, joy in fighting the right fight. He was a good writer, a good person and a good friend. He'll be missed on this side of the Atlantic too.

# YOU MUST BE JOKING...

Let's talk of graves and worms and... censorship of epitaphs. A Church of England vicar has banned the use of colloquial words like 'Dad' and 'Mum' on headstones in his graveyard at Freckleton in Lancashire, England. His ban has been upheld by a church court. Other unacceptable words include 'Grandad', 'Mom' and 'Grandpa'. The vicar, the Rev Stephen Brian, defended his decision as being in the interests of 'all who believe there ought to be some minimum standard for what is acceptable'. Previous vicars of Freckleton clearly had different standards: headstones already in the graveyard refer to Dad, Mum, Grandad and Grandma.

Connoisseurs of the absurd will have welcomed the recent decision by the European Commission of Human Rights, that the British government ban on broadcasting the voices of those who support terrorist groups in Northern Ireland does not breach European law. The ban has been a rich mine of farce: last autumn, for instance, Prime Minister John Major complained that the actors who dub the voices of banned politicians are doing such a good job of 'lip-synching' that you can hardly tell that it's dubbed. It's also rumoured that one of the actors who regularly impersonates Gerry Adams is used to provide the voice-over on government anti-terrorist advertisements.

Hospital radio stations aren't often in the news, but reports that some refuse to play Frank Sinatra's 'My Way', and that others just fade out the bit about 'and now the end is near', featured in the UK national news in August. Sensitivity to patients also restricts the playing of the theme from *Mash* ('Suicide is painless') and 'Tell Laura I love her', purportedly the dying words of a crash victim. It seems the proposed banning of Tony Bennett's 'I left my heart in San Francisco', was purely a joke.

'ET'

# Media moguls & megalo- mania

(LEFT) CAMERA PRESS
(THIS PAGE) PETER CLARKE

MILEN RADEV

**LEO BOGART**

# Consumer games

Control over mass media, in every advanced democracy, has steadily moved into fewer hands. How, if at all, does this imperil the free flow of information? Concentration and globalisation are universal features of today's industrial world. In the oil, automotive, soap, tobacco and drug industries, a smaller number of international companies wield ever greater market power. Propelled by growing capital requirements and by the incessant demands of capital markets for larger profits and more efficiency, companies in every field of enterprise buy out, merge and consolidate. They cut deals with competitors, seek to pre-empt or crowd out upstart rivals, exploit new technologies, identify and co-opt new ideas and fresh talent. In general, this development seems to stimulate productivity and economic growth, though it is sometimes accompanied by a disregard for broader social interests, a narrowing of consumer choice, the destruction of many individual smaller enterprises, and the disruption of innumerable individual lives. In most countries, the process is constrained by politically imposed restrictions on true monopolies, leaving the handful of large firms that dominate an industry — whatever their common interests and private arrangements — to struggle vigorously over market share. Corporations driven by their shareholders' expectations of continual growth must venture into unfamiliar terrain, thereby introducing new elements of volatility. In an era of ubiquitous technical innovation, markets that appear to be stable can be transformed by the sudden emergence of unexpected competition.

As one of the world's largest and fastest growing industries, mass communications shares all of the characteristics of the other fields of enterprise to which it often has important economic links. A small number of major advertisers account for a large percentage of the advertising revenues on which most media depend as their primary source of income. (In the United States, the top five senders account for about a quarter of all national advertising.) A small number of giant advertising agency groups place a growing share of these investments (four represent over half of US agency billings), and their major clients tend to set the ground rules under which media buying decisions are made for all the others. Retailing, the other main source of advertising income, shows similar concentration into large, centrally managed chains. So do the mechanisms of distribution — cable systems, booksellers, motion picture theatres, video and music stores. And media organisations themselves have been bound together into conglomerates (like News Corporation, Time Warner, Bertelsmann, and Matsushita's MCA) that cross the traditional boundary lines among individual media, and even the boundary lines between individual and mass communications. The line also blurs between the creative function of generating media content and the public-utility function of distributing it. In the age of telecommunications, the needs for capital are vast, the incentives to master exotic technology compelling.

Those who believe that this is the best of all possible mass media worlds can argue persuasively that, in the past few years, every advanced country — including those in which broadcasting is still a state monopoly, or in which state television holds a privileged position — has seen an explosion of media choices, that new channels of communication are constantly opening, and that the intense competition for audiences and talent is driving the media system forward in ever greater fulfilment of popular demand. In this resplendent universe of ever-expanding possibilities, enterprises arise and exist to serve a great variety of tastes and interests. The market, with its sensitive measuring mechanisms, is highly responsive to those interests, providing the public with the optimum array of publications and programmes that match its desires.

To question this thesis requires us to face the direct question of whether the market for mass communications is exactly comparable to the market for detergents, analgesics or other consumer products in which manufacturers either make what the public will buy or perish. If it is, then the present arrangement of things is probably all for the best. The long-run interests of the public may not always be served by catering to its immediate appetites, as in the case of demand for tobacco, liquor or candy. If it is legal to consume a product, why should it not be acceptable to sell it too?

**The information that individuals absorb becomes part of the culture that everyone shares in ways that have different consequences than choices in toothpaste or breakfast cereal**

But is the consumption of ideas and images really no different from the consumption of goods? The ideas and images that the mass media disseminate shape collective life, form social values and determine the course of history. The information that individuals absorb becomes part of the culture that everyone shares in ways that have different consequences than choices in toothpaste or breakfast cereal.

Universal education is generally accepted to be a prerequisite of a civilised society, and it is ruled by standards that transcend what most children are instinctively predisposed to learn. Free and democratic exercise of choice would mean the demise of geography and algebra as school subjects, so education is not usually considered to be an appropriate arena for the uninhibited play of market forces. Mass media are, at the least, as important as schools in determining national character and destiny, and the market is just as flawed a guiding mechanism.

The objectionable features of commercial culture were deplored long before they were enhanced by the mighty power of international media conglomerates. Scoundrels, charlatans and cynics have abounded among media entrepreneurs since Gutenberg went bankrupt. What is different today is that the goals of corporate profit leave less and less

room for idealism, inspiration, risk, iconoclasm and defiance of the status quo. The strong moral and creative impulses that fire journalism and the arts are subordinated to the demands of the quarterly earnings statement. The springs of information have increasingly been overwhelmed by the flood of electronic entertainment, where the greatest profits are to be found. Throughout the corporatised media world, there is a sameness to the criteria of success, to the view of the public, to the denial of responsibility. In today's giant communications empires, the media lords, their bureaucrats and their hired talent all regard themselves as instruments of that higher force, popular demand. But it is a demand that they themselves create — by publicity, promotion, and most of all, by the regurgitation of the familiar and the formulaic — while they purport to follow it.

In a film of Rainer Fassbinder's, there is a nightmare vision in which a single company runs all of Germany's media from an antiseptic office tower. Even Josef Goebbels in his heyday didn't go that far. How few owners, controlling what percentage of a nation's mass communications, constitute a menace to democracy? This question is not easily answered, but sooner or later it must be addressed.

# DAVID WALTER

# Winner takes all

**The incredible rise — and could it be fall — of Silvio Berlusconi**

In 1993, there was a real feeling of hope around in Italy. The country had been misgoverned for most of the past 40 years by the old *partitocrazia,* a system which involved frequent changes of government in which the same cast of characters moved round and round the scenery. On the understanding that the only real opposition, the Communist Party, could never be allowed to govern, the other parties colluded to split the spoils of office between them. The political establishment had its fingers in every pie. Millions of Italians depended on party patronage for their jobs, from chairmen of nationalised industries to receptionists in the party-run hotels.

A rare area where the Communists were allowed a share of the action was television. They controlled one of the three networks of the public television corporation RAI. The other two were in the hands of the Socialists and the Christian Democrats.

The old parties had become steadily more corrupt, until at last the chance came to bust the system. It was taken by a group of examining magistrates, led by Antonio di Pietro, who began in 1991 to plumb the depths of an almost bottomless well of sleaze. Beginning with a kickback scandal involving an old people's home in Milan, they drew up a list of suspected fraudsters that read like a Who's Who of Italian politics. The wave of scandals led to pressure for the electoral system to be changed, in the belief that this would lead to *l'alternanza,* an alternation of parties in government which would lead to a cleaner democracy. By 1993, a new system was in place which differed so much from the old one that it became known as the Second Republic, the First Republic dating from post-World War II reconstruction being deemed to have died an undignified death. The Christian Democrats and Socialists who had dominated the old system were completely discredited, and fresh political forces emerged. Favourites to win were the reform Communists, the PDS. There was also a respectable new centrist party led by Mario Segni, who had spearheaded the campaign for electoral reform, and the maverick populist Northern League under Umberto Bossi.

In the event, all these new players were outflanked by the late entrant into the race, the media mogul Silvio Berlusconi. Berlusconi possessed a weapon which no other party leader in any other Western democracy has been allowed to wield. He was the owner of three commercial television channels, plus three more pay-TV stations and a number of newspapers and magazines. With the average Italian watching four hours of television a day, the power which Berlusconi had as a candidate for the post of prime minister was unprecedented.

**The campaign also managed to peddle two myths... the first that Berlusconi was a new force in politics... the second that he was a highly successful businessman who would achieve equal success in running the country**

In the crucial period before the electoral campaign proper opened, he used this power to devastating effect. When he launched his new party, Forza Italia, the event was given four hours of prime time on the most popular of his networks. It was promoted shamelessly thereafter on the cheap and tacky variety shows which fill so much of the airtime which he controls. The scantily clad 14-year-old girls who perform song and dance routines on *Non e la Rai* would break off to plug Forza Italia. There were endless campaign spots too in the advertising breaks. The result was that within a month of the party being formed, it had 20 per cent of the vote in the polls.

During the campaign itself, there were strict new controls on the allocation of television time between the parties, and an impartial watchdog to ensure fairness. It was too late. By now the battle had already been won. The other parties could not compete with the slick packaging of the marketing men in Berlusconi's Fininvest corporation, who had been drafted en masse into his political party. Fininvest funds were poured into the party too, helping to secure it an opulent suite of offices in the historic city centre of Rome on the inappropriately named Humility Street.

The Berlusconi propaganda was based on intensive opinion polling. The candidate's technique was to find out what the people wanted and then to promise it to them, even if that entailed promises which contradicted each other. The campaign also managed to peddle two myths which were of great importance to the final result. The first was that Berlusconi was a new force in politics. In fact, he had very close relationships with the old politicians, especially the Socialist former prime minister Bettino Craxi, who was best man at his wedding. It was Craxi's influence which enabled Berlusconi to build up such a monopoly in commercial television. The second myth was that Berlusconi was a highly successful businessman who would achieve equal success in running the country. The truth was that his business empire was facing crippling debts. Some believed that his political candidature was merely designed to save his future in business.

Berlusconi was careful not to expose himself to much hostile questioning during the campaign. RAI was now out of the hands of the political parties: a reform of 1993 had attempted to put it on the same footing as the BBC in Britain, under the supervision of an independent board who became known as 'the professors'. Forza Italia spent the campaign accusing RAI of bias. Berlusconi's chief of staff, General Caligaris, remarked that, while in the old days RAI was split between the parties, now it was worse; the whole thing was controlled by Communists. Berlusconi refused to debate with the opposition on RAI, although he did consent to one discussion on one of his own channels.

Those parts of the media not controlled by Berlusconi reacted in outrage at his behaviour. The veteran journalist Indro Montanelli, who had edited the Berlusconi paper *Il Giornale*, deserted him to found a genuinely independent paper, *La Voce*. The deputy editor of *La Repubblica*, Giovanni Valentini, wrote that to make Berlusconi prime minister would be the equivalent of putting the state railways in the hands of a man who only ran trains for himself and his friends and family. Berlusconi, however, had muddied the waters even for his opponents. Just as he could be accused of using the media which he controls for promoting his political interests, so they too could be accused of using politics as a pretext for attacking a commercial rival.

Berlusconi himself may have underestimated the strength that his media domination would give his party. Knowing that he could not win on his own, he had formed two separate coalitions with the Northern League and the neo-fascist National Alliance. He could perhaps have negotiated a share-out of seats more favourable to his own Forza Italia. When he won the election, he became prime minister, but the Northern League was stronger in parliament. It was his other partners, the neo-

PETER CLARKE

fascists, however, who caused the most alarm abroad. Their leader, Gianfranco Fini, maintained that Mussolini was a great man; one of his backbenchers called for Italy to recover lost territory in Slovenia and Croatia; another demanded concentration camps for homosexuals. A spurious attempt in April to rewrite history by rehabilitating the wartime fascists on Berlusconi's TV channel brought tens of thousands onto the streets of Milan in protest.

There was great anxiety at RAI about the Berlusconi victory. Having already secured half the outlets on Italian television for his interests as a businessman, Berlusconi now had the means to secure the other half for his role as prime minister. RAI was in a weak condition, with heavy debts, which could be used as a convenient excuse for any restructuring which the prime minister might choose to impose.

Berlusconi stated early in his period of office that it was the role of state television to support the elected government of the state, a remark which he later partly retracted but which seemed to represent his true feelings on the matter. RAI was struggling to maintain its new-found impartiality. Two of its channels tended towards obsequiousness to the prime minister, while the third allowed itself occasional acts of irreverence. It took great pleasure in screening an embarrassing old film starring Berlusconi's actress wife Veronica Lario as a lesbian. It was not long, however, before Berlusconi moved in to clamp down on his old rival. He forced the 'professors' to resign on the grounds that their financial reconstruction plan was inadequate. He then intended to impose a new board himself. At this stage, however, the Italian President, Oscar Luigi Scalfaro, stepped in. He had been pressed by the opposition parties to prevent Berlusconi gaining a complete monopoly over the media. There was a compromise: the board would be appointed by the speakers of the two houses of the Italian parliament.

Since both houses are in the hands of Berlusconi's coalition, it was not that much of a compromise. Four of the five new directors appointed are sympathetic to the government. In a sense, the old *partitocrazia* has been restored. Instead of a carve-up between Christian Democrats, Socialists and Communists, control of RAI is now divided between the new coalition partners, Forza Italia, the Northern League and the neo-fascists. The neo-fascists are keen to purge RAI employees whom they suspect of left-wing sympathies. Star presenters like Lilli Gruber, who used to be strongly identified with the Socialists, are in danger of losing their position. Claudio Dematte, who headed the board of the 'professors', has said: 'It is clear that a new era is beginning, which is heading towards government control of public broadcasting'.

Once in power, Berlusconi relinquished day-to-day control of his business empire, which included the construction company Edilnord and the Standa supermarket chain as well as his media interests. He did not, however, distance himself nearly sufficiently. He was open to the charge of conflict of interests at every turn. His position became all but untenable when senior executives of his companies including his brother Paolo were charged with corruption. In July, he attempted to impose a decree which released remand prisoners like those facing corruption charges from prison. While there is a case to be made for reducing the high numbers of those detained pending trial in Italy, Berlusconi's motives were suspect and his methods more so. It was a reform which most felt should have been carried out by proper act of parliament, not by prime ministerial fiat. The suspicion was that the decree was an effort to keep his brother out of jail and to save his own reputation. The outcry from the magistrates involved in the *mani puliti* (clean hands) anti-corruption campaign that had laid low the traditional parties, as well as from much of the public, was so great that the decree had to be withdrawn. The prime minister's image was shattered.

**His domination of the media, which was such an asset to him during his campaign, is proving his biggest liability**

At his villa near Milan the following Sunday, Berlusconi held a crisis meeting which included his political chief of staff Gianni Letta and defence minister Cesare Previti, both former business aides. Was this a private get-together, a government occasion or a company meeting? The three were impossible to disentangle, and all but the most loyal Berlusconi henchmen took the view that things could not go on like this. He was attacked not just by the opposition but by his partners in his increasingly fragile coalition as well.

Berlusconi came under overwhelming pressure to make a clean break with his companies. He promised to establish a system similar to the 'blind trusts' which operate in the USA, and he coupled the promise with a proposal to set up an anti-trust watchdog commission chosen by the President of Italy. The President, emerging as less and less of a rubber-stamp as time goes by, declared that the proposal was unconstitutional and postponed further consideration until the autumn. With his partners in the neo-fascist party and the Northern League expressing further reservations, Berlusconi was forced to offer further concessions. He survived a parliamentary debate on the eve of the summer recess, but the issue will return to plague him as the autumn wears on. His domination of the media, which was such an asset to him during his campaign, is proving his biggest liability.

The series of debacles have served to weaken the prime minister enormously. He had tried to run the government like his business, in an autocratic way which did not allow for democratic consultation, let alone consent. He has discovered that this does not work in a democracy, even in one as fragile as Italy's. Even loyalists in the grassroots of his own organisation, the so-called Forza Italia clubs, are protesting about his methods. They have had no say in the selection of candidates for national, local or European elections. The party's standard-bearers, mostly employees of Berlusconi's companies, have been imposed from above.

The hope for Berlusconi's opponents is that the dictatorial ways of a media mogul will quite rapidly be seen to be completely inappropriate to running a government in a democratic country. Berlusconi has already lost a great deal of his support. Many believe that he will not have the patience to stay in politics much longer. His bandwagon had looked unstoppable for a while; now he may choose to step off it before it hurtles over the edge of an Appenine cliff. Alternatively, he may be deposed by his coalition partners, particularly the Northern League with its considerable parliamentary strength. The country may have a second chance to create a Second Republic where there is a genuinely free media.

PETER CLARKE

# Interview: Indro Montanelli

*At 85, Indro Montanelli is the grand old man of the Italian press. Today he edits what another journalist has called 'the nearest thing to an independent paper in Italy'. Sitting at his desk, crouched behind the same Olivetti typewriter that he started out with 70 years ago, he was writing a leader for* La Voce, *Italy's newest daily paper, which he recently set up in Milan. Fifteen years ago he started* Il Giornale, *resigning as editor last Christmas, after a row with his proprietor, Silvio Berlusconi. For 15 years, Berlusconi was the ideal proprietor. It was only when he developed political ambitions that he started to interfere with the editorials, says Montanelli. He was interviewed by Joanna Coles.*

**IM:** It started to go wrong from the day he decided to go into politics. I got down on my knees in front of Berlusconi, I got down on my knees in order to pray him not to go into politics, to beg him not to go into politics. I went from supplication to anger, I bashed my fists on the table. I said to him if you go into politics, you are crazy, they will cut you into little pieces. I said this three years ago. In any case do not hope for *Il Giornale* to support your politics.

*JC: Did he want* Il Giornale *to support his politics?*
At this point, a very dirty game started. He said nothing direct to me, I've always been on fairly good terms with him. But he started to telephone directly, my staff, my writers. He kept saying to me that I was free, I could do what I wanted, that he wouldn't interfere, but he played this game behind my back. One day, without telling me, he came to the editorial offices of *Il Giornale*. He called a meeting of the journalists without telling me and said to the journalists who were at the meeting: 'I know that you are complaining about the economic conditions in this paper' — and they really weren't very good — 'if you want to improve them you will have to change the editorial line of the paper, and the language of the paper'. At this point I went to Mr Berlusconi and I said this is an intolerable interference: it is the sign that you are losing your head. I wrote my goodbye to the readers of *Il Giornale*, and I handed over my resignation. The last thing that Silvio Berlusconi said to me was, 'You have not understood that I am tired of being Silvio Berlusconi: I want an heroic life'.

*How did you feel resigning from a paper that you had set up?*
Like a father losing his son. I was called a few days later by Giovanni
Agnelli, who is practically the owner of *Corriere della Sera*, and also by the
editor, and was offered the editorship of *Corriere della Sera*, with a great
deal of kindness and a great deal of courtesy. This would have been my
big return, but I had to find a home, a roof, to house the journalists who
wanted to come with me from *Il Giornale*, and I couldn't bring them to
*Corriere*.

*So how many journalists left with you from Il Giornale?*
Fifty — and they're all here at *La Voce*, which is financed by public
shareholders.

*And how many people buy it?*
We sell on average 120,000 copies a day.

*And how pervasive do you think Berlusconi's influence is on the Italian media?*
The Italian press is owned by the large industrial and economic groups.
Big companies, obviously, are always pro-government policy. And
therefore it's always favourable to the government, or whatever the
government is doing. This is the real reason why I didn't want *Corriere
della Sera*. I don't want any owners.

*Do you think the Italian public share your concern about who owns the media?*
No.

*And what do you think that says about Italian democracy?*
Italian democracy? It's a beautiful dream — it has always been a beautiful
dream in Italy.

*When he was your proprietor in the good years, when he didn't interfere
editorially, what was he like as a man? Did you enjoy his company?*
Very pleasant man. He's an actor. I never believed anything Berlusconi
told me. He's a liar. But he's fun, he's sympathetic, he's full of ideas, of
imagination, and he's extremely courageous in what he undertakes.

*Excerpted from* Mediumwave *with the permission of BBC Radio 4*

# CHRISTOPHER HIRD

# Reach for the sky

**More than anyone, the science fiction writer Arthur C Clarke foresaw the coming of a technology which would be no respecter of national frontiers. But the freedom of information promised by direct satellite broadcasting is being thwarted by media monopolies and broadcasters' willingness to accommodate reactionary governments**

The scene was the Banqueting House, Whitehall, London. The date 1 September 1993. Three hundred members of the British media and political establishment were gathered to eat, drink and listen to Rupert Murdoch — if not the largest, certainly the best known media magnate in the world. Despite the evening's £1 million estimated costs, he was 'relaxed' (*The Times* — a newspaper he owns), 'cocky' (*The Financial Times* — a paper he once tried to take over) and 'jubilant and caustic' (*The Independent* — a paper he was trying to mortally damage through a price war).

Murdoch was cocky because in three years he had brought his family-controlled business — News Corporation — back from the verge of bankruptcy; he was caustic because he had proved his many detractors wrong and he was relaxed because he was the centre of attention. As he circulated among the guests, Cabinet ministers, newspaper owners and editors and television executives hung on his every word, as they had to a speech which he had just delivered.

Murdoch was unveiling a new programme schedule for his British satellite television station. The programmes were not, in truth, up to much: largely repeats of already made films and television programmes; there was barely a new programme idea to be seen. And the hype was out of all proportion to the size of his business — just 15 per cent of British homes could receive satellite programmes.

But Murdoch was a man worth listening to. He had gambled most of his business empire on his European satellite venture. He had just spent a further US$525 million buying his way into Asian satellite television. In theory he now had access to more than two-thirds of the world's population. And it was an access unrestricted by tiresome governments.

In his speech Murdoch developed his theme: 'The technology is galloping over the old regulatory machinery'. He presented such developments in a benign light — the revolution in telecommunications posed a threat to totalitarian regimes, allowing the 'information hungry residents of many closed societies to by-pass state-controlled television.' In Murdoch's view of the world, satellite television put the consumer in the driving seat.

Some at least of Murdoch's audience must have been struck by the undeliberate irony of what he said. Murdoch is a man interested in power and the power of the media to change the world. 'That's the fun of it, isn't it? Having a smidgen of power', he once said. And, on another occasion: 'Monopoly is a terrible thing, until you have it.' And wherever in the world you looked, satellite television was in the hands of a small number of companies — in Britain, for example, just one.

The choice satellite television offered reflected the preferences of its owners — preferences driven by the large amount of media product they already owned and needed to sell over and over again to get a return on their investment. In a telling aside to his own newspaper, when talking of a possible channel showing pornographic films, Murdoch said: 'I would not have it.' Again, the apparently uncontroversial sentiment obscured an important and less palatable truth — the choice was not the consumer's, but Murdoch's. His choice did include showing viewers the film *Death Warrant*, in which all manner of horrifying violence to humans is shown.

As to the wider responsibility with which Murdoch would discharge his ownership of this industry, his audience at the Banqueting Hall had only to read that morning's newspapers. His quality newspaper in Britain (*The Times*) had just cut its price from 45 to 30 pence — an act which would undoubtedly increase its already massive losses, but an act which might also deal a mortal blow to his competitors.

At the time, the price cut was justified by talk of British papers being overpriced in a recession, but most commentators recognised that Murdoch's company News Corporation could afford the losses, whilst its financially weak competitor, *The Independent*, could not. As Peter Bottomley, deputy chairman of the Conservative back bench media committee caustically remarked: 'It is the general rule that if you are running a loss making newspaper, you try to maximise revenue, not minimise competition.'

But Murdoch had more than just *The Independent* in his sights. He believed that, by international standards, Britain has too many national newspapers. He saw the day when he would face only one real competitor in the broadsheet market — *The Daily Telegraph*. Executives at *The Telegraph* understood this only too well; during 1993 and 1994 *Times* senior executives aggressively poached some of their key people. But, unlike *The Independent*, *The Telegraph* was part of a large group and was in a position to fight back in kind, cutting its own price if it wanted to.

For months it chose not to. But early in 1994, two things happened: *The Independent* was saved by Mirror Group Newspapers and *The Telegraph's* average daily circulation fell below one million for the first time in more than 40 years. Murdoch decided on another decisive move — the price of *The Times* was cut again — to 20 pence. *The Telegraph* had now to follow suit. The price cut will cost it tens of millions of pounds in lost revenue every year.

Although Murdoch continues to lose millions as a result of his price cuts, his company can afford it — many of his other interests elsewhere in the world are making money. Perhaps the best hope for his British newspaper's competitors is that he will make an enormous miscalculation in his ambitious plans for satellite television — a passion which nearly destroyed his business only four years ago.

One of the high points of Murdoch's evening at the Banqueting House in September 1993 was an interview — conducted by satellite — with the science fiction writer, underwater explorer and visionary Arthur C Clarke. Clarke, more than anyone, saw the coming of satellite television. In 1945 he realised that a satellite 23,300 miles above the earth would be able to pick up radio signals from one part of the world and beam them back to another. He foresaw a technology which would be no respecter of national frontiers.

Over the next 30 years, things developed much faster than Clarke expected. By the 1970s, more than 170 countries around the world communicated with each other by satellite but, as the dishes needed to receive the signals were so large, direct broadcasting to people's homes was not feasible. Within a few years, however, technological developments had both reduced the cost of satellites and the size of the dish. Suddenly direct broadcasting by satellite (DBS) was a possibility. One of the first companies to try it was Murdoch's News Corporation.

In 1983 Murdoch invested in a US satellite business which aimed to capture the 30 million US homes which did not have cable. It was a disaster — costing him US$20 million: the promoters had underestimated the resistance to large dishes and the competition from the US network television stations which, transmitting through the air, did not need a cable to get into people's homes. Even now, few Americans get their television by satellite.

There is an important distinction to be made between the technology in the skies and the distribution system on earth. In the days when satellites were expensive to build, put in orbit and maintain, and dishes were large, only governments and massive corporations could fund and use them. Technology has made it possible for every home to receive a message from a satellite, but the extent to which this happens depends crucially on existing patterns of television viewing and the regulatory structure in any individual country.

In the USA, loyalty to the big networks (of which there are now four, one owned by Murdoch) is strong. Cable — with dozens of channels — reaches most homes. In addition, the regulatory framework in the USA has, over the years, inhibited some of the normal features of capitalist development in the media. Concentration has been controlled and vertical integration prevented. In short, there are few reasons for US television viewers to invest in a dish and few ways for satellite companies to achieve the financial economies which would enable them to price their established competitors out of the market.

This does not mean that satellite has no influence — the immensely successful CNN news service needs satellites to send its images from all over the world. But once in the USA these images are distributed to viewers through cable. So for the ambitious satellite operator, the promising markets are those which are unregulated or undeveloped in television terms; or both.

When, in 1983, Murdoch was defeated in the USA, one of the most promising markets seemed to be Europe. Back in 1977 European governments — seeing what satellite technology could mean — had carved up the frequencies between themselves. For the next six years the British regulators painstakingly tried to put this agreement in place,

PETER CLARKE

eventually allocating the right to transmit satellite television programmes to a British company.

In retrospect, it was the last act of the regulated age of broadcasting, in which governments handed out lucrative monopolies. The BSB consortium was composed of some of the grand old names of British broadcasting and one French partner, and they believed the Thatcher government would guarantee them the time they needed to make a return on their investment.

But satellite was not like other television. As Murdoch has remarked — 'in the end technology can get past politicians and regulators.' After a brief flirtation with the official approach, Murdoch decided to go it alone. Luxembourg — which was not a party to the 1977 agreement — had launched its own satellite and Murdoch rented space on this to launch his service — Sky — before BSB got on the air. It was an immensely expensive gamble, costing many hundreds of millions of pounds. In the end, facing bankruptcy, he was forced to merge with BSB — which had proved equally costly for its shareholders.

MILEN RADEV

But, also in retrospect, it is clear that the British adventure was a diversion for Murdoch. Indeed, the whole of Europe is — at the moment — waiting to see how satellite will catch on. Sky News — Murdoch's impressive competitor to CNN — is available in 33 European countries. But very few people in these countries see it.

Most satellite services have to be paid for by the viewer — they are not financed by advertising income. In most European countries viewers have been brought up on a cheap form of television — advertising or government financed. Many do not see why they should spend more money to get satellite programmes. The Murdoch strategy of buying the right to popular sports programmes aims to give his services a unique product that people will be willing to pay for. The Murdoch newspapers' policy of attacking the licence fee principle — replacing it by pay-as-you-view — is aimed at undermining one of the main established competitors to satellite television.

In Europe today the technology does exist to beam an almost unlimited number of television programmes into people's homes — to find an outlet for all the films and television programmes which the US movie houses and television producers own. But satellite is only one way of distributing these media products and, for the time being, viewers are still attached to the conventional 'distribution systems'.

There are forecasts that by the end of the century half the homes in western Europe will have satellite dishes, but no-one knows if this will happen. At the moment, anyone who subscribes to a satellite channel in Europe will, by and large, receive an unending diet of old British and US television programmes and films. Satellite television has not yet established the virtuous financial circle in which large numbers of viewers generate large revenues to invest in competitive programming, which, in turn, attracts large numbers of viewers. The more lucrative markets for the satellite giants lie elsewhere.

STAR TV is a Hong Kong-based television company, founded and financed by one of the old established trading companies — Hutchison Whampoa — and Hong Kong's richest tycoon, Li Ka-shing. Its avowed strategy is to 'control the skies' in satellite broadcasting over an area from Japan to Turkey, encompassing the giant markets of India and China. At the moment, it transmits five free channels — one of which is BBC news — and is financed by advertising. Unlike the West, these countries are extremely promising territory for the new television entrepreneurs.

In many of these countries most of the population do not have televisions and those that do can only watch state-controlled networks. Satellite brings to these countries series such as *Neighbours,* the frank sexual discussions of the *Oprah Winfrey Show* and a constant supply of films in Hindi, Chinese and a number of other regional languages. As one Western commentator remarked after visiting India, it is as if the 1950s, '60s and '90s were all happening at the same time as commercial satellite television brought the sexual revolution to these countries.

It is not a prospect which pleases the establishment of these countries. In India Natwar Singh, vice-chairman of the Indira Gandhi Memorial Trust, has bemoaned the fact that 'satellite television has destroyed our serenity, our silence and our privacy', complaining that children read less, watch more and get fat. In Malaysia — where foreign ownership of television companies is banned — the prime minister has complained that foreign interests in the satellite stations will distort news coverage. And in China, since last October, ownership of a satellite dish can lead to a fine or imprisonment.

What has provoked much of this concern is the presence of Western investors and programme makers in the satellite companies. STAR's only real competitor at the moment is Television Broadcasts. Owned by the Malaysian businessman Robert Kwok and Sir Run Run Shaw it will broadcast programmes from Ted Turner's Cartoon Network, Time Warner and the Discovery Network. And since last August, 64 per cent of STAR has been owned by the ubiquitous Rupert Murdoch.

At the moment there is something of a stand-off between the satellite companies and the governments in the countries to which they plan to transmit programmes. All the Western investors have realised that they need local partners to help deal with local regulators. Murdoch's News Corporation has reassured the Malaysian prime minister that they mean no harm. A spokeswoman promised him 'a service which governments in the region will find both friendly and useful' — casting a rather odd light on Murdoch's claims that satellite is the enemy of authoritarian governments. STAR are in talks with the Chinese government about the satellite dish ban — Murdoch has an entrée here as his Fox Studios recently signed a deal with the government to supply films.

If, as Murdoch claims, technology can get past politicians, why are the companies so concerned about them? The blunt fact is that satellite is still a highly risky venture and the companies need the governments to ensure they make a profit. Until now the STAR services have been free and often distributed not by dish but by cable. In India, for example, corner shops stick a dish on their roofs, string cable from posts to adjoining houses and charge consumers US$5 a month for the service. As a result cable is spreading fast in the urban areas.

This poses a problem for the satellite operators. First, there is a real difficulty in measuring audiences — which they will eventually need to do to entice advertisers onto their services. But second, and more important, for their paid-for services planned for the future they need one of two things: a well regulated cable network or direct broadcasting to people's homes. To achieve either of these they need the co-operation of governments. In the West, satellite operators have already found that pirate operators are making the decoding equipment needed to receive the paid-for services, depriving them of important revenue. This sort of activity will be even more difficult to control when they are serving nearly 40 countries, often thinly populated and without the basic technical infrastructure that satellite businesses need.

This is where the interests of the satellite companies and the politicians converge. The Chinese are opposed to dishes because of the difficulty of controlling them; they favour cable. Television Broadcasting's strategy for its paid-for channels relies on cable distribution.

The satellite companies may want to keep governments sweet for another reason: nearly a dozen regional satellites are to be launched in the next two years; STAR and Television Broadcasting will soon face competition. Contrary to its rhetoric, competition is not something capitalism embraces. Its central paradox is that all businesses survive by taking risks and then strive to eliminate risk. Satellite television — like other media businesses — wants market domination, if it can get it. That the media is regulated by politicians only adds to the opportunities to control the risk content of the venture.

Together these developments provoke a degree of caution in our view of satellite television. There is no doubt about its technical capacity to beam the same message into millions of homes around the world. But not all viewers want the same message and, as long as advertisers want to reach viewers, or viewers have to pay, this will be a restriction on satellite's growth. In both the USA and Europe viewers show a real preference for new, nationally produced programmes. However, it is obviously easier for a satellite to avoid government regulations so long as the target population has access to a dish. Governments that wish to devise a media strategy that counters the monopoly tendencies of satellite development may find that the best course is to combine policies which encourage domestic programme-making and diversity in the skies with low costs of entry to the satellite.

In other words, the opposite of what Murdoch says is true: satellite and dictatorship are natural allies; and it is the regulatory framework of the liberal democracies at which he so often sneers that can ensure diversity and plurality in broadcasting.

*(Chart overleaf reprinted with the kind permission of* Asiaweek)

PETER CLARKE

| | AsiaSat1 | Palapa B2P | Intelsat 508 | |
|---|---|---|---|---|
| **Transponders** | 24 C-band | 24 C-band | 24 C-band | |
| **Launch Date** | April 1990 (not operational after 1995) | March 1987 | March 1984 | |
| **Channels** | MTV (STAR) Music videos<br>BBC (STAR) News & documentaries<br>STAR Plus Entertainment<br>Prime Sports (STAR) International sports<br>Chinese Channel (STAR) Mandarin programs<br>Zee TV Hindi & Urdu entertainment<br>Children's Channel*<br>Asian Business Channel*<br>Movie Channel*<br>Asian Movies* STAR pay-TV channels, due in early 1994<br>Yunnan TV-1 Chinese provincial<br>Guizhou TV-1 Chinese provincial<br>Pakistan TV-1 Pakistan regional<br>CCTV-4 Chinese government<br>Myanmar TV Burma government (b/w)<br>TV Mongol Mongolian government | CNN International Global news<br>Home Box Office Asia* Movies & entertainment<br>ESPN International* International sports<br>ABN Asia Business News<br>RCTI Indonesian commercial<br>RTM-1 Malaysian government<br>TV3 Malaysian commercial<br>ATVI Australian international<br>CFI French overseas<br>SBC Singapore international<br>TVBI Hong Kong international<br>ABS-CBN* Philippine commercial<br>AN Teve Indonesian commercial<br>GMA Philippine commercial<br>People's Network Philippine government<br>TPI Indonesian commercial<br>SCTV Indonesian commercial<br>Nine Net Australian commercial | CNN International Global news<br>ESPN International* International sports<br>Network Ten Australian commercial<br>ABC Australian government<br>Channel 9 Australian commercial<br>World Net/ C-SPAN U.S. government<br>Deutsche Welle TV German government<br>NHK Japanese government<br>RFO Tahiti French overseas<br>Nine Net Australian commercial<br>TBS Japanese commercial<br>Fuji TV Japanese commercial | IBC<br><br>IBC<br>IBC |
| **Owners** | CITIC (China), Cable & Wireless (Britain), Hutchison Whampoa (Hong Kong) | Indonesian Government | International Satellite Consortium | |
| **Reception Area** | China, Japan, Taiwan, Hong Kong, ASEAN, Indochina, South Asia, West Asia | ASEAN, Indochina, South China, Hong Kong, Taiwan, Eastern India | Japan, Taiwan, Philippines, Hong Kong, South China, Australia | |

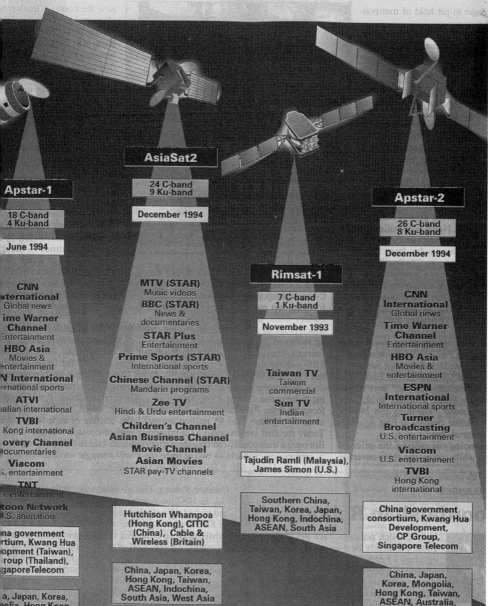

## AsiaSat2

Apstar-1

**18 C-band**
**4 Ku-band**

**June 1994**

CNN
**International**
Global news
**Time Warner**
**Channel**
Entertainment
**HBO Asia**
Movies &
entertainment
**ESPN International**
International sports
**ATVI**
Australian international
**TVBI**
Hong Kong international
**Discovery Channel**
Documentaries
**Viacom**
U.S. entertainment
**TNT**
U.S. entertainment
**Cartoon Network**
U.S. animation

China government
consortium, Kwang Hua
Development (Taiwan),
CP Group (Thailand),
SingaporeTelecom

China, Japan, Korea,
Mongolia, Hong Kong,
Taiwan, ASEAN,
Indochina

**24 C-band**
**9 Ku-band**

**December 1994**

**MTV (STAR)**
Music videos
**BBC (STAR)**
News &
documentaries
**STAR Plus**
Entertainment
**Prime Sports (STAR)**
International sports
**Chinese Channel (STAR)**
Mandarin programs
**Zee TV**
Hindi & Urdu entertainment
**Children's Channel**
**Asian Business Channel**
**Movie Channel**
**Asian Movies**
STAR pay-TV channels

**Hutchison Whampoa**
**(Hong Kong), CITIC**
**(China), Cable &**
**Wireless (Britain)**

China, Japan, Korea,
Hong Kong, Taiwan,
ASEAN, Indochina,
South Asia, West Asia

## Rimsat-1

**7 C-band**
**1 Ku-band**

**November 1993**

**Taiwan TV**
Taiwan
commercial
**Sun TV**
Indian
entertainment

**Tajudin Ramli (Malaysia),**
**James Simon (U.S.)**

Southern China,
Taiwan, Korea, Japan,
Hong Kong, Indochina,
ASEAN, South Asia

Apstar-2

**26 C-band**
**8 Ku-band**

**December 1994**

CNN
**International**
Global news
**Time Warner**
**Channel**
Entertainment
**HBO Asia**
Movies &
entertainment
**ESPN**
**International**
International sports
**Turner**
**Broadcasting**
U.S. entertainment
**Viacom**
U.S. entertainment
**TVBI**
Hong Kong
international

**China government**
**consortium, Kwang Hua**
**Development,**
**CP Group,**
**Singapore Telecom**

China, Japan,
Korea, Mongolia,
Hong Kong, Taiwan,
ASEAN, Australia,
West Asia, India

## The Sky's the Limit

[Satellit]es have come a long way since the U.S. [r]ocketed SCORE aloft on Dec. 18, 1958. The [lov]e bird had one voice channel. By 1989 the [...]VI series could carry 33,000 conversations [simulta]neously. When satellite signals are [compresse]d, 100,000 conversations are possible. [Motio]n pictures demand more space, so the [...] birds now carry 144 channels at most.

Again, digital compression will allow extra video capacity. Transponders relay and amplify signals. Satellites use two kinds: C-band, which creates a big "footprint" but needs big dishes and Ku-band, which produces a small footprint and requires small receivers. Some broadcasts are "free-to-air," and anyone with a dish can catch them. Others are "encrypted," so a decoder is required.

# TED TURNER

PETER CLARKE

# The mission thing

**While the US congress was debating whether to continue China's Most Favoured Nation status, and Clinton was going back on his election promises, CNN's boss in Hong Kong was appealing for a laissez-faire approach to human rights**

I come from a country that wants to tell other countries what to do. I don't know why it is. I don't think we're the only country that way. Britain has been that way at times in the past. I don't think any country is in a position to tell any other country what to do. I'm a great believer in living and let live. I certainly have my own philosophy on how a country ought to be run; and I haven't ever found a country that was run that way, including the one I live in now. I know we talk a lot about human rights in the United States; but other countries could hit the ball right back across the net to us and say: 'Well, what about the right to have a home?' We have a large homelessness problem in the United States. Other countries don't have as large a problem. But nobody ever throws that one back at us. What about the right to be safe? We have the highest crime and murder rate in the world in the United States. It's not safe to go outside in a lot of our major cities. Even in the daytime. That could be interpreted as a human right as well.

I'm a firm believer that if you want people to mimic you you don't tell them that that's what they ought to do. Just go ahead and do your thing and do it in such a way that you are more successful and happier than they are; and people will come along with you.

We never came out here and told people how to run a television station. We just came out here with our little satellite CNN International, and now everybody's copying it. So, it's the perfect proof that it works. Build a better mousetrap and the world will beat a pathway to your door.

I wish I could bring some brilliant new perspective on the situation out here. But this area of the world has developed so much over the five years since I was last here that I have no way of knowing if the TNT [Turner Network Television] and Cartoon Network are going to be popular. We could all lose our buns out here.

CNN International was profitable for a number of reasons. One, we already had the product; all we had to do was purchase the transponders and the satellites to get here. Second, we had a market with television stations. In fact that's our number one revenue producer in this area. We also knew there was a very large group of English language people who travel both for business and tourism and we knew there was a market in the hotels. So advertising was just a plus. There wasn't really any advertising to start with, and there's not much advertising today. But because of the revenues we get for service from our broadcast affiliates in the area and revenues from hotels, and our extremely low cost because our programme is already advertised because of coverage in the United States, it was basically not too difficult to make a profit with CNN International.

With TNT and Cartoon, we're going to be using library product we've already paid close to US$2 billion for, but it's basically product that isn't generating revenue in this area, or very little, at the current time, so we don't have a lot of downside there.

CNN International has been in the region since 1982 in Japan and Australia, creating less stir in those past 12 years than one other company has in six months. We are pioneers; and our philosophy has been and continues to be that we always want to come in where we're wanted, and we never try to force our way or force anybody in any way, shape or form. That will continue to be our policy and we intend to take the same approach with TNT and Cartoon Network. Our new acquisition of New Line and Castle Rock gives us access to approximately 30 new theatrical movies a year to help freshen our library of around 3,000 older films and we're very excited about that. We will be distributing those films theatrically out here, where it's appropriate, and also on video. And, as a demonstration of our commitment to the area, we now have six bureaux in Asia: Beijing, Bangkok, Seoul, Manila and New Delhi. With the opening of our production centre here, we'll be opening a Hong Kong bureau as well.

It's estimated that with our current satellite set-up, we are in about nine million homes in the region via four satellites. With Apstar 1 this year and with Apstar 2 next year, we and a gang of four others will give STAR a real run for its money, we believe. We hope to continue to be good neighbours. I try to operate as much as possible the Golden Rule: by treating people the way I'd like to be treated if the circumstances were reversed. We will continue to do that.

Entering the satellite business is not very difficult. It doesn't require much. All you have to do is

PETER CLARKE

purchase a transponder, and be able to provide programming at a reasonable cost so you don't go broke before there is enough coverage to make it work. But, there are so many people in the business, both here, in Europe and in the United States that I really do think it's going to put a lot of pressure on the networking people.

One good thing about satellite networking is that you can send out a number of language tracks, even though dubbing in all those languages is not inexpensive. It's better with movies and cartoons which you can run over and over, because they only have to be dubbed once and you can use them again. It's an extremely interesting field. I've certainly enjoyed my association with the television business.

It's been a real kick to have been a pioneer. You think the days of the explorers have come to an end and yet this whole satellite global television business is a relatively new business, and there is a chance to brave new trails and go where people have never gone before. It's exciting and, like almost everything, is good in a way and bad in a way.

---

### Turner Broadcasting System

operates from its regional headquarters in Hong Kong in partnership with Wharf Cable and Asia Television Network (ATV). The former is now in 30,000 homes and carries CNN International; TNT and Cartoon Network for Asia will be launching later this year, with, says Turner, 'quality-oriented movies and cartoons from our library, some documentaries and other programming' adding, 'TBS has a long-term approach and commitment to this part of the world.'

---

If we want to survive we have no choice in this world today but to start thinking internationally, like we're citizens of the world. That's another new concept.

I think we need to test the phrase 'the Third World.' First, because two-thirds of the [world's] people live in the Third World, it's really the first world. And second, the word 'foreign' to describe other countries and other people on the planet is an outdated term. Five hundred, four hundred, even one hundred years ago, the world was foreign. It was far from one place to another. But now it's not. We're all neighbours in the world today, and within 24 hours you can get to any place on the earth, and with satellite television you can go anywhere on the earth in a fraction of a second. So it's time to stop thinking that other people on the earth are foreigners and start thinking that they're neighbours.

The problems that we have today, environmental problems and other problems, have got to be solved collectively. And this time, this station is not going to survive at the expense of another nation. We're either going to survive together or we're going to perish together. I think global television can help that. And that does not mean that individual nations have to give up their languages or their cultures or their religions. That is not necessary. All of us are citizens of our neighbourhood, and we work for the improvement of our neighbourhoods, and our neighbourhood schools and places of worship and so forth. And we're all citizens of a district or state that we live in. And also citizens of a nation we live in. And we love our countries, and we love our states and we love our neighbourhoods and we love our little families — the smallest unit. And there's no reason we can't carry that one step further and love the world and the other people around it as well.

We've got to stop killing each other and beating each other on the head. We've got too many sophisticated weapons today to make that practical. What we really have to do is start acting like educated, civilised human beings. And more and more, that is occurring. The end of the Cold War was a tremendously heartening thing to happen. It is discouraging to see so many civil wars breaking out after the Cold War ended. But they're trying for peace in the Middle East and it's already been achieved for the most part in Central America. So there are things to be excited and encouraged about and there's still a tremendous amount of work to do. No group of people has a greater responsibility or a greater opportunity to change these ways of doing things than the people here in the television and communications business. All of us have a tremendous social responsibility to our nations and to the people and all the creatures on this planet to programme at least part of our networks with information that will create a sense of brotherhood and global citizenship.

*Speech at 1994 PAN Asia cable and satellite TV conference, Hong Kong.*

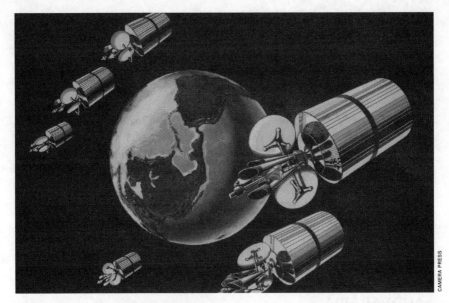

CAMERA PRESS

# Down with the dish

Many countries, particularly those whose governments have reason to fear the free flow of information from the skies, have been attempting to keep out the evil dish. Outright banning is less common than attempts to control the import and price of the dishes or the imposition of a state-controlled licensing system at prohibitive cost.

There is a good deal of confusion surrounding the whole subject; in most cases it is already too late to stem the flood. Haphazard legislation has resulted in confusion — in which case the law is either broken with impunity or the state has ceased any real effort to implement it — or in acrimonious debate between those who wish to benefit from the technology — or maybe just escape the tedium of local programming.

Contrary to the common view, it is not just the affluent who are affected. In Iran, hundreds of mini-cartels have been organised so that people who cannot afford to buy a dish on their own can share a communal one. In India, one dish hooked to the national grid in a remote village or urban ghetto draws a crowd who willingly pay a couple of rupees each for the joys of STAR.

All attempts at banning have had limited success: the latest strategy, particularly in south east Asia, is a more frontal approach to the pedlars of satellite rather than to the technology. It is not too difficult, it seems, to persuade the Murdochs, Turners and others that the quid pro quo for the advertising revenue is co-operation on programming guaranteed not to offend the incumbent government or, as it is most often expressed, 'local sensibilities'.

Or to doctor the offending image. This can go to ludicrous lengths. In Iran, for instance, during the World Cup, prerecorded satellite broadcasts of the matches were re-transmitted on state TV but with the scantily clad crowds in the US heat replaced by another phantom crowd suitably clad in all concealing winter coats.

The last resort is to set up one's own satellite system, programmed exclusively and in conformity with local codes, by only what the state wishes its citizens to see. The Gulf countries, which are most anxious to protect their citizens without offending their princes, are among the few with the money to get involved at source.

## SAUDI ARABIA
Satellite viewing boomed in Saudi Arabia during the Gulf War in 1990-1991 when Saudis discovered Cable News Network's (CNN) coverage of the war on their doorstep. Over one million watch satellite television, via around 150,00 dishes.

In March this year, the government banned the import and use of satellite dishes. In July, owners of dishes were ordered to dismantle and re-export them, or face confiscation and stiff fines of around 500,000 rials (US$130,000). So far the order seems not to have been enforced.

But Saudi already plans to extend its control over foreign broadcasting by setting up an officially sanctioned satellite and cable television network. The contract to develop, install and operate the system by 1995 has been given to ARA International, based in Riyadh, the parent company of the London-based Middle East Broadcasting Centre (MBC). This network will be available via the latest technology — microwave multi-directional system (MMDS) — using a small, difficult to detect antenna and decoder. Censorship will be pre-transmission; and advertising revenue will remain within Saudi-owned companies. Since the present banning appears to include MMDS decoders as well as dishes, the new technology could herald the end of the satellite ban in the Kingdom.

## CHINA

Though satellite reception was banned in 1990, the import and sale of satellite dishes was not prohibited until October 1993. Dishes are officially allowed only for those who need to use satellite transmissions for work, such as state-run news organisations and government departments. In 1992 shops in Shanghai and Beijing were fined for selling dishes. No one seems deterred and the dishes are still on sale.

China launched its own satellite, Apstar 1, in July with a second satellite planned for December. PanAmSat's PAS-2, also launched in July, offers even more channels. Chinese-language broadcasts and the disappearance of BBC World Service Television from STAR TV this year may also make satellite television more palatable to China's leaders.

## BURMA

The government has yet to take action to enforce its ruling that all satellite dishes must be registered by their owners by 30 August 1993. The purchase of dishes after this date was technically illegal and rendered out of the reach of most Burmese by the artificially high cost of the dish and the exorbitant charge for a licence.

## SINGAPORE

Singapore is heavily involved in the expansion of satellite technology in the region; Viacom International's MTV and Time-Warner's HBO have their regional bases in Singapore. Nevertheless, foreign broadcasts are banned if the content 'offends good taste or decency' or disturbs public interest. It is also an offence to sell satellite dishes with which to receive the broadcasts, or to publicise or advertise on a banned satellite service. Dishes are allowed for businesses that need them but not for individual households.

In Colombia, where there are an estimated 300,000 satellite dishes, the government order to register dishes was widely ignored. Morocco taxes dishes at 5,000 dirhams (US$70) per month. Taiwan's popular local cable television network uses satellite dishes to pick up foreign broadcasts — but is not licensed.

*Philippa Nugent*

# TOM FAWTHROP

# Chinese shadows

**New communications technology played a vital role in overthrowing Thailand's military government. No wonder the Chinese are getting nervous**

By the end of 1993, 30 million-70 million Chinese viewers were watching everything from *Tom and Jerry* cartoons dubbed into Chinese to American soaps and BBC World Service TV on satellite. The sudden exposure of a critical mass of the population to such a diverse range of foreign influences alarmed the authoritarian regime in Beijing which moved swiftly to ban the installation of satellite dishes.

The potential for new information technology to jolt dictatorial regimes and contribute to their defeat is well established. In the pro-democracy movement of Tiananmen Square, fax machines helped to thwart official censorship. A more dramatic illustration of its power was shown in Bangkok in May 1992 in the aftermath of the Thai military's massacre of the pro-democracy march that sought to oust General Suchinda Krapayoon.

The military regime ordered all Thai TV channels to operate strict censorship on all footage of the bloodshed. However, Bangkok's fast-expanding business elite with their Motorolas and their satellite dishes saw the real story courtesy of BBC TV, CNN and Japanese NHK. Within 24 hours their VHS tapes recorded from the satellite channels were being sold like hot cakes on the still blood-stained streets of Bangkok.

In short, the old techniques of mind control and censorship were rendered useless as the new technology of mobile phones, fax machines, and video were deployed to disseminate information, counter government lies, monitor troop movements and organise further protests and demonstrations. The Suchinda government was forced to resign and democratic elections took place a few months later.

But as the satellite revolution sweeps all in Asia before it, governments

China's consuming passion

are doing their best to co-opt its subversive potential. In the wake of the democratisation in Asia that has seen the downfall of the Marcos regime in the Philippines and the liberalisation of South Korea and Taiwan, remaining one-party systems show varying degrees of nervousness over the effect of foreign satellite TV being beamed directly at their citizens. China and Malaysia, however, are the only two countries that have passed legislation to ban the private ownership of satellite dishes — although both governments are aware that it may be impossible to enforce it.

China banned unlicensed ownership from April 1994; penalties range from US$900 for individuals to US$9,000 for businesses plus confiscation of the dish. *World Satellite Almanac* estimates that in Malyasia there are 26,000 dishes; in China, analysts say, there are now between 600,000 and one million. The ban has come too late to be effective.

Aware of this, China is developing an alternative strategy to retain its control of information. It is already influencing programming through business deals with the satellite networks and, with 1997 in mind, increased control over Hong Kong-based satellites like STAR TV.

During the next decade Asian skies will be humming with new satellites. Asia Sat1 (HKK STAR TV) is currently competing with Indonesia's Palapa B2R and B2P, Thailand's recently launched THAICOM and US/Malaysian-owned RIMSAT. In the next two years a

Chinese consortium will launch two Apstars whose shareholders include Beijing's Ministry of Telecommunications. They will attempt to apply Chinese censorship regulations to all Apstar clients — a position that is being contested by US broadcast executives.

While BBC World Service TV has been snuffed out of the STAR TV network beamed over China since the end of April by its dominant shareholder, Rupert Murdoch, BBC sport and non-controversial foreign programming continues to flood the Chinese market. Fast-expanding cable TV in China is mostly supplied by Hong Kong's TVB which owns the world's largest Chinese-language programme library. TVB director Fung Shung admits that 'we don't do news, and everything we sell to China is pre-censored'. TVB's seemingly inexhausible diet of B-grade Kung Fu and Chinese gangster movies now dominates the insatiable viewing habits of southern China. The opiate serves Beijing's interests in maintaining a docile and stable information order (SIO). At the same time China's TV networks are trying to make more entertaining programmes which reflect 'tradition and Chinese values'.

Although Rupert Murdoch bought 63.6 per cent of STAR TV, founded by billionaire Li Ka-Ching, he gained only 48 per cent of the STAR TV licence. Li retains of the signal and the programming. The Hong Kong government has already conceded to China's approval for broadcast licenses and the future of Hong Kong-based satellite companies after 1997 is uncertain.

Singapore hopes to reap the benefits of nervous investors. Both Asian Business TV and TVN Zealand opted for a Singapore-based satellite. Like China, Singapore also runs a tightly controlled domestic press, limits circulation of foreign journals and at times bans them completely. But despite its controls, Singapore wants the technology that furnishes the satellite revolution and is therefore prepared to play host to *Asian Business News* (Dow Jones group — the *Asian Wall Street Journal* on air). But with a ban on individual ownership of dishes, the citizens of Singapore remain so far uncontaminated by this foreign news production.

For Singapore it is business as usual — luring international media companies away from Hong Kong with 1997 beckoning, but making no concessions to an open society. Singapore information minister George Yeo admits 'the fact that we cannot effectively censor the objectionable is not a reason to legitimise it. While we may not have the means to prevent satellite TV we can make it very difficult for the broadcaster.'

# SAFA HAERI

# A fate worse than Saudi

**Even the dreaded dish is better than playing follow-my-neighbour**

The fate of satellite dishes has been at the centre of one of the hottest public debates in Iran this year.

It all began with a confusing statement by interior minister Ali Mohammad Besharati on the legal status of the ubiquitous satellite aerials that sprout from roofs and window sills and allow the Iranian public unlimited — and uncontrolled — access to programmes ranging from education to hard porn from around the world.

There are no official statistics, but it is widely believed that there are already more than 500,000 houses in Tehran equipped with locally produced dishes. Prices range from US$4,000 to US$200 at the floating rate of US$1 to IR2,500, according to the aerial's capacity and the technology involved.

Unlike Saudi Arabia, which has banned the dish outright, Iran is pondering a number of solutions to the undesirable impact of satellite TV: follow the Saudi example, legalise the dishes, leave the situation as it is — ambiguous.

Besharati's first tack was to declare the dish 'illegal' and order its removal. The minister is close to the leader and strong man of the regime, President Ayatollah Ali Khameneh'i, known for his antagonism to all things Western or non-Islamic.

After criticism that outlawing the dish could have a negative impact, the minister backed off, claiming he had been misunderstood. 'Dishes are not illegal, but their use needs regulation. The cabinet is considering the matter and a law will be adopted within two months,' he told the semi-official English-language daily *Tehran Times*.

This in turn was met with outraged uproar from conservative mullahs and their press campaign for a complete ban on the dish, which they described as 'anti-Islamic'. 'No!' proclaimed *Jomhuri Eslami*, a reactionary paper owned by Ayatollah Khameneh'i and directed at the hard-line Islamists. 'The authorities are unanimous that satellite-beamed programmes are harmful and immoral and must be harshly dealt with.'

Other papers, led by the daily *Abrar* and with wide public support, then leaped into the confusion created by the authorities. They initiated a debate and came up with an unequivocal 'yes' in favour of the aerial.

In an editorial under the headline: 'Closing eyes won't serve any purpose', *Abrar* urged the authorities not to be afraid of modern technologies. 'Those who look at the world realistically and with open eyes know full well that there is no way to fight modern technologies such as the satellite antenna. Today, they are large and visible; what happens tomorrow when they will be miniaturised? And what about millions of our citizens who live in border areas where they can receive neighbouring TV programmes without antennae? Have they not been corrupted?'

> 'In less than five years all new TV sets will be able to pick up all satellite channels. Then what will the authorities do? Shoot the satellites?'

Continuing its campaign, *Abrar,* which is close to the powerful bazaari merchant community, told the authorities that it was 'humiliating for a great nation such as Iran which in the past has contributed so profoundly to the world's civilisation to emulate the Saudi example'.

Ministers and MPs joined the debate on both sides. 'From a legal point of view, possessing satellite antennae is not a crime and, in any case, it's not possible completely to eradicate them, even if we bring in our entire army,' noted justice minister Hojatoleslam Esmail Shushtari. 'We cannot allow our people to be contaminated by harmful, corrupt TV products aimed at destroying our Islamic system', retorted a member of parliament.

The majority view was best expressed in 'Allo Salam', a widely read column in the leftist *Salam,* well known and much appreciated in Iran for its dissenting views: 'The interior minister says dishes must be banned because they have the "physical" power to corrupt. If this is so, then one has to arrest and execute every man and woman for they too possess the physical power of prostitution.

'Please tell the interior minister that the best way of fighting [Western] cultural aggression is to erect around Iran walls as high as the sky; to forbid people to go beyond them on pain of execution; to forbid travellers to bring in any foreign books, magazine or products on pain of the same penalty. Then he can rest assured that he has fought back the cultural onslaught.

'Ninety per cent of the programmes received by satellite are educational and highly useful. As to the other 10 per cent, those who are after such programmes can and will always be able to see them via videos.

'As an electronic engineer, I can assure you that there is no way to fight the dish. In less than five years, all new TV sets will be able to pick up all satellite channels. Then what will the authorities do? Shoot the satellites?

'Forbidding the dish will be a very unpopular law and removing them will obviously end up in clashes between the owners and the authorities. People will be killed. Do the government need to make the people even more angry than they already are?'

Iran 1890s: frontline against the future

# BERNARDO KUCINSKI

# Big, bigger, biggest

**The moguls of the Western world are not alone in imposing their will on captive audiences. Brazil's Globo empire is one of the biggest in the media world**

The popular camp calls him 'public enemy number one'; media professionals call him 'our Citizen Kane'; a British TV documentary says he goes 'beyond Citizen Kane.'

The truth is that Brazil's Roberto Marinho today runs one of the world's largest media monopolies. Besides his 50-station radio network, he runs an 85-station TV network (Rede Globo), six of which he owns, the Globosat/Net cable television system, operating 26 cable TV channels in Rio de Janeiro and São Paulo, the magazine and book publishing house Globo, and Brazil's second-largest circulation daily O Globo. He also owns, alone or in association with muncipal authorities, 1,500 Earth Reception Stations (ERT) or retransmission units, and has substantial stock in major advertising agencies and printing plants.

In contrast to major TV networks elsewhere in the world, TV Globo produces most of its own programmes and is the world's largest private producer of TV programmes. It is not only a horizontal media empire but a vertical monopoly, referred to in Brazil as a 'cross monopoly'.

The Globo group has subsidiaries in Latin America and Europe, among them Globovision, Seabay and Globo Europa; and substantial shares in financial, real estate, mineral and manufacturing companies. It is a key partner in telephone, electronic and telecommunication companies, including NEC do Brasil. It is now entering another joint venture with major Brazilian groups to launch and operate three communication satellites covering the whole of Latin America.

Roberto Marinho gets most of Brazil's US$3.9 billion expenditure a year in advertising. In the 1992 financial statement, the Roberto Marinho group declared just over US$2 billion net revenue. Marinho's communication empire has a massive audience hegemony. His TV broadcasting attracts, on average, 63 per cent of all TV sets in Brazil. His nearest rival is the Sistema Brasileiro de Televisão (SBT) with an average 22 per cent audience; others get each around 6 per cent or less each of the remaining market.

The five top-rated TV programmes in Brazil are all by TV Globo. SBT's top-ranking programme gets only half the audience of Globo's least popular programme. Brazil's TV audience is estimated at 80 million people, more than half the population. Even in the most remote shanty towns, where people hardly get a decent meal a day, there is always a TV antenna pointing up to the sky.

Roberto Marinho is Brazil's most powerful man and exercises his power without scruple. Globo's distorted reporting of the 1989 presidential election was instrumental in defeating the Workers Party leader, Luis Ignacio 'Lula' da Silva. This time, with Lula once again in the lead for the October presidential elections, Marinho is again using his media hegemony to promote the candidacy of Fernando Henrique Cardoso in an effort to pre-empt Lula's succession to the presidency.

Globo has much to fear from Lula. Most of Marinho's 'cross monopoly' has no solid legal base. Brazil's regulations do not permit such a concentration of concessions, many of which have expired and are waiting renewal. His cable TV companies were operating before cable TV was regulated. Lula's manifesto proposes to break the media monopoly and to implement the 1988 Constitution's articles forbidding media concentration and establish rules for wavelength concessions and media plurality.

Roberto Marinho's career was made under the protection of the military regime that took power in 1964. Since then, he has remained loyal to the plan of the country's elite to replace the military by a limited and controlled version of democracy in which the mass of the people must listen rather than have a say.

Yet the extent to which big brother Globo can manipulate people is an open question. President Collor, who defeated Lula with Globo's help in the 1989 presidential elections, was removed after a massive popular movement that neither TV Globo nor any other media could stop. It is also clear that what operates in Brazil as the main instrument of social control today is not Roberto Marinho alone, but an entire hierarchy of journalists, editors, reporters, TV and radio producers and artists, who collude in the system and enable it to operate.

# CLIVE HOLLICK

# Media regulation and democracy

**Contrary to the general view, regulation can be the defender of free speech and the forces of the marketplace the chief threat to a plurality of view. But new technologies demand new forms of regulation and government intervention may be the best way of ensuring the plurality of voice on which democracy depends**

'The regulation of broadcasting by government is tantamount to censorship and is therefore undesirable. In the past, technology strictly limited the number of broadcasters and created a natural monopoly which had to be regulated.

'Technology has now opened up the airwaves, removed the monopoly and is allowing an unlimited number of broadcasters to flourish. With such a benign and open technology, regulation is redundant and undesirable.

'Oh, and by the way, it is no longer possible for governments to regulate broadcasting because satellite technology is beyond the control of national government.'

This beguiling case against regulation is being advanced by the usual suspects — large multinational media groups who find the regulation of ownership and content inconvenient and restricting. The case for the deregulation of broadcasting chimes with the free market approach of many governments and provides a convenient alibi for their failure to tackle the monopolistic and anti-democratic nature of some major media groups which, as it happens, also provide them with important political support.

The case for regulation must be made afresh and must address the consequences of technological development. Regulation has both liberating and restricting aspects. Restricting when it seeks to restrain powerful commercial forces bent on securing market dominance and relishing the power and influence in society offered by a dominant share of voice. Liberating in its efforts to promote a diversity and range of choice and a structure which can foster cultural and democratic values.

Foremost amongst the public goods which must be protected by government are the commitment to freedom of speech, diversity of view, consumer choice, absence of state political or editorial control, fairness in general political debate and news coverage and the protection of national and regional cultural identities.

The rise of major world media corporations and their enormous potential to influence political events is now ringing alarm bells in many countries. President François Mitterrand used an interview with five European publications to criticise the 'media marketing' which helped to elect Silvio Berlusconi. 'This is an approach which we are not used to and which appears fearsome to me,' he said. 'There is a serious risk of perverting democracy'. Signor Berlusconi is now embroiled in a heated debate over his continuing direction of private media interests and his parallel responsibility for state media.

**Regulation has both liberating and restricting aspects. Restricting when it seeks to restrain powerful commercial forces... Liberating in its efforts to promote a diversity of choice**

In the UK former Conservative party treasurer Lord McAlpine's comments after the 1992 General Election struck the same theme. 'The heroes of the campaign,' he said, 'were the editors of the Tory press. This was how the election was won.' The force of his words was strengthened by Neil Kinnock's endorsement of the truth of that assessment.

Successive governments — of all political colours — have sought to protect those public goods by supporting public service broadcasting and by controlling the extent of media ownership by any one private company. All terrestrial broadcasters in the UK are subject to public service and programme obligations and complex ownership rules which have together created a structure for the industry in which quality and diversity has flourished free from political partiality and beholden to no

PETER CLARKE

particular interest group. To protect the public good governments should ensure that all media organisations, whether terrestrial, satellite or new telecommunication technologies, are subject to the same rules and compete on a level playing field.

The only way to guard against the erosion of freedom of expression and diversity of view — values which lie at the core of democracy — is to ensure and sustain a plurality of voice. Monopoly media ownership is the main threat to the diversity of view and the current ineffective and illogical anti-monopoly legislation in the UK provides a feeble defence against this threat.

So it is encouraging that, in Europe, governments are now recognising their responsibility to ensure a common approach to the construction of the European and national audio visual marketplace. The playing field in Europe is one where regulators already recognise that the games to be played are both commercial and cultural.

Governments must develop a new definition of monopoly which reflects the modern media world and which covers all forms of media. Broadcasting and media markets should be defined by reference to two characteristics, first, geographical — for example global, national, regional and local — and secondly, sectoral — for example newspapers, radio, terrestrial television, cable and satellite.

The optimal measures for monopoly would seem to be outputs such as newspaper circulation, share of television and share of radio listening. There is no long-term logic for different regulation of terrestrial and satellite television. As far as the viewer is concerned television is television however delivered and media regulation should aspire to be technology-neutral.

**Governments must develop a new definition of monopoly which reflects the modern media world**

A crucial element in the measurement of market power is the weighting applied to the relative influence of a particular medium. While the formula for weighting the relative influence of each medium will inevitably be controversial, a simple addition of listeners, viewers and readers ignores the fact that television is the most potent form of communication.

Anti-monopoly rules would, then, set maximum levels of market share for sectoral and for each geographic market. The conventional measure in the UK of maximum market share of 25 per cent is an appropriate measure for the geographic and sectoral markets but a lower figure, probably under 10 per cent, is the maximum of the total share of national media that any single privately owned organisation should be allowed to control.

In the absence of such a transparent set of rules the media industry will continue to muddle along with the current incoherent and illogical regulations which are prey to political and commercial manipulation and offer scant protection for the overriding public interest of plurality of ownership.

The UK should follow the example of others and appoint a single regulator for all types of broadcasting to replace the current confusion of regulatory bodies. A single regulator would protect the BBC from the real, or imagined, pressures from the government of the day that is currently responsible for setting the level of its annual funding.

Regulators in all countries would also have to tackle the emerging problem of access to multi-channel systems. At its most extreme, a cable system could make only one news channel available to its customers and so deprive them of a diverse range and choice of news coverage. In the USA it is the stated intention of several influential religious channels to use their televisual pulpits to promote their chosen political agenda and to support like-minded candidates for office. As such channels become available internationally the US and other governments will have to grapple with the problem of maintaining political balance and impartiality in the face of an onslaught of highly professional political campaigning by the Reverends Graham, Robertson and their ilk.

**Complex technical change should not divert governments from addressing the more predictable consequences of the enduring human instincts which drive media organisations**

The claim that technology makes regulation more difficult, even impossible, is a fallacy. On the contrary, it makes it easier. At the heart of satellite and cable technology is a highly sophisticated subscription payment system. Any interruption to the flow of funds to the broadcasters would quickly lead to blank screens. The threat from pirate satellite broadcasters is greatly exaggerated; international regulation, for instance the European Union's steps towards a comprehensive media policy, is likely to thwart such endeavours.

Rapid and complex technical change should not divert governments from addressing the more predictable consequences of the enduring and straightforward human instincts which drive media organisations. The quest for market domination and the desire to wield influence and control are familiar and enduring characteristics of these organisations. Governments must defend the public interest by protecting and sustaining freedom of expression, diversity of view, plurality of ownership and consumer choice, safe in the knowledge that media companies are unlikely to go hungry.

# MATTHEW HOFFMAN

# How big was my village

**The freedom and diversity of information offered by the technology of the global village could founder on the concentration of political and commercial power in the hands of the world's media moguls**

About 30 years ago the Canadian writer Marshall McLuhan coined the then fashionable term 'global village'. In his book *Understanding Media* he argued that the phenomenon of ever-widening accessibility to the lifestyles of various cultures through the 'cool' medium of television was breaking down the boundaries that separated societies and forming a new globally extensive polysemous environment. In the New York City art world in the 1960s, I recall a combination of art forms came together to celebrate McLuhan's vision by projecting images from around the world on the translucent walls of a geodesic dome to a passive audience lying inside lulled by the sound of exotic musical droning. The medium was truly the message as the chaos of overlapping and unrelated imagery cancelled out any more coherent narrative. But in this small moment of 'underground' art there may be a hint of how the high hopes many now hold for the development of 'cyberspace' on the Internet may develop.

A persuasive element in the vision of a benign global village was the belief that new technologies, such as video and audio cassette, would allow everyone to create and distribute their own documentaries or works of art to anyone who wished to have them. In fact, although some small-scale production has proceeded this way, the economics of mass distribution has generally defeated the development of this ideal. Part of the problem has been financial: television, whether broadcast or cable, is similar to other businesses in that economies of scale allow the big battalions to offer the customers more for their money and, through mass-marketing, to advertise the availability of their product. As in retail sales generally, there has been a concentration of ownership and a concomitant uniformity of product: CNN was hailed as a start-up, cable-TV rival to the news services of the big broadcast companies; but despite its global span, there is an evident US 'spin' to its news values that flattens as much as it enriches the diversity of global reporting. The concentration of political and commercial power in the hands of such media groups as Murdoch's News International is well documented.

Nonetheless, despite the failure of previous visions of a new diversity of material in the print and visual media — desktop publishing was the latest bubble to burst — there are factors in the exponential growth of communication by computer and modem that give one pause to reconsider the old hopes. There are now, we are told, 30 million people 'on-line' and more joining daily. Members of the 'human rights community', such as *Index* and Amnesty, have been using bulletin boards, electronic-mail and conferencing systems to communicate among themselves and to alert others to abuses that require publicity. It is said, for instance, that e-mail played a large part in keeping the world informed of Russian resistance to the 1991 coup against Gorbachev.

There is a gopher site in New Jersey (gopher.iia.org), run by the Digital Freedom Network, that, subject to the limits of copyright and editorial discretion, is making banned texts available to anyone on the Internet. And there is a project being coordinated by Gary Sick of Human Rights Watch in New York that hopes to have a gopher site running soon which will 'bring all together in one place' the work of such leading human rights groups as his own, Amnesty, PEN, and *Index on Censorship*. A gopher site is a 'place' in cyberspace where you can find and place information, provided you have the appropriate hardware and software. It is one of the key facilities available on the Internet.

But for some, the hopes for Internet go far beyond facilitating communication between like-minded people — even though this is not

Germany 1988: the wonders of technology

necessarily benign. In the July/August 1994 issue of *Index,* a German journalist says that 'neo-Nazi efficiency has improved dramatically now that they're using an electronic communication network'.

First, they stress security. The Internet was originally created by the US military to provide a means of communication in the event of a nuclear war: there is tremendous redundancy in the system, information is held in duplicating 'mirror sites' all over the network, and messages are divided into packets that go every which way so that both interception and interference with the contents of the system as a whole are well-nigh impossible. On the other hand, monitoring of individual telephones is still possible. And, of course, privacy is difficult to maintain in a system where the whole point is communication.

Second, there is the notion of unlimited freedom. In a recent issue of *The New Yorker,* John Seabrook writes: 'The net is, fundamentally, about free speech ... [It] poses a fundamental threat not only to the authority of the government but to all authority, because it permits people to organise, think, and influence one another without any institutional supervision whatsoever.' It is said that traditional communication is either of the form one-to-many, or one-to-one; but the Internet allows a new form of many-to-many. This is meant to be an epitome of democratic life, or even working anarchy.

Unfortunately, anarchy has its pitfalls, particularly a tendency to fall into a Hobbesian form of all-against-all. The phenomenon of 'flaming' is one instance of that: a flame is a sort of unsolicited verbal assault from one user to another across the net. Another pitfall, much worried about as the Internet grows and grows, is the babel of too many voices. The talk now is of 'filters' to allow one to cut out the flame-throwers and to sift the wheat from the chaff before it arrives on one's screen.

At this point a lesson from McLuhan's global village may become relevant. The failure of that village was, I believe, in the failure to appreciate how particular is each village: until, if ever, all societies — and even persons — share common values and loyalties, attention will focus primarily on the most powerful exponents of each culture's way of living. The reason some newspapers, for example, sell many copies to loyal audiences is that they are edited in accordance with a set of (usually unspoken) assumptions. Chauvinistic newspapers, such as Murdoch's *Sun,* with its famous 'Up yours! Delors!' headline, unsurprisingly sell best of all. Unfortunately, the more some people get to know about other people, the more they dislike them.

**The net is, fundamentally about free speech... [It] poses a fundamental threat not only to the authority of the government but to all authority**

The Internet will come of age when the pressures towards its commercialisation succeed; at that point the equivalent of editors in journalism and producers in the performing arts will come aboard. They will command high salaries for relatively rare skills and a method will be found to remunerate them from the user's pocket. They will bring order to the chaos and give it point and shape; but hierarchies will reappear, and I fear many-to-many will become many-from-one, again.

Internet is not quite a new world, it's the same old one intensified. It is salutary to recall, however, an article by Andrei Sakharov, in an early issue of *Index,* that predicted the demise of the Soviet system. Sakharov argued that prosperity requires access to information, and information widely spread is a great deterrent to tyranny. This insight was proved true in the Soviet Union. Perhaps the Internet, for all its limitations, will help it continue to prove true wherever people log-on in order to find out what's going on.

# NEWS REVIEW

ANTHONY HYMAN

# One death more or less

*The young Kabul-based BBC reporter, Mirwais Jalil, was kidnapped and brutally murdered by gunman on a road close to Kabul on 29 July. He was returning from an interview Gulbuddin Hekmatyar had given to Italian journalist Ettore Mo for the Italian daily* Corriere della Sera

There are different ways of seeing this death of a gifted and hugely likeable young man of just 25. It could, and surely will, be asked why one more death should matter, in a war where 1.5 million Afghans have already lost their lives.

Journalism is a notoriously dangerous profession in time of civil war when such strong passions are roused.

That is the narrow, cynical view. This murder does matter. The victim was a brave man doing a vital job in keeping the world, but primarily his own people, informed about day-to-day realities of life and politics in Afghanistan through the BBC radio.

I got to know and respect Mirwais in Afghanistan earlier this summer. He never carried a gun, only his tape recorder and microphone. He had plenty of courage and energy. If millions of ordinary Afghans regularly

listen to BBC broadcasts, and trust their accuracy, it is because of the reputation for objectivity won by the reporting of Mirwais Jalil, William Reeve, and earlier Kabul correspondents of the BBC.

This murder could have a serious impact on international attitudes towards Afghanistan. Those who are weary of the problems and challenges of peacemaking in Afghanistan — and there are many such both within and outside the United Nations — can use it as further proof that the country is reduced to such anarchy that nothing more can, or should, be attempted from outside to affect events or improve the situation.

By many Afghans, as well as outside observers, Mirwais Jalil's murder is interpreted as a deliberate warning — not only to the BBC but to journalists in general — to stop criticism of the armed groups currently holding power. Because Jalil was abducted and brutally murdered in a corner of Afghanistan under the control of Gulbuddin Hekmatyar's *Hizb-i-Islami* it is natural enough that many will conclude the murder was done on the orders of Hekmatyar, nominal prime minister of the country. But if past experience is any guide, no arrests or trials are likely to be held, and this charge will remain unproven in any court of law.

The international lesson which will almost certainly be drawn from this cowardly murder of an unarmed man may well reinforce the stereotype common, but not exclusive, to the West, that the Afghans are peculiarly violent and treacherous people. What the leader of one armed group may have done will be blamed on the Afghans in general.

Since 1 January, with what looks like an endless cycle of destruction and general anarchy in the capital, international attitudes towards Afghanistan have visibly hardened. The mayhem in Kabul obscures the progress towards the peaceful rebuilding of the country in Herat and in other provinces now at peace, as well as the return of over one million Afghan refugees from Pakistan and Iran. There is a real danger that those few international organisations still working in Afghanistan may rethink the dangers to their personnel and reduce, or even close down, their operations. In Kabul, a small number

of trained experts, expatriates as well as Afghans, are keeping the city's essential services going. There, as in other Afghan cities, the International Committee of the Red Cross (ICRC) and a few other humanitarian organisations are giving vital help to scores of thousands of victims of war.

The desperate plight of the Afghan people needs to be regularly and accurately covered in the media if governments and humanitarian organisations are to help with reconstruction and assist in bringing about an end to the war.

On 17 August, Ettore Mo, Baquer Moin, head of the BBC's Persian Service, and other BBC journalists discussed the difficulties of reporting from Afghanistan at a press conference in London's Foreign Press Association. Afghanistan's media have virtually collapsed, along with the disintegration of the state. No newspapers are published in Kabul and most trained journalists, along with the rest of the educated elite, have fled to Pakistan, Iran, Western Europe and elsewhere. Various radio operations are mounted in parts of Afghanistan and in the region, but they have little credibility among Afghans.

The press conference announced a plan to found a trust fund in memory of Mirwais Jalil for the training of young Afghan journalists in the hope that they will continue to keep their people informed in the tradition that has come to be associated with the BBC. Reliable estimates claim 80 per cent of the Afghan adult population listen regularly to its broadcasts.

Promises of funding have already come from the BBC, Reuters, *Newsweek,* Oxfam and several other aid agencies.

GIL GONZALEZ-FOERSTER

# Time for change

*Three years after its return to democracy appearances in Bangladesh are deceptive. The media remains under strict government surveillance*

'The press enjoys total freedom in Bangladesh,' says Minister of Information Nazmul Hudda without a moment's hesitation. Given the diversity of publications available in the country's capital, Dhaka, his assurances seem justified. Particularly given that General Ershad banned something like 693 titles in his nine years as head of state.

On closer examination, however, this freedom turns out to be little more than a facade. Everyone acknowledges that things have improved since 1991, but obstacles in the way of the press are still plentiful. Journalists are arrested for reporting on corruption; editorial offices are attacked; photographers are beaten up when covering demonstrations; newspapers are banned.

In typical dictator fashion, President Ershad planned to demolish the press through censorship. His democratically elected successor since 1991, President Khaleda Zia, has a different style: direct censorship is out, self-censorship in. Telephone calls in the middle of the night from the Ministry of Information may be a thing of the past, but journalists are kept well aware of the unwritten rules which they breach at their peril. For the most part they observe the taboos.

While journalists acknowledge the improvements, they are far from satisfied. The state retains its monopoly on the import of newsprint and its allocation. It also finances 80 per cent of all newspaper advertising. Depriving an unruly paper of one or the other — at worst both — is tantamount to financial ruin.

Advertising is allocated by the DFP (Department of Films and Publications), answerable to the Ministry of Information. Officially, this is calculated on a pro-rata basis related to circulation with a minimum requirement of 6,000 copies. In reality, the two state-owned newspapers get the lion's share, despite having a circulation only just over the minimum and far less than their independent rivals. The same applies to the mouthpiece of the ruling Bangladesh National Party (BNP). According to a parliamentary report quoted in 1993 by NGO Development Features, of the Taka 23 million (cUS$5,000,000) of the advertising budget paid out between January and May 1993, *Dainik Bangla* and *The Bangladesh Times* received Tk6.2 and Tk4.2 million respectively. In the same period, the fundamentalist, pro-Iraqi, newspaper, *Dainik Inqilab*, received Tk2.6 million, and *Dainik Dinkal*, also owned by the ruling party, Tk1.9 million. *Dainik Al-Amin, Dainik Samachar* and *Dainik Sakti* shared Tk2 million — substantial sums for publications that cannot be found on newsstands.

The CCHRB (Coordinating Council for Human Rights in Bangladesh) confirms that 'state advertising is used as a weapon against any newspaper critical of the government'. On 6 April, the daily *Janakantha,* with a circulation of 100,000 and 470 employees, lost its state advertising for publishing an article on six political personalities, including Minister of Energy Khandokar Mosharraf Hossain. 'We'll need to sell 50,000 extra copies to recoup the loss,' says the paper's director, Mohammad Atiqullah Khan Masud, a wealthy industrialist. Fortunately, he can afford to replenish the coffers of the newspaper with the profits he makes in his other, more lucrative, activities.

Another trump card in the hands of *Janakantha* is its distribution system. In a country where the road infrastructure is less than adequate, *Janakantha,* which prints at five presses distributed across the country, is the only daily newspaper on sale country-wide each morning, rather than midday.

In a country where 60 to 70 per cent of the population is illiterate, the print run of even the most popular papers is little more than 150,000; sales revenue alone would not keep them in business. More than anything else it is the need for government advertising that keeps journalists in line — and the government safe from criticism.

> **More than anything else it is the need for government advertising that keeps journalists in line and their government safe from criticism**

In the audio-visual sector virtually nothing has changed in the last three years. State-owned television (BTV) and radio have no competitors. BTV broadcasts CNN and BBC programmes for up to six hours daily; even this is not free of censorship. In December 1992, for instance, a CNN report on clashes in northern India following the destruction of the Ayodhya Mosque by Hindu militants, was replaced by a test card.

State-owned television continues to dominate national news; such political debate as occurs is tightly controlled by the government. On just one day, 30 January 1994, during the electoral campaign, the BNP were given 58 minutes on TV; the main opposition party had to make do with one minute.

While there is no law prohibiting the creation of private television stations, state approval is needed for use of the telecommunications network. It took veteran journalist Enayatullah Khan over a year to get clearance for the launch of his private press agency, UNB (United News of Bangladesh). In 1993, the authorities cut off the agency's satellite link for 40 days, on the pretext that it had failed to pay its bills. UNB is in direct competition with the official press agency BSS. Foreign embassies claim UNB is a more reliable and independent source than the official agency, a fact that does nothing to endear it to the government who would prefer to see it close.

According to Golam Rahman, professor of journalism at Dhaka University, media law, which largely dates from colonial times, is totally outdated. The defamation clause, for example, still forbids criticism of the president, prime minister and the leader of parliament.

Journalists themselves, however, have a lot to answer for, according to S Kamaluddin, Dhaka corespondent for the *Far Eastern Economic Review*. 'There is press freedom here, but it is damaged by the lack of professionalism, by sloppiness, among many journalists.' Others quote many instances of this, particularly those involving a cavalier lack of responsibilty among the local press corps. 'Freedom of the press goes hand in hand with responsibility,' says Kamaluddin, 'and many newspapers abuse that freedom.'

*Translated from La Lettre of Reporters sans Frontières by Nathalie Vartanpour-Naalbandian*

ADEWALE MAJA-PEARCE

# Press intimidation

*Three years in power has dampened the government's initial enthusiasm for free speech. With elections looming, things can only get worse*

Ethiopia is a poor country. In Addis Ababa, the capital, there are an estimated 40,000 street children in a city of only 3 million inhabitants. Many of the children are orphans. Their parents were killed by Colonel Mengistu Haile Mariam for a reason which he might have believed in once upon a time but quickly forgot once the blood began to flow. Mengistu now lives in considerable splendour in Harare, Zimbabwe, and has resisted all efforts to repatriate him back to his homeland to face charges. The present government of Ethiopia has promised to institute a series of human rights trials — the first in the continent — against the Colonel and his boys, but nobody believes it's really going to happen as the government itself appears less and less convinced of its utility. Three years of power has taught them the value of keeping things hidden away in dark corners. All kinds of things, because you never know. That was why the official press, represented by the parrots in the offices of *Abeiotawi Democracy* (Revolutionary Democracy) chose to remain silent over circulation figures and number of staff employed and ownership, exactly the kind of banal information you might expect to find in a decent directory. The more's the pity. Ethiopia can hardly afford yet another debilitating exercise in tyranny, but how to break the vicious cycle is a question that can only be answered by those who are silenced in the interests of a self-justifying cabal intent only on its own pleasures.

Following the fall of the Mengistu regime in May 1991, and with it a decade-and-a-half of terror in which parents of the executed were required to pay for the bullets that killed their children, an estimated 60 publications appeared on the Ethiopian scene. Most of them were eight-page weeklies with small staffs and few resources; all of them were initially encouraged by the victorious Tigrayan Peoples' Liberation Front and its political wing, the Ethiopian Peoples' Revolutionary Democratic Front (EPRDF), to help build the new society in which all the funda-

mental freedoms were to be guaranteed. Three years later, the news is not good. The triumphal liberators of a proud and ancient people seem less certain about the wisdom of unfettered criticism, and have opted to follow the seductive path of their predecessors in order to guarantee their own continued power beyond February next year, when the much-postponed elections are scheduled to take place.

According to a recent report by the Ethiopian Free Press Journalists' Association (EFJA), the credible alternative to the official Ethiopian Journalists' Association, about half the independent publications have been forced to shut over the last 12 months. The methods for achieving this are familiar enough: beating up news vendors and seizing their goods under the pretext of 'cleaning the streets'; arbitrarily jacking up the cost of printing in a country where the government has a monopoly of the printing presses; charging a camera-

man with 'contempt of court' for taking a photograph in the course of a trial of a fellow journalist and sentencing him to four months' imprisonment. But the most common is to 'concoct all sorts of petty charges as a result of which editors and publishers of the private press are too often obliged to appear before the Central Criminal Investigation office'. The subsequent 'investigations' have little or nothing to do with the assumed offences — 'disseminating false information'; 'inciting social unrest'; 'interfering with religion' — but for 'discovering the political leanings of the journalists and the publishers', a crime thought to have been abolished by those who fought a civil war for that very reason, but who now detain said journalists and publishers for anything up to six months at a time in order to ensure, amongst other things, that they are unlikely ever to publish again.

Given the economics of publishing in a country pauperised to the point of famine by bad politics, two missed deadlines can mean bankruptcy. It's unlikely that so many publications could have survived the initial euphoria of an unfamiliar freedom, or even that such a restricted market could have coped with those that were left, but the 1992 Press Law — 'A Proclamation to Provide for the Freedom of the Press' — also

**The intimidation of the independent press is supported by a vicious propaganda campaign in the government-owned papers**

contains provisions, in the words of the EFJA report, 'to put a brake on the progress of free expression in Ethiopia'.

Article 20 of the Press Law allows for prison sentences of between one and three years, or a fine of not less than Birr 10,000 (US$1,600) and not more than Birr 50,000, or both, for contravening the relevant sections of Article 10 of the Proclamation. This states that any 'press product' should be free from 'any criminal offence against the safety of the State', 'any defamation or false accusation against any individual, nation/nationality, people or organisation', 'any criminal instigation of one nationality against another', and 'any agitation for war'. In other words, disseminating false information, inciting social unrest, and interfering with religion, but only as defined by the authorities.

Articles 15 and 16 of the same Proclamation enjoins the Prosecutor of the Central Government, or of a region, to present his case against the erring journalist to the Central High Court, or to the regional court, within 24 hours. The court, for its part, 'shall render its decision within 48 hours'; the decision of the court 'shall be executed within 72 hours unless a stay of execution is ordered by an appellate court'. All things being equal, you should be out within the week. The following were detained on 9 February this year, and were still in detention on 27 April: Meleskachew Amha and Birhana Mena, editor-in-chief and publisher, respectively, of *Dewel;* W Giorgis W Michael, reporter, *Muday;* Tenker Tereda, Belayneh Asegu, Feleke Alemu, editorial staff, *Meqdella;* Eyob Demeke, acting editor-in-chief, *Wakt.* In the same period, three editors were imprisoned for between one and two years, and four others were fined between Birr 500 and Birr 15,000. One editor-in-chief, Mesfin Shiferaw, was declared missing. Article 15 of the Press Law also states that the prosecutor of the Central Government, or of a region, 'shall be legally liable for any unjustified exercise of his powers under this Article'.

There is no evidence that the prosecutor, in this case of the Central Government, was aware of his responsibilities with regard to the provisions of the Proclamation. The journalists, for their part, understood well enough the futility of holding any government official responsible for their illegal actions, which would only draw unnecessary attention to what is already a highly visible career.

The intimidation of the independent press is supported by a vicious propaganda campaign waged in the pages of the government-owned publications: 'the private press are falsely accused of siding with real or imagined opposition forces, of not publishing materials favourable to the EPRDF, of being irresponsble, unobjective, etc.'

## IVES MARIE CHANEL

# No news is bad news

*Rumours of intervention abound but the military does its best to ensure that the facts don't get out*

Dejean Belizaire, one of the senators voted in during the 18 January 1993 elections carried out under the military after their deposition of President Jean-Bertrand Aristide in the September 1991 coup, has declared all-out war on the Haitian press. Confirming what Haitian journalists had feared since the imposition of the state of emergency two days earlier, he announced on the private station Radio Metropole on 14 June that 'the state of emergency, declared two days earlier, gives the government greater powers to control the press.'

The new offensive had been foreshadowed by a government communiqué of 13 May warning the media against the use of 'excessive language'.

The *junta's* information minister, Jacques Saint Louis, has reopened the official radio and television stations after a gap of over six months. The new broadcasting chiefs, appointed on 23 May, are both known as apologists for Duvalierism and for their close links to the military. Shortly after their appointment, 101 employees were dismissed from television;

35 more lost their jobs at state radio.

The audiences for state radio and TV have, in any case, dropped off substantially; residents of Port-au-Prince have other alternatives in the form of five new television stations (Télémax, Télé 13, Union, Haïti Monde and Eclair) and six new FM radio stations that have taken to the air over the last two years. Five independent radio stations have been closed since the coup — Antilles, Galaxie, Cacique, Haïti Inter and Phalanstère (which stopped broadcasting on 3 January this year, after armed men confiscated equipment from the station in Gonaïves, about 90 miles north of the capital.

The level of physical attacks on reporters has declined slightly, but caution is still the order of the day. The combination of self-censorship and paucity of sources — journalists are confined to official sources and agency despatches — are the main problem. But Liliane Pierre Paul, programme director for Radio Kiskeya, says a campaign of telephone threats has dogged the station since it opened on 7 May. Pierre Paul, an eminent journalist who was expelled from the country by Duvalier in November 1980, has also suffered, throughout June, from verbal attacks by the neo-Duvalierist director of Radio Liberté, Serge Beaulieu.

Life for journalists is even tougher in the provinces; most reporters have simply dropped out of circulation, finding it impossible to find work when local stations are closing and those based in the capital are having to deal with their own financial and security problems. Most seek refuge in Port-au-Prince or apply for political asylum abroad.

The main regional radio stations now carry only music and sports news. Journalists working for two stations based in Saint Marc, Digital FM and Radio Saint Marc, which have resumed news broadcasts, confirm the need for self-censorship.

The US blockade is also taking its toll. In the town of Jacmel, the four radio and three television stations have been unable to broadcast since the hydroelectric turbines that feed the town stopped working in May. Increased running costs, caused by the scarcity and high price of fuel, together with dwindling financial returns, have forced station directors to shut up shop. According to a survey carried out in April on behalf of UNICEF, in seven of the country's nine departments the US station Voice of America is the principal, if not the sole, source of information for those unable to receive FM broadcasts from the capital.

Venel Remarais, director of the Haitian Press Agency (AHP) and editor-in-chief of the country's most

**The state of emergency won't make any great difference because the press has always been under threat here**

important Creole-language weekly, *Libète*, says the new decrees are 'arbitrary acts by an illegal government' and regrets that journalists have been slow to respond. 'The really serious thing,' he says 'is that some journalists from the independent press are carrying on a kind of collaboration with the de facto [a terminology recently banned by the regime] government.' Max Chauvet, the director of the country's most important French-language daily paper, *Le Nouvelliste*, believes 'the declaration of the state of emergency won't make any great difference since the press has always been under threat here, and because we're living in a state of complete illegality.'

The embargo is still an everyday preoccupation, even for those stations in the capital which have been able to resume their normal programming with the resumption of a regular electricity supply. And even if the recent tightening of the embargo has not had a dramatic impact on the broadcast media, production costs for newspapers remain exorbitantly high. Max Chauvet argues that the procedures governing exemptions from sanctions for the press are not clear enough. In fact, the exemptions as framed by the UN only apply to the foreign press corps in Haiti and to publications destined for local libraries; but not at all to the local press.

GRALIP, an independent campaigning body for press freedom grouping Haitian freelance journalists, fears that the military's take-over of the media could leave the country with no formal journalistic structure. It is more than systematic self-censorship and the regime's control of circulation that is whittling away room for manoeuvre, they claim. The closure of papers and radio stations seriously limits their ability to get out the news and is eroding the public's right to information, says GRALIP.

*Translated from* La Lettre *of Reporters sans Frontières by Adam Newey*

FRANÇOIS MISSER AND YVES JAUMAIN

# Death by radio

*If Rwandan crimes against humanity ever come to trial, the owners of Radio des Mille Collines will stand at the head of the accused*

'By 5 May the elimination of the Tutsis should be finished.' The message broadcast at the end of April on Radio-Télévision Libre des Mille Collines (Thousand Hills Television and Radio, RTLM), encapsulates the incessant stream of hate speech that poured from the station once the death of the Rwandan president, Juvenal Habyarimana, was announced on 6 April 1994. Two hundred thousand died in three weeks; hundreds of thousands more as Hutu militias combed the countryside in advance of the Tutsi army of the Rwandan Patriotic Front (RPF); thousands more of the million-plus refugees, forced into haphazard flight by the threats of retribution from their own government should they stay. Survivors of the massacres say the extent of the killing and the uncontrollable size of the subsequent exodus would not have happened without it.

RTLM was the propaganda arm of the Hutu government and its extremist allies, prepared long in advance of April. Once the flight carrying President Habyarimana and President Cyprien Ntaryamina of Burundi had been shot down near Kigali, RTLM moved relentlessly into the attack, not only against the Tutsis but also against opposition Hutus — people demanding implementaion of the Arusha peace agreements of August 1993 which would have instituted a measure of power-sharing between the majority, governing Hutu and the minority Tutsi.

RTLM was launched in August 1993 to counteract the propaganda of the Rwandan Patriotic Front's Radio Muhabura. Those who backed it were part of the ruling inner circle, some with close links to the extreme Hutu nationalist party, the Coalition for the Defence of the Republic (CDR). Joseph Nzirorera, spokesman for Habyarimana's political party, the National Republican Movement for Democracy and Development (NRMD); Agatha Kanziga, wife of the dead president; Seraphin Rwabukumba, businessman and father-in-law of one of Habyarimana's sons, and Felicien Kabuga, a businessman known for his friendships within the far right Hutu movement. In Kigali, this group is discreetly referred to as 'Habyarimana's wife's clan'. Nzirorera and Rwabukumba have also been accused of belonging to 'Reseau Zero', death squads implicated in the massacres, accusations they continue

ROBERT KING/CAMERA PRESS

to deny.

The moving spirit and ideologue behind the radio was Ferdinand Nahimana, pseudo-historian and architect of the genocidal Hutu ethnic mythology. This former head of Radio Rwanda, now a refugee in Zaire, was personally involved in the nation-wide broadcasting of a call to violence which led to the death of 300 people in the Bugesera region in March 1992. During massacres in neighbouring Burundi in October and November last year — the first signs, largely ignored by the West, of a recurrence of the Hutu/Tutsi slaughter that has periodically plagued both countries since independence — Radio Rwanda and RTLM handed their microphones over to the most extreme faction of the exiled Burundi government in Rwanda, allowing them to advocate violent resistance to the Tutsi enemy. As in Kigali in April, this was the incitement that kicked off the wholesale killing.

RTLM is sited near the presidential palace, in premises guarded by the 'interahamwe', Hutu militiamen acting as a presidential guard, mostly from Bushiru in the north, Habyarimana's home region. According to the former governor of the National Rwandan Bank, Jean Birara, the radio station received its electricity supply directly from the presidential buildings. Destroyed by RPF bombing around 25 April, RTLM was on the air again three days later, courtesy of the government-owned Radio Rwanda's second channel.

Belgian nationals and the UN peace-keeping force were among its early targets. As early as autumn 1993, George Ruggiu, a Belgian invited to Rwanda by Eugene Nahimana — spokesman for the NRMD in Belgium and a relation of Habyarimana — attacked the French-language papers over the RTLM airwaves and initiated a campaign of violence against the Belgian government, which supported the Arusha agreement, and Belgian soldiers in the United Nations Mission for Aid to Rwanda (UNMAR).

The campaign came to a head with the death of Habyarimana: Ruggiu blamed the UN peace-keeping force, maintaining that 'they must be deported [because] they were providing the RPF with arms'. He added that 'Belgian para-militaries were going to invade the country.'

'One Belgian each' was the slogan adopted by RTLM. Instructions allegedly broadcast by RTLM included information on the handling of grenades and different methods of killing the 'enemy' — Tutsis, opposing Hutus and Belgians. The deaths of six Belgian civilians and 10 members of the UN peace-keeping force at the hands of the Presidential Guard led to an investigation of Ruggiu by Belgian police. In a fax sent on 2 May from the Rwandan army headquarters, Ruggiu denied that he was implicated in their deaths and defended RTLM, describing it as a 'radio of the people'.

*Translated from* La Lettre *of Reporters sans Frontières by Carmen Gibson*

# MINORITIES: CRIMEAN TATARS

**STEPHEN MULVEY**

# A lunatic's revenge

In his 'state-of-the-nation' speech to the Russian parliament on 24 February 1994 President Boris Yeltsin said that Russia, as the legal successor of the former Soviet Union, bore responsibility for Stalin's deportations, and had a duty to eradicate the consequences of 'those terrible events'. His apology to those who suffered, however, extended only to 'citizens of Russia'. Like Khrushchev before him, Yeltsin turned a blind eye to the plight of a large category of victims of deportation, among them the Crimean Tatars, who are not members of the successor stateFifty years ago this summer the defeat of Nazism was assured by Allied military offensives. But against the background of this military success, a human catastrophe took place in Eastern Europe — on both sides of the rapidly changing front line. The early summer of 1944 remains one of the most ambiguous and contradictory moments in European history.

While Oskar Schindler choked on the smoke of burning flesh at Plaszow, and the Auschwitz furnaces blackened the sky at an ever-increasing rate, Stalin was taking a lunatic's revenge on his own people. The Soviet army revealed Majdanek to the world, but some Nazi camps were simply taken over, the same barbed wire used to imprison ordinary Soviet citizens on 'liberated' territory. As part of this process, entire nationalities were deported from Soviet Europe to Central Asia. For many of these people, as for the Crimean Tatars, this turned out to be half a century of exile.

On the night of 18 May 1944, Tatars in the Crimea were woken and

Bakhchisarai: the palace of the Khans

given 10 minutes to leave their homes. More than 180,000 people, jammed into goods wagons, were subjected to a suffocating 20-day journey to Uzbekistan. Survivors recall being forced to push their dead from tiny windows as the train crossed the scorching Central Asian steppe.

The Crimean Tatars — descendants of Gothic tribes and the Mongol Golden Horde — regard this deportation as genocide. They claim that nearly half the population (46 per cent) died in transit, or from hunger and disease in the first 18 months of exile. Recently opened Soviet NKVD (secret police) archives — if they can be trusted — point to a death toll nearer 25 per cent, perhaps 45,000 people, in the first five years. A lower figure but still a shocking one.

The Soviet model for persecution on grounds of nationality had been set in 1937, with the exile of ethnic Koreans from the Soviet Far East, on grounds of 'spying for Japan'. After the German invasion in 1941, Stalin's fear of conspiracy only increased, resulting in the deportation of more than a million ethnic Germans to Central Asia. Ethnic Finns from the Leningrad area followed them in 1942. But it was military success that led to the most frenetic period of deportation, helped along by the enthusiasm of the NKVD chief, Lavrenty Beria.

By the end of 1943 the Red Army had regained enough territory for him to oversee the deportation of the Karachai from the Northern Caucasus and, a month later, the Kalmyks, from the southern Russian steppe. In February 1944, he returned to the Caucasus to expel the Chechens and Ingush — a population of some half a million. A surviving letter from Beria to Stalin, written at this time but published only in 1990, shows him volunteering to deport the nearby Balkar people at the same time — an idea Stalin evidently welcomed. The same thing happened in Crimea. Having dealt with the Tatars, Beria offered to deport Crimea's Armenian, Bulgarian and Greek population as well. They were on their way before the end of the month.

The standard pretext for deportation was alleged collaboration with the German occupying army; the Crimean Greeks, accused of 'reviving private trade', were an exception. Given their bitter experience of Stalinism, from the purges of 'bourgeois nationalists' in the 1920s to the terror of the late 1930s, the scale of Tatar collaboration was smaller than might have been expected. When the news of their deportation was made public two years later, it was implicitly recognised that active collaborators were in a minority. The many were blamed for failing to prevent the anti-Soviet activities of the few — an accusation that could equally well have been levelled against the peninsula's majority population of Russians and Ukrainians.

Once in Uzbekistan, the Crimean Tatars, like other deportees, were put to work, mainly on collective farms. They were obliged to register with the police at frequent intervals, and had no freedom of movement, attempts to escape being punishable by 20 years' hard labour. This regime, described as 'special settlement', was one of several forms of exile, quite distinct from the Gulag labour camps. At its peak, before Stalin's death in 1953, special settlement accounted for more than 2.75 million people. While Stalin's successors began to dismantle the system, they nevertheless strove — until 1956 — to perpetuate the myth that the deportations had been, as Beria said, 'necessary'. However, while the deported peoples of the Caucasus were allowed to return home in 1957, the Crimean Tatars had to wait another 30 years. Even their official rehabilitation, in September 1967, occurred on paper only. The rehabilitation decree referred to them, significantly, as 'Tatars formerly resident in the Crimea' who had 'taken root' elsewhere. The Tatars were asked at their workplaces to express gratitude for this acknowledgement — after 23 years of exile — that they were actually guiltless. Meanwhile, the entire mechanism of the state, including the internal passport and registration laws, was exploited to prevent them from going home, presumably because of fears that Tatar claims for compensation, or for the return of confiscated property in Crimea, could sour the party atmosphere in a region that had become a holiday 'riviera' for the Soviet elite.

It was only with the advent of perestroika that the Tatars got the chance to resettle in Crimea in any significant numbers. More than 65,000 returned in a two-year period starting spring 1988, and another 50,000 in the year after that. By March this year roughly 280,000, somewhat over half the estimated Crimean Tatar population on the territory of the former Soviet Union, had returned. Nearly all of these returnees were obliged to become squatters on unoccupied land, because of the refusal of local authorities to provide any sites for new Tatar settlements. Their tent villages and shanty towns were frequently bulldozed or torn down by riot police. More than once Tatars doused themselves with petrol, and threatened to ignite it, to persuade police to leave them in peace.

Opposition to Tatar resettlement has tended to be strongest along Crimea's southern coastal strip, where the holiday resorts are concentrated. Many Tatars who were expelled from this area in 1944 have been forced to settle elsewhere. The Tatar struggle for land culminated here in October 1992, in the oddly named village of Red Heaven (Krasny Rai), near the seaside town of Alushta. The arrest of a number of Tatars during a routinely violent police attempt at dispersal led to a counter-attack on the Crimean parliament the next day, by stone-throwing Tatar demonstrators. Most of the building's windows were smashed, and shots were reportedly fired from inside, before Tatar leaders successfully appealed for calm. The detainees were promptly released, and since that time the main obstacles to resettlement have become economic rather than legal or administrative.

Tatar settlements today tend to be characterised by half-finished buildings, with families living in basements for lack of funds to complete the upper floors. Building materials are increasingly costly and scarce. Those Tatars remaining in Uzbekistan find that the sale value of their houses has plummeted because of the large numbers of non-Uzbeks wishing to leave the country and the general economic chaos. The only state aid for resettlement comes from the impoverished government of

Ukraine, of which Crimea has formally been a part since 1954. Part of this money, the Tatars allege, is siphoned off by Crimean authorities for other purposes. Demands for compensation appear to have gone largely unheard. Few Tatars have even bothered to appeal for their former homes to be returned to them, realising that this is a vain hope.

The main priority for Tatar leaders at present is to ensure that all those who wish to return from Uzbekistan are able to do so. Although the influx has been slowing, another 70,000 or so are expected in the next couple of years. It seems likely that the Tatar population will then stabilise at around 12-13 per cent of the peninsula's total population of 2.75 million. Great importance is also attached to the return of mosques, and the opening of schools teaching in the Crimean Tatar language, a process which is beginning.

The greatest potential for controversy, however, arises in the political field. During the latter half of their period in exile the Tatars

Ilver Ametov: member of Tatar mejlis

campaigned tirelessly for the re-establishment of a Crimean autonomous republic, the initial creation of which in 1921 had led to a period of national rebirth. In Tatar settlements in Central Asia, police had to cordon off statues of Lenin on the anniversary of the republic's creation, to prevent Tatars laying wreaths. Unexpectedly, however, Crimea's Communist leaders re-established the former autonomous republic themselves, early in 1991 — but with no intention of re-introducing any 1920s-style positive discrimination in favour of Tatars. The Tatars' demand was accordingly recast as a demand for self-government that was embodied in a proposal for a power-sharing constitution, published later that year.

When the Crimean parliament adopted its own constitution in mid-1992, this draft constitution was more ignored than rejected. The Tatars were forced to change tack again, and this time began to press for a quota of seats in the new Crimean parliament. An initial demand for 22 seats out of 98 was whittled down in negotiations with the authorities to 14 but, even so, was rejected by the parliament in September 1993. Once again, the Tatars achieved their goal by resolute protest. After a series of large-scale Tatar demonstrations, and railway line blockages, the Crimean parliament conceded the 14-seat quota in mid-October. It became a reality during elections to the Crimean parliament in March 1994.

This parliamentary quota represents the only political step forward that the Tatars have made in more than 50 years, and is already under threat following the election of a Russian nationalist, Yuri Meshkov, in Crimea's first presidential elections this January. While President Meshkov is prepared to lobby for more state aid for Tatar resettlement — from Russia and Uzbekistan, for example, which have so far provided no funds at all — he describes the quota as a 'barbarous' departure from democratic norms, and has often hinted that the quota could be abolished. Officials at the Crimean parliament claim that it was only introduced for one term of four years, and thereafter 'it probably won't be necessary'.

Bakhchisarai: home at last

Given the present tendency in

Crimea to vote along national lines, and since they do not make up more than 20 per cent of the population in any constituency, the resettled Tatars would have little chance of gaining even one seat in an election conducted according to the strict 'democratic' principles favoured by Meshkov. Before the quota system was introduced there was one Tatar deputy in the Crimean parliament, the millionaire businessman Iskander Memetov. He was gunned down during this year's election campaign.

Just as menacing, from the Tatars' point of view, is Meshkov's insistence that the Tatar *mejlis,* or 'parliament', elected in 1991, should give up its claims to be a political body representing the entire Crimean Tatar community. His demand that it should either register as a 'social organisation' or disband has led the veteran dissident Mustafa Cemiloglu to warn of the possibility of 'yet another spiral of confrontation'.

One notable aspect of the Crimean Tatar campaign, over the last half century, has been the emphasis on peaceful, constitutional methods of struggle. One indication of this is the huge quantity of letters, appeals and petitions sent to Soviet authorities: by 1975, they were said to fill 207 volumes. However, some Tatar leaders now admit the possibility of a more radical movement emerging, as a reaction to the more confrontational attitude of the new Crimean leadership. Hints of this potential radicalisation have, perhaps, already been seen in the protest actions of the autumns of 1992 and 1993. Analysts do not rule out the possibility of confrontation between Tatars and the Crimean authorities triggering a wider conflict involving both Ukrainian and Russian security forces — though there is no shortage of other, perhaps more plausible scenarios, which could deliver the same outcome in Crimea. During times of tension between the Ukrainian and Crimean authorities, such as the present, relations between the Ukrainian government and the Tatars typically grow warmer. Whether Ukraine would ever go so far as to risk an armed conflict on their behalf is, however, another matter.

On 23 February this year, Russian president Boris Yeltsin, expressing his condolences to the Chechen and Ingush peoples on the 50th anniversary of their exile, described the deportations as 'delayed-action time bombs' in inter-ethnic relations. The bloody conflict between Ossetians and Ingush was the most dramatic example of this, he said. The even bloodier war between Abkhazia and Georgia is another. The legacy of Stalin's wartime revenge on his own people has not yet worked itself out; the Crimean Tatars could become one more of its casualties.

# Scheherazade 2001

'Art is a healing power in Sarajevo. It is not a luxury for us, something that interests us when all other work is done. Art is a fundamental component of every-day survival for us.'

*Haris Pasovic*

**ILONKA VERDURMEN**

# One more night...

'Listen,' said Scheherazade to the Sultan on her wedding night, 'will you permit me to tell you a story?' 'Willingly,' he answered. So Scheherazade began

It is with this sentence, referring to the Scheherazade of the *Thousand and One Nights*, that contemporary Scheherazades all over Europe have started their reading performances in the past few months.

The plan was born at the 'Artists for Sarajevo' meeting in January 1994 in Amsterdam. Haris Pasovic, director of the Film and Theatre Festival in Sarajevo, suggested organising a series of tales to be told simultaneously in Sarajevo and other European cities. Scheherazade, in the stories of that 1001 nights, saves her own life and that of the young women of the town by telling stories. She cures the King of his insanity and ends his barbarous practice of beheading his brides the morning after the wedding. Her stories put an end to the death and violence around her.

Now the time has come for the Scheherazades of 2001 to use the healing power of story-telling again. Authors such as AS Byatt (GB), Julian Barnes (GB), John Berger (GB/France), Nedim Gursel (Turkey/France), Peter Nadas (Hungary), Gianni Celati (Italy/GB), Claudio Magris (Italy), Dubravka Ugresic (Former Yugoslavia/Germany), Margriet de Moor (Holland), Boris Cosic (Former Yugoslavia/Germany) wrote a story especially for Scheherazade 2001 or sent in a story of their choice that had not been published elsewhere.

On Friday nights, after the regular performance, audiences in Sarajevo and in other cities in Bosnia and in more than 50 theatres in Holland, Belgium, Germany, Bulgaria, Spain and Moscow, were invited to stay and listen and participate in the project. The same stories were published and broadcast in theatres, magazines and on radio all over Europe.

Every week a fax from Sarajevo was sent to Amsterdam, where the project was coordinated in De Balie Theatre, describing the events of that week, to keep audiences informed of daily life in the besieged city. These so called 'stories of the day' were translated and distributed to the participating theatres and were read with the stories.

On 15 April Mirza Halilovic, who coordinated the Scheherazade Project in Sarajevo wrote:

'I am very glad to inform you that Scheherazade 2001 started on 8 April in Sarajevo, Zenica and Tuzla very succesfully. It was a great event. That night was a night when artists, writers and audiences from Europe became closely connected with us. The healing energy of art was once again shown by this action. I hope the night was great in all other European theatres too. Audiences in Zenica, Tuzla and Sarajevo were delighted. They support our action with their hearts. I hope our cooperation lasts for a long time...'

By now the second part of the project has been completed. Students from theatre schools in Holland and Belgium went to Sarajevo this summer to work with students from the Theatre School in Sarejevo.

These workshops were based on the themes Scheherazade offered, such as the struggle between the one who has power, and the one who has the power of imagination.

For the visiting students their stay turned into a lesson in Sarajevo Survivalism. It was an extraordinary experience for them to share, at least for a limited period of time, daily life in Sarajevo, and to share their knowledge and theatre know-how with the students there.

In September Haris Pasovic and his troupe of professional actors will give performances in Paris and Amsterdam (possibly in London and Hamburg as well) of a play based on 'In the Country of Lost Things' by Paul Auster and their own piece *Silks Drums II* based on the principles of Noh theatre.

**Out of Sarajevo**
An evening of readings from Scheherazade 2001 with Julian Barnes and *Guardian* journalist Maggie O'Kane takes place on 22 September 1994 at 7.30pm at the Voice Box, Royal Festival Hall, South Bank Centre, London SE1. Slobodan Blagojevic, Dubravka Ugresic and Hamdija Demirovic will read from the latest issue of *STORM* magazine, 'Out of Yugoslavia', at the Voice Box at 7pm on 29 September.

*All illustrations to the following stories by Geoffrey Keeling*

# IRFAN HOROZOVIC

# The Bosnian bull

He didn't notice the Butcher approach. Images of the world took on hazy shapes in his drowsy eyes. That made the blow all the more terrible. His head suddenly felt severed from his body, fertility from foreboding, his tail powerless against all former and future leeches.

Never had that little bull felt as big as now, with this growing pain.

He was not dead. Murky, dark senses were aroused when the steel jaws began to bite, tear and chew, when his flesh, his life became food, food for the insatiable tooth, food which watches itself being eaten! He saw the towns through which his flesh was being hauled. He saw the villages in the eyes of his raped shepherdesses. He saw the destroyed houses and the old men who resembled scorched tree stumps which glow in the night. He saw the throngs of people streaming into exile like blood from his body.

He saw. And he tried to stand up.

The game had only just begun.

Just like the Spanish theatre of sacrifice, his little meadow became peopled with observers, supporters and advisers. The loud scream produced a sudden hush. The medicinal herb he had unconsciously

bitten into, its juice mixing with his own blood, took his attention away from the spear-throwers who were approaching with their quivering muscles, taking aim at his pulse, his arteries, his heart. The iron rhinos made for his stomach and shoulder blades. Their riders held charts of the bull's flesh, reproduced at the Great Butcher Shop. They knew who would get the ribs, who the shanks, who the legs and the tail, who the heart, who the eyes, the brain and the tongue. They knew and they quarrelled.

Drawing his strength from unplumbed memory, the bull rose to his feet. In that same instant, the iron, toothed horn knocked him down, and pinned him to the ground, to the trampled secret grass. Now he resembled a living monument who served as a target for the steel birds which fired their vapours at him from the very firmament above. He no longer heard a thing. No shouts of delight or of displeasure. He did not notice how the iron rhinos had been removed so as not to block the view while the performance of the steel birds was on. Only the one pinning him down remained, while the others circled around, waiting for their moment to come.

Finally, his head slumped, his chest, his legs.

The butchers quarrelled over the various pieces, they threatened each other with their teeth and toothed horns, they cited the promises and secret agreements made in the Great Butcher Shop. The observers joined in the fight. The supporters created an unbearable racket, completely covering a dark sound which emanated from the bull's severed head, from his slit throat. It was a death rattle in which one sensed something like memory, something like the trumpet of a parallel world, something like birth.

The decimated bull rose to its feet.

He stood there like that, awkward and desperate, trying to understand.

After their initial surprise, the butchers, the iron rhino masters, the steel bird drivers, and the observers all rushed in. The butchers killed the severed pieces which still clung to the body, if only in foreboding; they cut up the bones, the nerves, directing their knives at the foreboding itself.

The bull stood there and screamed.

The observers, the supporters and the advisers returned to their places behind the fence and continued watching the show which defied every known rule. They watched the killing which emerged from the killing, the killing which turned into the next killing, the killing and decimation, the decimation and killing. They watched and they waited. Time stopped. Time stopped behind the fence. The pulse of pain.

Everybody waited to see the little decimated bull knuckle under, its magnificent horns of a herbivore raised to the sky.

© *Irfan Horozovic* © *Translated by Christina Pribichevich-Zoric*

## A S BYATT

# Dragon's breath

Once upon a time, in a village in a valley surrounded by high mountains, lived a family with two sons and a daughter, whose names were Harry, Jack and Eva. The village was on the lower slopes of the mountains, and in the deep bowl of the valley was a lake, clear as crystal on its shores, and black as ink in its unplumbed centre. Thick pine forests grew in the shadow of the mountain ridges, but the village stood amongst flowery meadows and orchards, and cornfields, not luscious, but sufficient for the needs of the villages. The peaks of the mountains were inaccessible, with blue ice-shadows and glittering snow-fields. The sides of the mountain were scored with long descending channels, like the furrows of some monstrous plough. In England the circular impressions around certain hills are ascribed to the coiling grip of ancient dragons, and in that country there was a tale that in some primeval time the channels had been cut by the descent of giant worms from the peaks. In the night, by the fire, parents frightened children pleasurably with tales of the flaming, cavorting descent of the dragons.

Harry, Jack and Eva were not afraid of dragons, but they were, in their different ways, afraid of boredom. Life in that village repeated itself, generation after generation. They were born, they became lovers, they became parents and grandparents, they died. The villagers made a certain traditional kind of rug, on handlooms, with a certain limited range of colours from vegetable dyes they made themselves — a blood-red, a dark blue with a hint of green, a sandy yellow, a charcoal black. There were a few traditional designs, which hardly varied: a branching tree, with fruit like pomegranates, and roosting birds, somewhat like pheasants, or a more abstract geometrical design, with discs of one colour threaded on a criss-crossing web of another on the ground of a third. The rugs were on the whole made by the women, who also cooked and washed. The men looked after the livestock, worked the fields and made music. They had their own musical instrument, a wailing pipe, not found anywhere else, though most of them had not travelled far enough to know that.

Harry was a swineherd and Jack dug in the fields, sowed and harvested. Harry had a particular friend amongst the pigs, a young boar called Boris, a sagacious creature who made cunning escapes and dug up unexpected truffles. But Boris's playfulness was not enough to mitigate Harry's prevailing boredom. He dreamed of great cities beyond the mountain, with streaming crowds of urgent people, all different, all busy. Jack liked to see the corn come up, green spikes in the black earth, and he knew where to find ceps and wild honey, but these treats did little to mitigate his prevailing boredom. He dreamed of ornamental gardens inside high walls surrounding huge palaces. He dreamed of subtle tastes, spices and fiery spirits unknown in the valley. He dreamed also of wilder dances, bodies flung about freely, to music on instruments he knew only by hearsay: the zither, the bongo drum, the grand piano, tubular bells.

Eva made the rugs. She could have woven in her sleep, she thought, and often did, waking to find her mind buzzing with repeats and variations, twisting threads and shifting warp and weft. She dreamed of unknown colours, purple, vermilion, turquoise and orange. She dreamed of the sea, which she could not imagine, she dreamed of salt water and tasted her own impatient tears. She was not good at weaving, she made her tension too tight, and her patterns bunched, but this was her task.

The first sign may have been the hunter's reports of unusual snowslides in the high mountains. Or maybe it was, as some of them later claimed, dawns that were hectically rosy, sunsets that flared too crimson. After a time it became quite clear that the rim of the mountains directly above the village, both by day and by night, was flickering and dancing with a kind of fiery haze, a smoky salmon-pink, a burst here and there of crimson and gold. Below this flaming rim the white of the snow was giving way to the gaunt grey of wet rock, and the shimmer — and yes, steam — of new water.

They must have been afraid from the beginning: they could see well enough that large changes were taking place, that everything was on the move, earth and air, fire and water. But the fear was mixed with a great deal of excited interest, and with even a certain pleasure in novelty, and with aesthetic pleasure, of which many of them were later ashamed. Hunting-parties went out in the direction of the phenomenon and came back to report that the hillside seemed to be on the move, and was boiling and burning, so that it was hard to see through the very thick clouds of ash and smoke and steam that hung over the movement. The mountains were not, as far as anyone knew, volcanic, but the lives of men are short besides the history of rocks and stones, so they wondered and debated.

After some time they saw on the skyline lumps like the knuckles of a giant fist, six lumps, where nothing had been, lumps that might represent objects the size of large sheds or small houses, at that distance. And over the next few weeks the lumps advanced, in smoke and spitting sparks, regularly and slowly, side by side, without hesitation or deviation, down the mountainside. Behind each lump trailed a long, unbending tube.

Some brave men went out to prospect but were forced back by clouds of scalding steam and showers of burning grit. Two friends, bold hunters both, went out and never returned.

One day a woman in her garden said: 'It is almost as though it was not landslides but creatures, great worms with fat heads creeping down on us. Great fat, nodding bald heads, with knobs and sprouts and whelks and whorls on them, and nasty hot wet eyes in great caverns in their muddy flesh, that glint blood-red, twelve eyes, can you see them, and twelve hairy nostrils on blunt snouts made of grey mud.' And after conversations and comparisons and pointings and descriptions they could all see them, and they were just as she said, six fat, lolling, loathsome heads, trailing heavy bodies as long as the road from their village to the next, trailing them with difficulty, even with pain, it seemed, but unrelenting and deadly slow.

When they were nearer — and the slowness of their progress was dreamlike, unreal — their great jaws could be seen, jaws wide as whales and armed with a scythe-like horny or flinty edge like a terrible beak with which they excavated and swallowed a layer of the earth and whatever was on it — bushes, fences, haystacks, fruit trees, a couple of goats, a black and white cow, a duckpond and the life in it. As they approached, the cloud of ash came before them, and settled on everything in the houses and gardens, coated the windows, filmed the wells. It stank, the ash, it was unspeakably foul. At first they grumbled and dusted, and then they gave up dusting, for it was no use, and began to be afraid. It was all so slow, that there was a period of unreal, half-titillating fear, before the real, sick, paralysing fear took hold, which was when the creatures were close enough for men and women to see their eyes, which were rimmed with a gummy discharge, like melting rubber, and their tongues of flame. It was not clear that the worms exactly saw the human beings. The human beings were not on their scale, as small creatures that inhabit our scalps, or burrow in the salad leaves we eat are not visible to us, and we take no account of them.

The tongues of flame were nothing like the brave red banners of painted dragons in churches, and nothing like the flaming swords of archangels. They were molten and lolling, covered with a leathery transparent skin thick with crimson warts and taste-buds glowing like coals, the size of cabbages, slavering with some sulphurous glue and stinking of despair and endless decay that would never be clean again in the whole life of the world.

When it was almost too late, the villagers began to snatch up their belongings at random and move into the forest where life again became

monotonous, boring even, since boredom is possible for human beings in patches of tedium between exertion and terror.

Harry and Jack finally went with some other young men, out in the direction of the village, to see from close quarters the nature and extent of the devastation. They found they were walking towards a whole wall of evil-smelling smoke and flame. A pig shot out of the smoke, panting and squeaking, and Harry called out, 'Boris!' and began to run after his pig, which snorted wildly and charged back into the darkness, followed by Harry, and Jack saw pig and human in sooty silhouette before he heard a monstrous sucking sound, and an exhalation of hot vapours and thick, choking fiery breath which sent him staggering and fainting back. When he came to, his skin was thick with adhesive ash and he could hear, it seemed to him, the liquids boiling and burning in the worm's belly.

For a moment he thought he would simply lie there, in the path of that jaw, and be scooped up with the cornfield and the hedgerow. Then he found he had decided to roll away, and little by little, rolling, crawling and scrambling, he put patches of space between himself and the worm. He lay for several hours, then, winded and sick, under a thorn-bush, before picking himself painfully up, and returning to the camp in the forest. He hoped that Harry too would return, but was not surprised, not really surprised, when he did not.

And so it dragged on, for weeks and months, with the air full of ash and falling cinders, with their clothes and flesh permeated by that terrible smell, until little by little the long loathsome bodies dragged past, across the fields and the meadows, leaving behind those same furrows of rocky surface, scooped clean of life and growth. And from a hilly point they saw the creatures, side by side, cross the sandy shore of the lake, and without changing pace or hesitating, advance across the shallows, as though driven by mechanical necessity, or by some organic need like the periodic return of toads or turtles to a watery world to breed. And the great heads dipped to meet the lake surface, and where they met it, it boiled, and steamed and spat like a great cauldron. And then the heads went under the surface, which still boiled, puckered and bubbling, as the slow lengths of the long bodies humped and slithered, day after day over the sand and down through the water to the depths, until finally only blunt, ugly butts could be seen, under the shallows, and then one day, as uncertainly as their coming had been established, it became clear that their going was over, that the worms had plunged into, through, under the lake, leaving only the harsh marks of their bodies' weight and burning breath in the soil, the rock, the vegetable world crushed and withered.

When the villagers returned to look on their village from a distance, the devastation seemed uniform: the houses flattened, the trees uprooted, the earth scored, channelled, ashy and smoking. They wandered in the ruins, turning over bricks and boards, some people finding, as some people always will, lost treasures and trivia in the ashes, a coin, half a book, a dented cooking-pot. And some people who had vanished in the early chaos returned, with singed eyebrows or seared faces, and others did not. Jack and Eva came back together, and for a moment could not work out in what direction to look for the ruins of what had been their house. And then, coming round a heap of fallen rubble they saw it there, untouched. Jack lifted the stone under which the key was always kept, and there was the key, where it had always been. And Jack and Eva went into the house, and there were tables and chairs, fireplace and bookcase, and Eva's loom, standing in the window, at the back of the house, where you looked out on the slopes and then up at the peaks of the mountains. And there was a heavy humping sound against the back door, which Jack opened. And when he opened it, there was Boris the pig, hanging his head a little, and giving off an odour of roast pork, with not a bristle on his charred rind, but with pleasure and recognition in his deep-set little eyes.

When they saw that the pig had by some miracle, or kindness of luck, escaped the dragon-breath and the fiery tongues, they hoped, of course, that Harry too would return. They hoped he would return for days and months, and against their reasonable judgment, for years. But he did not.

Eva dusted her rug, which was lightly filmed with ash, since it was at the back of the house, and the windows were well-made. She saw the colours — red, blue, yellow, black — as though she had never seen colour before, and yet with disturbed pleasure at their familiarity. An archaeologist, finding this room, and this rug on this loom in it, say two thousand years later, might have felt intense excitement that these things were improbably intact, and intense curiosity about the workmanship, and about the even daily life that could be partly imagined around the found artefacts. Eva felt such amazement now, about her own work, the stubborn persistence of wood and wool and bone shuttle, of the unfinished tree with its squatting pheasants and fat pomegranates. Jack too felt delight and amazement, walking repeatedly across the house from the windows which opened on smouldering devastation to those from which you could see the unchanging mountains. Both embraced Boris, restored and rescued, feeling his wet snout and warm flanks. Such wonder, such amazement, are the opposite, the exact opposite, of boredom, and many people only know them after fear and loss. Once known, I believe, they cannot be completely forgotten; they cast flashes and floods of paradisal light in odd places and at odd times.

The villagers rebuilt their village, and the rescued things in the rescued house stood amongst new houses in whose gardens new flowers and vegetables sprouted, and new saplings were planted. The people began to tell tales about the coming of the worms down the mountain, and the tales too were the opposite of boredom. Some things they made into tales, and some things they did not speak. Jack told of Harry's impetuous bravery, rushing into the billowing smoke to save his pig, and nobody told the day to day misery of slowly diminishing hope of his return. The resourcefulness and restoration of the pig were celebrated, but not his inevitable fate, in those hard days. And these tales, made from those people's wonder at their own survival, became in time charms against boredom for their children and grandchildren, riddling hints of the true relations between peace and beauty and terror.

© *AS Byatt. This story will appear in a new collection of stories* The Djinn in the Nightingale's Eye, *published by Chatto & Windus in November 1994.*

CLAUDIO MAGRIS

# The mistake

Towards the end of August we were in the habit of visiting the
Professor at Ilirska Bistrica, Villa del Nevoso, during the brief period
between the two wars in which Italy's eastern border ran through that
zone — the frontier with Yugoslavia, which is now the frontier between
Slovenia and Croatia. The Professor is both the true lord and the faithful
servant of Monte Nevoso, which rises above the Slovene town of Sneznik
with its endless forests, its clearings where, at dawn, all of a sudden a
buck or a wolf might appear, and the passing of its time engraved in the
growth-rings of the trees which framed not only the forest paths but also
the years of our lives. It was as if our visits to these forests were not just
occasional periods of vacation, but rather an uninterrupted rhythm and
continuity reflected in the growing trees, their coming to maturity, their

changing colour and their eventual fading to nothingness.

The Professor was our 'Leather Stocking'. He showed us the hidden dens and secret pathways used by animals, he took us to view the slow, regal death throes of some ancient tree as it returned peaceably to a state of nature, and he told us old stories of hunters, stags and bears — the destinies and fortunes of men and animals, stories into which flow and merge, as if in one last echo, the histories of all the peoples and empires that have passed through these forests. Every grand passion is meticulous; it seeks perfection and precision. The Professor's love of the woods was more than just their magical dawns and sunsets, the adventure of seeing a wounded wolf, the smell of the first snow in the air; it was also a concern for the detail of small daily things, an attention paid to the forest with the same care that a housewife looks to see where things need dusting, or where a leaking tap needs mending.

The Professor was already over eighty when Marisa Madieri described him going round the Nevoso, repainting the signposts where paths crossed, redrawing maps, gathering grotesque-shaped roots, and giving way to sudden bouts of anger if he should happen to take a wrong path in the forest (in which event — undignified, but fortunately rare — he would tell his amiable and loquacious wife to keep her opinions to herself).

The Professor was a Slovenian, educated in the old Habsburg Austria, and with me he always spoke a ceremonious and antiquated German which tended towards the use of indirect forms. For example, one day, as we were proceeding cautiously into a clearing that was frequented by boars, he said: 'I told my wife, "Ask the esteemed professor whether by chance his respected consort prefers her *gubaniza* with or without grappa"...'

In his company, one penetrated truly to the heart of the forest — a forest in which it is desperately difficult to make your way, even when you're right in the middle of it, because more often than not seemingly invisible and impassable barriers block your progress, and the forest, despite being so close — in fact all around you — remains inaccesible.

A few months ago we visited him again, partly because it would be unthinkable to spend a summer without going to the Nevoso for the pleasure of his company, but partly because, seeing that I was thinking of writing a story about the Nevoso and its bear, I needed circumstantial details, a few basic facts and names, the kinds of things which have no intrinsic importance in themselves, but which are necessary, like a choice of musical key, in order to vary or reinvent the reality that you're wanting to narrate — particularly if you follow Svevo in believing that life, even in its most non-apparent details, is highly original, often more original than the imaginings of a writer, and that a due attention and respect for the truth of men and things is the premise of good story-telling.

The Professor, who by this time was ninety-two, had been in bed for some weeks with a circulational disorder which was making it hard for him to speak. He was feverish and sweating, obviously tired, but his eyes were still alive and cheerful, imparting a tenderness to a face that had been sculpted over the decades into an expression of severe authority. Next to his bed were a number of bundles and packing cases, into which his wife — following on a request that had been expressed haltingly, but with that same tone of incontrovertible authority — had the task of gathering and ordering his things — his books, his collection of strange-shaped roots, a deer's head and a stuffed marten, paintings, drawings and photographs of the mountain, letters, documents and curios — all of which were then to be disposed of. The Professor was clearing out his life, emptying it of things that he loved and that he had collected with a passion bordering on obsession. He was bringing order into his life and renouncing all the things that had adorned it. Rather like the Habsburg emperors in the Baroque era, who, before they could be welcomed into the Crypt of the Capuchins, had to strip themselves of the titles and badges of their authority.

Having provided me punctiliously with the details that I was seeking, the Professor gave me a postcard of the Nevoso. On the back of it were printed — in Slovenian, obviously — some verses (he was also a poet, and penned verse in the nineteenth-century style, about rustling forests and distant peaks). Raising himself on the pillow with the assistance of his wife, with the aid of thick spectacles he translated the verses into German, in a large, trembling hand.

When we finally left him, that small card with its four verses in German seemed to us like a kind of last testament, a definitive seal. But even nonagenarians can spring surprises and give the lie to the doctor's baleful prognostications. Two or three weeks ago a letter arrived, written in German. From the large, wavering handwriting on the envelope it was immediately obvious who had sent it, but it gave no hint of the firm, albeit mortified, observations that were contained therein, written in a venerable old hand that was tremulous but rigorous in its logical and syntactical sequence, its punctuation, its spelling, spacing, and paragraphs. 'Most esteemed professor, when you last came to visit us, I gave you some of my poetry, which I translated into German for you. My wife, who was observing at my side as I wrote, maintains that I wrote *das Berg* instead of *der Berg* ['the mountain']. If this is the case, I would ask you to correct this lamentable error, and to forgive me. I have been suffering from circulatory disorders, and am subject to momentary bouts of amnesia, and if I did make such a mistake, I must blame it on my condition. Now I am better. I have been out of bed, and have been for a short walk in the woods.'

It would have been unthinkable for the Professor to have let himself pass away without having corrected the mistake, and having clarified, for himself and for the world at large, any doubt on the matter. He must have spent a couple of months turning it over in his mind, trying to remember if he really had used *das,* the neuter article, instead of the masculine *der,* or whether his wife had been mistaken (she, presumably, must have been vexing him on the matter in the course of the two intervening months). Passion derives from a love of life, but also stimulates it, and thus, spurred by his annoyance over a mistake in grammar and his strong desire to correct it, the Professor had refound his strength, had got up from his bed, and re-made contact with a little of his forest, his world and his life.

Correctness in language is a precondition for moral clarity and honesty. As Karl Kraus, the apocalyptic Viennese writer, never tired of saying, dishonesty and breaches of trust are the inevitable result when people start playing with grammar and syntax, putting the subject in the accusative or the object in the nominative, shuffling the cards and switching roles between victims and guilty parties, altering the order of things and attributing events to causes or motivators that are different from their actual ones, abolishing distinctions and hierarchies and producing instead a misleading jumble of concepts and sentiments that deform the truth.

Language is a grating placed over the subterranean discharges of the irrational, and our so-precarious life depends on it almost in its entirety. For this reason, even a single comma in the wrong place is capable of bringing about disasters, sparking fires that may destroy the forests of the Earth. But the Professor's story seems to say that, by respecting language, or rather truth, life is also made more substantial, one stands a little more firmly on one's feet, and one is better able to take a short walk to enjoy the world, with that sensual love of life which is all the more relaxed when it is free from the entanglements of self-deception and deceit. Who can say how many things, how much pleasure and delight, we owe, without realising it, to the corrections of our teachers' red pens when we were at school?

© *Claudio Magris.* © *Translated by Ed Emery*

## JULIAN BARNES

# Hamlet in the Wild West

A few years after the end of the American Civil War an English theatrical troupe arrived in a small town in western Missouri. It was the sort of town where most people had two occupations: the saloon-keeper ran the stables, the sheriff was also the gunsmith, while the schoolteacher accepted travelling gentlemen as paying guests, provided they were clean and generous. This would have made the English actors feel at home. Being themselves few in number, they were constantly obliged to double up their parts: no sooner had a villain been shot than he had to reappear as the priest and bury himself. Whether they were playing comedy, melodrama or tragedy, the actors found themselves changing costumes and accents as often as if they were in a French farce.

On the night of my story, the English troupe was due to play *Hamlet*. This always caused an extra strain, since on the Atlantic crossing their *jeune première*, their Ophelia, had been courted by the ship's captain, who told her such terrifying stories of the American mid-West that she immediately accepted his proposal of marriage. The captain exercised his traditional maritime right to conduct a wedding ceremony, and so on this occasion he too doubled up, as civilian authority and bridegroom. The other members of the troupe stood around the captain's cabin doubling up their emotions: they all pretended, and some felt, true happiness for the young actress, but were at the same time extremely annoyed that Ophelia would now have to be played by one of two fifty-year-old sisters.

However, the farther they got from New York, the less it mattered, since few of their audience had ever seen *Hamlet* before, and many had never been to the theatre. Everything therefore seemed both miraculously strange and absolutely normal: Shakespeare's language, the extravagant costumes, the non-existent scenery. So was the fact that the play lasted no more than an hour and had been reduced to its key scenes: the ghost of Hamlet's father, the murder of Polonius, the madness of a middle-aged Ophelia, the plotting of Claudius, the gravedigger scene, and the final duel.

The theatre in that Missouri town was much like this theatre, except that by day it was a drinking saloon; the seats were like your seats, except that they were uncomfortable and insufficient in number; the audience was like you, except that some of them wore guns, and none of them knew the plot of *Hamlet*. After three months on the road, the English actors had learned which sections of the play to emphasise, which to slow down, which to eliminate. They had also got used to the fact that the audience constantly voiced their reactions to the play, like a modern family around a television set. Even in its simplified form — tragedy thinned to melodrama — the story of Hamlet still excited and enraged the audience, made them tender and made them sad. The ghost of Hamlet's father walking headless while carrying his own skull in his hand was always a great success; the killing of Polonius behind the curtain moved some to shout at the injustice, others to laugh raucously. The refusal of Hamlet to kill Claudius while the king was praying was approved by most, yet baffled some. And the final sword-fight and massacre always brought a climax of shouting, encouragement, protest and dismay.

It was a hot night in the saloon, and the audience was even more rapt and vocal than usual. The account of Ophelia's death was heard in tranced silence, the plotting of Claudius with even more disapproval than usual. Claudius made an extravagant display of poisoning the tip of Laertes's sword, and with great gestures of evil played up to the hissing from the audience. The sword-fight began, and reached the moment when Hamlet was about to receive his fatal injury. Laertes was poised, his poisoned sword aloft, and just about to slash at the defenceless prince, when a cowboy in the audience rose to his feet and shot Laertes dead. Whereupon the cowboy siting next to him got up, loudly protested that his friend had plugged the wrong villain, and shot Claudius dead as the king lolled on his throne.

The sheriff, who was also the gunsmith, disarmed the two cowboys, and the surgeon was called. It was fortunate for the English actors that pistols at this time were much less accurate than they subsequently became in Hollywood. So once things had calmed down, Laertes, who had been lying dead for several minutes, opened one eye and climbed to his feet. Claudius also returned from the dead, although he had received a

flesh wound in the upper arm which required cauterising and bandaging by the surgeon. In subsequent performances Claudius turned this to his advantage, playing the king as an old soldier still troubled by a war wound.

Justice being swift in that time, the trial of five men took place the following day. The two cowboys were charged with attempted murder and causing an affray; while three actors — Claudius, Laertes, and even Hamlet himself— were charged with inciting an affray. The five men sat in the dock guarded by the sheriff, who was also the gunsmith. Evidence was heard that the cowboys had been completely sober the night before; that they had never previously seen a play; and that they honestly believed themselves to be defending Hamlet's life. Witnesses declared them to be of previously good character. The other three defendants, being actors, were presumed to be of previously bad character.

The judge, who was also the surgeon, was a veteran of the American Civil War. He was a wise man who did not consult his law books very often. He knew that justice is often best achieved by a leap of the imagination rather than by the dogged rivalry of fact. He also understood the duality of human nature. He knew that our friends may become our enemies, but that the logical counterpart of this is that our enemies may in time become our friends, and that this is our only hope as a race. His judgment, there, did not strictly accord with the state law of the territory of Missouri. He found the two cowboys not guilty of attempting to murder Claudius and Laertes on the grounds that, Claudius and Laertes being figments of the imagination, they could not be murdered except by other figments of the imagination. On the charge of causing an affray, he found the cowboys guilty: they were ordered to be run out of town, and once out of town, to be brought back and rewarded out of municipal funds for their public-spirited behaviour. Hamlet, Claudius and Laertes were all found guilty of inciting an affray: they were first to be rewarded out of municipal funds for their self-restraint in not fighting back when shot, and then punished by being run out of town in the direction of their next engagement.

The judge, who was also the surgeon, believed in the maxim that justice must not only be done, but also be seen to be done. He therefore had not just a second but also a third occupation, as proprietor of the local newspaper, which the following day came out with a special edition. The crime correspondent, who just for that issue was doubling as the theatrical critic, recounted as if he had been present the events of the previous twenty-four hours, offering special praise for the skill of the surgeon and the wisdom of the judge. Before being run out of town, the English actors brought several copies of that newspaper. Hamlet was my great-great-grandfather, which is how I am able to tell you this story tonight.

© *Julian Barnes*

## BORA COSIC

# Reading Hamsun

Recently, travelling through Italy, I noticed that I aroused the suspicions of my Italian companions simply because I happened to be holding a strange book in my hand. Where, asked my Italian friends, did I get the idea of choosing this moment to read Hamsun's old book, which may have lost its relevance? I tell them it hasn't and explain, imprudently, that it is about human hunger as a universal phenomenon. My companions, however, do not understand my theme, and take me to the Campo dei Fiori, a marketplace overflowing in every respect, where flowers, as well as edibles, have been sold for centuries.

Loath to explain any further, I nonetheless today diligently record my hunger for this book, which had been left behind on the bookshelf of my one-time home, and note how I finally sent for my old book through a valued hand. I always irritate my companions by reading some sort of book when I travel, especially as it hardly ever has anything to do with my trip. I must be a particularly contrary kind of person because I see every phenomenon in a highly distorted way, and such people should probably never travel; indeed it would be best for them and for others if they simply stayed at home. Only I don't exactly know where my home is and where this staying at home could be done.

Although I thought I knew what I would find in my old book, which I read so long ago, I must say I did not know. It was a sort of intuition that had drawn me to its title, *Sult* (Hunger), a title which in itself aroused not unfamiliar impulses. Now, at last, I am reading this tale of hunger in the city of Christiania, at the end of the last century, but in it I find instances experienced by a friend of mine in besieged Sarajevo. The hero of the book I am reading picks up a splinter of wood in the street and begins sucking it, just to have something in his mouth. Again I say that apart from the theme of hunger, there are also other things in the book which have nothing to do with this basic theme. And then I say that my friend who came from the siege talks hardly at all about the hunger there but, strangely enough, just like Hamsun, does talk about all sorts of other things. About how people go from house to house as though they had work waiting for them in these houses, whereas they have nothing to do and no one to see there. In any town there's always this problem of not knowing what we are going to do at any given moment, but then a quintessential situation arises when all these questions about the incomprehensibility of life come to a head. So my friend talks about chores in her besieged city which would never occur to people in normal times, and yet she says madness is not the norm. This, then, is a story about people who would have every right to be crazy but, despite everything, are not. Madness somehow turns out to be the advantage of relatively happy people who live in normal circumstances, but when the circumstances themselves go mad, then all one has left is one's normality. My friend, who came out of besieged Sarajevo, made a guide for life in Sarajevo out of all this, just the way Michelin has its own guidebooks for many cities. In my madness I am now combining her Survival Guide-Sarajevo with Hamsun's book *Sult,* which I am reading. I want to find out what has happened to those small, everyday objects my friend left behind in her Sarajevo house, but then I realise I am asking the question of someone who has left everything he had in a pawnshop, forever. 'The actor Magelsen,' says our old story-writer, 'has my watch, an acquaintance bought the calendar in which my first attempts at poetry were printed, my cloak fell into the hands of a photographer. 'Nothing was lost, it had all merely

changed owners, conclusively. I tell this to my friends in Italy and they say these are terrible things, terrible. But, they say, why am I worrying my head over them when I am here, on safe ground, and when I don't want for the essentials of life? They say I am a real European gentleman and that perhaps such people should not have to dwell on these terrible matters. But I tell them that my known and unknown compatriots in a city under siege are also mostly European gentlefolk, only they have been forced to pawn the things and objects that could bear witness to Europe, to pawn them in a planetary pawnshop. And I tell them that there is not a city, European or otherwise, which could not find its finest details being swallowed up by such a pawnshop. Let them ponder that now, as they question me in Rome about my genteelness. Then, giving the book I am reading no peace, they proceed to ask me whether Hamsun is the writer who was condemned for treason by his own kin, and I say he is, and that, actually, he hadn't committed treason but rather had had in his head a treasonous idea, to wit that a foreign kin, that of the occupier, seemed to him more important than his own. Because of this he suffered vilification and condemnation from his own kin, and readers returned his books, including the one I am now holding, in droves. However, I too am despised and ostracised by my own kin, although I have not spoken out in favour of any foreign power, I simply think that my one-time tribe has subjugated itself and is thus keeping itself under some sort of self-occupation. Any country threatened with conquest hides some of its knowledge and values, so as to have them at hand later on. Only I don't know where such a country can hide its spiritual values if its own people have their minds set on conquering it and on holding it under such counter-spiritual conquest at length. Well, if that's the way things are, say my friends, then why not let such a people live in their self-occupation, and I say that is what I am doing. I am letting them live under their own occupation, except that I have removed myself from such self-occupation forever.

Now it is perhaps easier to understand why here in Rome I am reading my Hamsun, secretly delighting in his treason.

© *Bora Cosic*
© *Translated by Christina Pribichevich-Zoric*

ZORAN FILIPOVIC

# A season of hell

**Nothing has changed in Sarajevo...**

Hell is, by definition, a general place of *evil* where God sends the souls of those who have during their lives sinned so terribly and incorrigibly that there is for their sins neither forgiveness nor remedy. In that place their souls 'live' in eternal pain, making hard and unforgiving amends for the hard and unforgivable sins committed during the short life of man upon the earth. Sins that during their commission were limited and definitive in time, even if, sometimes, they lasted the whole of someone's life, are expiated in a time that is limitless, endless, definitive only in the knowledge of its existence in eternity. This place lies *somewhere* in the reign of eternal fire and where the souls of the condemned cry for *death* because it is so dreadful, so dreadful that it cannot be imagined, let alone described, and death seems to be the only escape from this hell, and yet there is neither death nor any other way out, because you only die once, and this hell is for *eternity*.

Sarajevo is a place of general evil. In Sarajevo there is no time. In Sarajevo there is no yesterday, in Sarajevo there is no tomorrow. In Sarajevo there is only now, a dreadful and remorseless now. To eat now, now to warm oneself, now to find and fetch water.... Until when?

It is hard to get to Sarajevo. The preparations for departure are filigree painstaking and lengthy, or the decision is made in an instant, come what may. One doesn't go there without a deal of trouble, without a dreadful and enormous need to be just there. Sarajevo is where you leave. Sarajevo is what you escape from. Departure or flight, the preparations are long and painstaking, anxious. Departure is discussed, openly or secretly, it is gone into, whether legally or conspiratorially, it is what is fantasised, dreamed of. Everyone wants to get out of Sarajevo. And those who say they would not want to, that they would rather stay, and they would too. These most of all. Leave. Disappear. For ever.

Sarajevo is a trap. Completely surrounded by chetniks, exposed to the mercy of the double, triple, quadruple enemy encirclement, of his infantry and his still more deadly and unpredictable artillery that fires indiscriminately, from time to time, and always scores a direct hit, because whatever they hit is a direct hit. Every shell fired from above, from the hills, means at least one life less below, in the city, and one place more in a shallow grave hurriedly scraped out of the stadium, a park or a car park, where people are now being buried because there has long, long since been not enough room in the cemeteries. They are buried in a hurry, with little groups that follow the killed (natural death has long since been a rarity) with no large gestures, without tears or mourning. The dry grey faces, a couple of them, the closest relatives, a shallow grave and the clay that sticks to the soles of your shoes, everyone throws a few clods of earth, a bunch of dried or perhaps even plastic flowers, and the simple marking that is knocked in above the heads: name, surname, year of birth and year of death, the grave-diggers with their shovels wipe the sweat from their foreheads while they throw in the soil, wipe it with their sleeves, there is little time, they don't talk, they don't rest. When they have finished that, they step aside, and say: 'Next.' They say it curtly and the spade is already throwing earth into some other, new grave, and some new, other group of people are saying farewell to their loved ones. Sarajevo is a trap. In Sarajevo there is nowhere to hide or take cover. Whichever part of the town you are in, or whatever street you are walking down, along whichever side, it is always the same. The probability that a shell will fall just here and that you will be the next victim is always the same. There is no rule. No good advice. There is no time of day when you can say: 'They have never shot at this time before!' They are always shooting. By night. During the day. In the morning. The streets are always full. During the day. People, looking for food and firewood. Waiting in queues for bread, and water. When a shell falls in such a place, it creates utter carnage, as it did then in Vasa Miskin Street, or not long ago at the brewery, where people were standing in line for water. This makes everyone in the city the same, equal. At night, when dark covers the city

> **Sarajevo is a trap. In Sarajevo there is nowhere to hide or take cover. Which ever part of town you are in, it is always the same**

and everything vanishes in the blackness, people desert the streets, the city empties. Only a few people, who needs must be bold, dare to walk at night. The night swallows things up. People disappear. Then the city is covered by the headlights of crazily hurrying cars. They drive murderously. Suicidally. On every one of them you can see some sign: Police, Military Police, Special Police. They are all some kind of police. Everyone who has money for fuel (7 marks a litre) or has some power or authority, drives auto-police.

Sometimes the fog comes down, and it's thick and heavy, and it lasts for days. The visibility is bad during the day, but hopeless at night. Torch-light, switched on in brief bursts, is almost no help. But just in case. The fog is so thick it pinches and saws at your throat. Then you have to go haphazardly, by memory. It happens that sometimes you get your legs caught in the downed cables of the tram-lines. One night I could feel blood on my shoes. Don't ask how and why I knew, I just knew, I could feel I was walking in blood. When I switched on the lamp, there was a great frozen puddle. The streets were still covered in snow, which was firm and frozen in other parts. In this place the snow was red and tacky. There were a couple of such puddles along this part of the pavement. It was in front of the Presidency building. That day a shell had fallen here and killed six people. Two sentries guarding the building had had their legs taken off with shell fragments.

On Sundays there is mass. Mass at 11 in the chapel of Catholic Theology. The chapel is full. People in uniform. HVO. Special police. Civilians. All believers. The clergy say it's like that at all masses, in the Cathedral and at the Franciscans. One Friday I went to a mosque, in Vase Miskin, not far from the Cathedral. At noon, prayers. At the entrance, the Imam asks me where I am from, he can see I am a stranger. I say, from Zagreb. One of us, he says, welcome. And the mosque is full, and there are uniforms there too. The army of B and H. Civilians. It is unbelievers who are shooting at us, we say later. If those up there on the hills were believers, they would not do that, they wouldn't shoot at us. No. A believer would not do it. They are pagans. Sarajevo is a trap. In Sarajevo, there are still living some hungry, frozen, dirty missed people, those whom shells and snipers have somehow missed or passed by. Counted according to our peacetime calendar, it has already lasted ten months. In their time, it is a question of years. With one blast everything has gone, your family, possessions and memories. Yesterday, they had everything. Today, everything has gone. Even time has gone. Only the now is left. A dreadful, anxious, everyday now. The birds that left the town in the autumn won't know their way back in the spring. They won't recognise it, and will continue straight on in some other direction. Those that get here all the same won't have anywhere to come to. The roofs they would have alighted on will not exist any more, the trees they would have lived in will have gone. There are only people and ruins and their terrible fate, with their now. Until when?

*Sarajevo-Zagreb, February 1993*

© *Excerpt from* A Season of Hell *(1994) First English translation*

It is four weeks now since I went to Sarajevo, God-knows-for-the-nth-time, and a full three weeks since I left Sarajevo God-knows-for-the-nth-time. Only this time the reason for my departure from the 'darkness' was different. I went to give back to Sarajevo whatever I had taken from it during my previous stays in 1992 and 1993. After more than six months of attempts and preparations, I managed to transport and prepare my exhibition, 'A Season of Hell', at the Art Gallery BiH. A moving meeting at the exhibition with the subjects of my photographic essay. Unusually crowded opening. Monsignor Vinko Puljic — the Archbishop Bosanski and Mrs Azra Begic open the exhibition. Moving speech, beautiful words. While they speak, I wonder whether I have deserved them. It is difficult to bear these beautiful words with so many eyes watching, knowing that every one in the audience deserves respect at least twice as large as this.

It is difficult to bear this Sarajevo, different from all the previous times. Like a Satyr's mask, from the windows of shops previously ravaged, rows of bananas, pineapples and kiwis leer at me... The shelves are filled with delicatessen from France, England,... beer from Austria, Holland, Denmark,... wine from Spain,... fashion accessories from Italy, shoes and clothing for all sizes and genders... The prices are lower than anywhere on this planet. Like a fairy tale. Like a dream, a nightmare. Sarajevo is living through its phase between war and — war?! Friends take me round town, saying: look at this, look at that,... I moonwalk behind them thinking, heretically; the war was better,.. The war was more truthful. What happens when the magic passes, when it stops and people wake up, or even worse, when those up on the hills wake up and everything starts again: the same hunger, the same cold, the same poverty and misery. What will happen? And even now, all this abundance, on the stalls and in the shops, who can afford it? Who has the money to buy anything? It was different before, the same for everybody: bad. And they all dreamt about the same things. These dreams are further than ever now, because they are at arm's length. It's impossible even to dream about it any more, because it just passes by in front of your eyes: like a guilty conscience. It is difficult when a person loses the capacity to dream as well, the last escape from brutal reality. This abundance is the abundance of the privileged.

My friends are taking me further, still showing me things. Look, they say, the tram is running! Yes, a moving target, I think, I do not want to spoil their joy, I know it will not last. Yes, I say aloud, nice. You see how it's all good now, how everything is better, they say — happy. Yes, I say, softly, hardly managing to open my mouth, while inside I am screaming... Enough! Enough! Nothing is good! Nothing is better! It's worse! Everything is worse — because it looks better!

Sarajevo is a trap. Sarajevo is a cage. Sarajevans cannot leave Sarajevo, nor enter it. Sarajevo is a golden cage. Now. Other people come to be photographed in Sarajevo. Anyone who cares about his image comes to have his photograph taken in Sarajevo. Statesmen, writers, philosophers, singers, jongleurs, circus people... Afterwards, they go home, to their friends, their governments and states. They hold press conferences, give interviews and say: 'You know, I was in Sarajevo', handing out their photographs: the people are impressed. Overnight they have become heroes of the media, who still haven't managed to get to those mythical places, but watch them, with envy, thinking: 'I will have my picture taken in Sarajevo, one day.'
**Sarajevo, August 1994**

*Translated by Vanessa Vasic.*

# Sarajevo: A season of hell

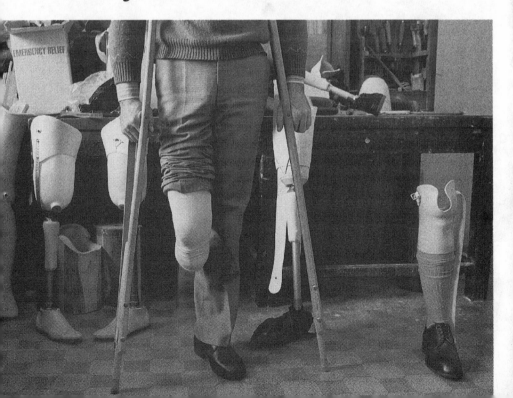

All photos by Zoran Filipovic, from A Season of Hell (1994)

# BOGDAN BOGDANOVIC

# Defending the city

## A letter to my Sarajevo friends

Entering my eighth decade plagued by nightmares of fire and blood, racked by mute but unrelenting pangs of conscience, agonised conscience, I find myself returning, for the last time perhaps, to the ideas of my youth, ideas I shall discuss in terms I have tended to overstate, in terms of the interplay between the essence of the city and the fate of the city. But going over what I once thought, concluded and deposited in the vain theoretical vaults of peace-time urban studies, I find it has taken on a new meaning; it throws new light on the issues it originally treated while relating to the unforeseen horrors of today.

I have thought a great deal — spoken, written, lectured and preached a great deal — about the mysterious 'essence and fate of the city', firm in the conviction that my students and I stood on the safe — that is, verbal — side of the concepts and categories involved. It never occurred to me I would live to see the fate of cities so dear to me subjected to outrages that our coddled theory never came close to predicting, let alone describing.

To be perfectly frank, my lectures were often charged with the kind of overwrought emotion professors bring to their pet themes and theses from the lectern, and there was no hypothesis too bleak for my students and me when it came to the fate of a city or of cities, European and worldwide, that is, of the new megalopolis. Catastrophic projections of world and urban blight were in fashion, and the dire forecasts had a kind of aesthetic titillation about them. A millenarian spirit plus a belief in the 'decline of the West' doomed the city — the universal city, Panurbium, so to speak. Emotionally charged metaphors like 'the extinction of the city' and 'the demise of the city' warned of the consequences of insidious growth, invidious wealth, the anonymous concentration of power.

Again I admit that I too entered into the spirit of things. Juxtaposing *urbs* and *logos,* I sought analogies between a decadent Rome and the gloomy perspectives of the modern *urbs* (by which I meant urban civilization as a whole). My texts depicted the cataclysm to come in cosmic proportions: the city exploding like the cosmos. Why not? The simile was tempting. 'We cannot help noting a certain parallel between the cosmos fleeting into muddled images beyond the reach of our senses and cities disintegrating like cosmic mist before our very eyes... The main reason our classical ancestors could draw sophistic analogies between the image of the world and the image of the city was that they saw a whole. I cannot see a whole. The only order I can perceive — the only order that is not perhaps entirely arbitrary — is the obvious similarity of two rent images' (*The City as a Symbol of Immortality and the Death of the City*, 1972).

Of course I was thinking in terms too emblematic, too allegorical: I was thinking in terms of the urban population explosion and afflictions of the megapolis. I never dreamed I would actually see the 'rent images', be forced to see them on my odious television screen; I never dreamed I would see cities once so close to me that I felt them somehow an integral part of my being — I never dreamed I would see them yielded up to the frightful technology of cold-blooded, virtually ritual massacre.

But there is something else in both my own 'cosmic catastrophical' ruminations and those of others that calls the value of what I have termed the coddled theory of peace-time urban studies into question, something that deeply disturbs me and forces me to re-examine everything I have written. Is it possible that somewhere beneath the surface, beneath all my chiliastic speculations, I had an inkling of horrors neither cosmic nor ecologic nor ecumenic but of a diabolically home-grown variety? Could I have somewhere deep down known that I knew what was awaiting us without wanting or daring to know?

How close to the truth I was in my obsessive hypotheses about the conflict between city builders and city destroyers, between urbiphilic and urbiphobic impulses in all periods, all peoples, all clans and hordes and ethnic groups, in each and every individual! How close I was to the truth — and how far!

Why, for instance, did I fail to note the hard boiled, self-indulgent city destroyers in our very midst? Only now, face to face with the horrors they have perpetrated, do I realise that these criminals — the men who scourged and ravaged Jericho, Sodom, Gomorrah and Troy, purging them in the name of ethnic and any and every purity, in the name of the supposed superiority of matter over spirit — that these criminals are not simply urbanological hypotheses.

Terrifying models for such crimes occur in classical texts, but now the criminals — savage, bestial men with names and nicknames people purposefully forget — are performing them before our very eyes, leaving behind the skeletons of Vukovar, Mostar, and, most recently, half of Sarajevo as well. What is next? Pristina, Novi Pazar, Skopje? Subotica and Novi Sad?

Interpreting my early urbanological texts today is like interpreting nightmares. If warnings there were, I paid them no heed: they must have been too deep in my subconscious, too disturbing. But this is no time to dredge up vague premonitions. Savage, bestial city destroyers with no conscience are hard at work gutting, sacking, murdering the population, burning archives and libraries, demolishing museums and houses of worship.

What does it mean to 'murder a city'? It means to snuff out its strength, stifle its metaphysical eros, its will to live, its sense of self; its means of scattering its memory to the winds, annihilating its past along with its present...

... What I would call the 'holy essence of the city' stems from the best in human nature, from moral beauty. 'We all still carry our immortal cities inside ourselves,' I wrote some twenty years ago... Of course you must have a city and have pride in it if you are to carry it inside yourself, and there are cities that cannot be murdered as long as a single urban being survives in them and carries it everywhere.

Which is why — my dear, hungry, wounded, much esteemed and much tormented friends — I admire you so and am with you as much as I can be in my old age, I am with you in your troubled, sleepless nights. Defending the city is the only valid moral paradigm for the future. It is a light that even the most humanitarian of humans — as much understanding as they may have for the rift between nature and man and the plight of endangered flora and fauna — are as yet unable to see, unable to understand.

The Mosque in Córdoba, Spain: the glory of Islam in Europe

## ABDULLAHI AN-NA'IM

# What do we mean by universal?

**Any concept of human rights that is to be universally accepted and globally enforced demands equal respect and mutual comprehension between rival cultures**

Human rights ought, by definition, to be universal in concept, scope and content as well as in application: a globally accepted set of rights or claims to which all human beings are entitled by virtue of their humanity and without distinction on grounds such as race, gender or religion. Yet there can be no prospect of the universal application of such rights unless there is, at least, substantial agreement on their concept, scope and content.

What is at issue — between those who support a universal concept and those who argue for a relativist approach — is how and by whom these rights are to be defined and articulated. Universality requires global agreement, a consensus between different societies and cultures, not the application of one set of standards derived from the culture and context of a particular society to all other societies. The normative system in one society may not necessarily be appropriate for other societies who need to elaborate their own systems based on their particular cultural context.

Hence the paradox in which the international human rights movement is presently caught: the concept and essential characteristics of currently accepted international standards on 'universal' human rights have been primarily conceived, developed and established by the West; they cannot be accepted and implemented globally by the peoples of other parts of the world unless they are seen to be valid and legitimate from their perspectives. If they are to be more widely accepted and implemented, they must be premised on a genuinely universal model rather than the universalisation of a certain culturally specific, 'Western', model. To attempt to deny or disguise the dilemma only plays into the hands of those who may wish to manipulate it and undermines the credibility of those who attempt to uphold the contested human rights norms by making them appear to reject what their own constituency sees as obvious and important.

The paradox can only be resolved by first acknowledging the historical facts and then by arguing that although the universal validity of these standards cannot be assumed or taken for granted, they are not necessarily or inherently invalid from the perspective of other cultures. The question of whether and to what extent there is fundamental and irreconcilable difference between a particular international human rights standard and the norms, values and institutions of any other culture, can then be debated internally and across cultures.

All cultures have an element of ambivalence and contestability in the sense that prevailing practices and institutions are open to constant challenge and change. Not only is this essential for the survival of the culture as a whole, it provides a range of debatable options, any one of which may prevail at a particular time. While a particular interpretation or perception of certain cultural norms and institutions may appear to be in fundamental conflict with existing international human rights standards, this does not make it impossible to articulate an alternative interpretation which may begin to resolve the conflict.

If dialogue is to broaden and deepen global consensus it must be undertaken in good faith, with mutual respect for, and sensitivity to, the integrity and fundamental concerns of respective cultures, with an open mind and with the recognition that existing formulations may be changed — or even abolished — in the process. Ideally, participants should feel on an equal footing but, given existing power relations, those in a position to do so might seek ways of redressing the imbalance.

Where the Islamic world is concerned it is important to appreciate the profoundly defensive and reactive mode of internal discourse and cross-cultural exchange. Following the failure of secular liberalism or national socialism in the post-independence era, Muslims are now channelling their frustration and powerlessness into radical and militant Islamic revivalism as an assertion of their right to self-determination. The insistence on one universally valid set of human rights, therefore, risks the sort of confrontation we have seen in the Rushdie affair and forces debate under the worst possible circumstances.

The value and validity of a given concept of human rights is neither necessarily diminished nor validated by the fact that it is historically or geographically specific. It may well be that the 'democratic way of life' which presupposes the existence and acceptance of a certain concept of individual human rights is superior to other forms of political life. However, there are many parts of the world in which Western conceptions of democracy and human rights have not taken root. Instead of simply asserting the inherent superiority of those conceptions in the abstract, it would be more constructive to examine the reasons for this failure in regions that might be more receptive to their own equivalent or corresponding concepts.

Individual civil and political rights are integral to fundamental human rights, as are economic and social rights and collective rights to development and self-determination. Support for this holistic and interdependent concept of human rights includes efforts to promote their legitimacy in all cultures of the world as well as the need to protest their violation by exerting pressure on offending governments to respect them.

The present dynamics of the international protection of human rights operates primarily through the monitoring by Northern organisations of violations in the South in order to lobby Northern governments to pressure Southern governments to respect the human rights of their own populations. A truly universalist dynamic of protection would rely on monitoring and advocacy by local constituencies within the South, such as those that exist in the North, as well as in both directions across the North-South divide. I am not suggesting the abandonment of international monitoring and advocacy as we know it today, but rather seeking to enhance its genuinely global nature by multiplying and diversifying its centres and axes through rooting and legitimating it in the cultures and experiences of all peoples.

Given general agreement that freedom of expression can be limited, by law, to protect the rights of others, we must then ask, which rights, when and how? Who is to articulate and enforce such limits, to what end and on what basis? Since I purport to present an 'Islamic' perspective, the basis and nature of claims of Islamicity is the key to the present discussion. Not only do such claims determine the conceptual framework which informs and conditions responses to the sort of questions raised here, they are the criteria by which others, whether insiders or outsiders, can understand and evaluate the substance, content and implications of the claim.

Religion is not excluded from the ambivalence and contestability that characterise all cultures. Even when a religion is, like Islam, believed to be founded on divine scripture and the traditions of the Prophet and other significant communities or personalities, the human interpretation of those sources remains significant. Given unavoidable differences in interpretation of textual sources in historical context, what the religion is believed to be at any given point in time, or to say on any specific matter, is the product of competing human perceptions and prevailing socio-economic factors and forces that have become the prevailing view.

To believers, Islam is primarily and essentially defined by the Quran and Sunna of the Prophet, but, historically, the interpretation and application of these has always been conditioned by the understanding of the Muslim community at any given time or place. While the traditions of early Muslim communities are believed to be authoritative, those who subsequently seek to invoke this authority are themselves similarly conditioned. What Islam means or says on any given matter is therefore what the Muslims of the time and place believe it to be. There is no

ALBERTO TESSORE: CAMERA PRESS

Senegal: the community will decide

other way for any religion, to have relevance to the lives of believers.

The dominance of a particular theological interpretation at any time is determined by a variety of factors. Historians may debate the relevance or relative significance of one factor or another, or speculate about the possibility of alternative results given a different set of factors, but the existence and nature of the process itself is beyond dispute.

During the second and third centuries of Islamic history, for example, there was a major debate between the so-called textualists and rationalists *(Ash'ariya* and *Mu'tazila)* on some fundamental issues of theology and politics which ended with the dominance of the former and suppression of the latter. One may debate why one view prevailed, or what might have happened under different circumstances, but the facts of the debate and its outcome are accepted by all historians of Islam. It is also clear that, although the *Mu'tazila* may not subsequently have won the day, elements of their approach and thought have survived and continue to be reflected in internal Muslim debates to the present day.

Whichever group or position a modern Muslim may support in that debate, the need to protect the freedom of expression which allows this sort of debate to take place cannot be denied. The same is true for any set of competing views in the past, present or future of Islamic experience. It is equally true that the winning side would want to curtail the freedom of expression of its opponents in the name of protecting and preserving the integrity of tradition and the stability of religious doctrine.

But since it is the totality of the community of Muslims of the time and place who have the legitimate right to decide which conception of the tradition is to be protected and preserved, and which religious doctrine should be maintained, freedom of expression remains of paramount importance. This conclusion does not yield definitive answers to the questions above — who is to articulate and enforce its limits, to what end and on what basis — but it does provide a clear presumption and orientation in favour of wider freedom of expression, and generally indicates by whom and how limitations may be set in practice.

This may sound exactly like a liberal justification of freedom of expression, but that does not make it necessarily non-Islamic. It is fully and coherently Islamic by virtue of its frame of reference, theological rationale and historical substantiation. This is perhaps the sort of overlapping consensus suggested by Jacques Maritain in a 1949 UNESCO study on the bases of an International Bill of Human Rights whereby different cultures come to a common understanding of the concept and its content, despite their disagreement on its justification.

The issue is not whether Islamic cultures, or any other cultures, are either inherently restrictive or tolerant of relatively greater freedom of expression. Such orientations tend to change over time. Neither is it a matter of citing textual sources or historical experiences as 'evidence' of greater or lesser 'Islamic' restriction or tolerance since texts are open to competing interpretations and historical experiences are susceptible to shifting characterisations. Reading the Quran and Sunna, one will find authority for liberalism as well as conservatism, and Muslim history gives clear examples of both tendencies. The matter is determined by the choices Muslims make, and the struggle they wage in favour of their choices, in their own historical context.

Secularism came to the Islamic world in the suspect company of colonialism, and is often confused with a particular experience of Western Christianity. Most Muslims believe there is a strong, organic link between Islam and politics since several verses of the Quran clearly instruct them to implement its dictates in their public as well as private affairs. The Quran and Sunna of the Prophet are also explicit in requiring

Muslim communities to enforce certain principles regarding taxation, commercial and financial dealings, penal sanctions and so forth.

Although Muslims have in fact lived under varying degrees of secularism for most of their history, the ideal of an Islamic state in full accordance with the *sharia* (Islamic law) has always been kept, even invoked, by secular rulers to legitimise their power. Nevertheless, if confronted today with a categorical and immediate choice between an Islamic *sharia* state and an openly and unequivocally secular state that relegates *sharia* to the purely personal and private domain, most Muslims would probably opt for the former since most find it extremely difficult openly to oppose the application of *sharia* in public affairs.

Without ruling out the possibility altogether, it seems highly improbable, given the present predilection for majority rule and self determination, that a strictly secular state could be sustained in the Islamic world today, at least in countries with an overwhelming Muslim majority. Whatever degree of secularism earlier authoritarian rulers like Ataturk of Turkey or Bourguiba of Tunisia were able to construct, the prospects of open secularism appear to be diminishing: the failure of post-independence secularism and nationalism gave Islamic fundamentalism its impetus. Using the tools of 'modern' political organisation, international finance and the technology of mass communication, Islamic fundamentalism is now confronting an increasing number of Muslims with a stark choice between the 'divine' law of God and the 'anti-religious' law of man.

In the present context, I see more hope in trying to expose the fallacy of that formulation and in constructing an alternative modern version of *sharia* based on a radical reinterpretation of Islamic sources — something I have tried to do in my book *Toward an Islamic Reformation* — than in openly arguing for Western secularism. *Sharia* is neither as divine as its advocates claim nor secularism as anti-religious as its opponents allege. Should that exercise fail, even on its own terms, it might still make a useful contribution to the development of a modernist Islamic moral philosophy fully consistent with the concepts and principles of constitutionalism and universal human rights. A modern Islamic moral philosophy is unlikely to achieve its desired objectives, however, unless it succeeds in fulfilling the dual function of presenting Muslims with a justification for setting *sharia* aside and providing them with sound foundations for a political and legal order they can accept as Islamic.

## The Rushdie affair in perspective

While I would maintain that the West has not overreacted to the *fatwa* on Salman Rushdie as a result of its own prejudices, I cannnot agree that the Muslim response is the act of a small minority of Shia fundamentalists. The Western reaction to a serious challenge to what most people around the world, Muslims and non-Muslims alike, hold to be fundamental and universal human rights is perfectly normal. And even though few non-Shia Muslims have spoken out in condemnation of the *fatwa*, the Shia response is shared by many Sunni Muslims.

The model can also operate through an alternative scenario whereby Islamic fundamentalism seizes power in a number of Islamic countries, is seen to have failed, and is replaced by a renewed drive for open secularism legitimised by a reconstruction of Islamic moral philosophy. I am convinced, however, that moral rights cannot be 'constitutionalised' in Islamic countries without some form of religious legitimacy.

Muslim responsibility goes much wider. Formalistic objections to the *fatwa* should not be allowed to hide the fact that its underlying justification in the *sharia* has not been challenged even by Muslims who would oppose this use of apostasy for procedural reasons. At the same time, simplistic condemnations of the Muslim failure to uphold universal norms of freedom of expression are equally inadequate and unlikely to succeed in mediating and resolving the issues.

The ultimate importance of the Rushdie affair is that it confronts the proponents of both sides with a serious challenge to their convictions. It casts individual freedom of belief and expression in global terms because of totally novel circumstances in human history. Whereas such issues have always been debated, mediated and resolved in relative privacy within relatively homogenous settings, they are now cast, and demand resolution, at a global, public and publicised level. This is happening at a time when global power relations are shifting away from gunboat diplomacy and the more recent superpower rivalries towards attempts to resolve conflict by mediation.

In this global and public confrontation, Muslims are required openly either to defend their belief in the validity of the *sharia* law of apostasy and its wider implications for freedom of belief and expression, or uphold the latter and thereby concede the invalidity of a law they believe to be divine. The 'Rushdie Defence Committees' and their constituencies, in turn, face the challenge of how to achieve their objective without frustrating the universality of human rights to which they claim allegiance.

I began with a discussion of relativity and universality, emphasising the need for discourse and dialogue to promote a global culture of human rights and break the current dependency of the South on Northern initiatives, priorities and resources. The course of the international advocacy of human rights will never be secure and consistent with its own rationale as long as 'Rushdie Defence Committees' are only set up in the North to pressure governments in the South.

There are potentially powerful and vigorous constituencies for universal human rights worldwide — including the Islamic world. But those constituencies can never be mobilised in a global project on purely Western liberal notions of individual civil and political rights. Along with other rights and new formulations of familiar rights, all human rights will only command genuine universal respect and validity through discourse and dialogue.

RACHAD EL KOUSSY: CAMERA PRESS

Al-Azhar, Egypt: the inviolate word

# SUBSCRIPTIONS 1994

## United Kingdom & Overseas (excl USA & Canada)

| | | | | | | |
|---|---|---|---|---|---|---|
| 1yr | UK: | £30 | Overseas: | £36 | Students: | £23 (Worldwide) |
| 2yr | | £55 | | £66 | | |
| 3yr | | £80 | | £99 | | |

❑ I enclose a cheque* or money order for **£**.................
(*Sterling cheques must be drawn on a London bank)

❑ Please charge **£**........ to my
   ❑ Visa/Mastercard
   ❑ American Express
   ❑ Diners Club

CARD NUMBER.....................................
.......................................................

EXP DT..................

SIGNATURE............................................

I have instructed my bank to send £..............
your bank account 0635788 at Lloyds Bank,
Hanover Square, London W1R OBT

NAME....................................................

ADDRESS................................................

I have sent £.............. to your Post Office
ational Giro account 574-5357 (Britain)

.......................................................
.......................................................

Also, you can send **Index** to a reader in the developing world — for only £18! These sponsored
ubscriptions promote free speech around the world for only the cost of printing and postage.

---

# SUBSCRIPTIONS 1994

## USA & Canada

*'Index has bylines that Vanity Fair would kill for. Would that bylines were the only things about Index people were willing to kill for.'* **BOSTON GLOBE**

| | | | |
|---|---|---|---|
| 1yr | US$ | $48 | Students: $35 |
| 2yr | | $90 | |
| 3yr | | $136 | |

❑ I enclose a cheque or money order in US$ for **$**.................

❑ Please charge **$** ........to my
   ❑ Visa/Mastercard
   ❑ American Express
   ❑ Diners Club

CARD NUMBER.....................................
.......................................................

EXP DT..................

SIGNATURE............................................

NAME....................................................

ADDRESS................................................
.......................................................
.......................................................

Also, you can send **Index** to a reader in the developing world — for only $27! These sponsored
ubscriptions promote free speech around the world for only the cost of printing and postage.

Index on Censorship
Lancaster House
33 Islington High Street
London N1 9LH
United Kingdom

Index on Censorship
c/o Human Rights Watch
485 Fifth Avenue
New York, NY 10164-0709
USA

# LETTER FROM MOSCOW

## JULIA LATYNINA

# Images of capitalism

About two months ago, just across the road from our flat, they shot the owner of a local restaurant. The Aist was originally a standard Soviet-style *stekliashka* — a 1930s imitation of an American fast-food bar. But in the first few months of perestroika it was privatised and soon afterwards became a meeting place for people widely suspected of affluence.

Its owners died unusually quickly, rather like wild flowers or Latin-American presidents, but in Russia the craving for gold is more intense than yearning for a quiet life. The last owner was dragged out of the restaurant in broad daylight and gunned down in the street. Two chance witnesses were shot at the same time, a young man and a girl who had been plying their wares in the kiosk opposite. They happened to be standing in the wrong place at the wrong time. Much like Russia herself.

This unremarkable incident took place in the very heart of Moscow, in an area littered with foreign embassies and privatised former Party buildings. Unlike most of the world's cities. Moscow is not divided into prosperous 'middle class' areas with private houses and well-kept lawns, and 'dangerous', or merely impoverished parts of town. Here, as in the sixteenth-century Caribbean, affluence — not poverty — is associated with crime. Thirty prominent bankers were killed in the streets of Moscow in the past year, including the chairman of the board of the Russian Agricultural Bank, Igor Likhachev. The head of the 'Most' financial group, Oleg Gusinskii, has said publicly that his organisation keeps 800 armed guards. The police have quoted a figure of 100 contract killings in Moscow last year.

In the West, a dramatic murder story will make the headlines, of course; but the bodies dug up in the former home of Frederick West are unlikely to have much impact on the British economy. The radical difference between modern Russia and the West is that in Russia crime is a prime form of economic activity.

One of the more unforgivable mistakes made by outside observers in the 1970s was their faith in the resilience of the Russian state apparatus. In fact, the Soviet state was never strong because it never functioned at the local level. 'In Russia, bad laws are redeemed by their negligent enforcement', as Pushkin used to say.

In the 1970s, the life of every Russian citizen was ruled not by a system of legislation but by an informal network of relationships. You scratch my back, I'll scratch Ivan's, Ivan'll scratch Petr's and Petr'll scratch yours. There was a socialist economy above and a primitive exchange economy below, similar to the system in the Tobriand Islands described by the anthropologist Bronislaw Malinowski. The main object of trade was not the goods exchanged, but the system itself: the relationships, the contacts and the influence.

**The Russian businessman is as far from his Western counterpart as Zhirinovsky's Liberal Democratic Party is from genuine liberal democracy**

The behaviour of every Soviet citizen, bureaucrat or dissident, was controlled not by the far-off, rusty mechanisms of state, but by the instant, insistent and inescapable reaction of close social allies. On meeting a stranger, bureaucrats and dissidents followed an identical pattern of behaviour. They would ring around their friends and make enquiries, without taking the slightest interest in their new acquaintance's formal status.

In contrast to the work of a church or a local city council, the activities of these small groups — whether of dissidents, bureaucrats or production workers — were directed against the state. After all, bribes can be viewed as a form of social protest too. And when the Soviet legal system disappeared, the sole foothold left to anyone with ambition was the system of relationships within these informal groupings, which promptly acquired mafia-like characteristics.

The dissolution of the Soviet Empire has been a process similar to the fall of any centralised mediaeval state. Its own officials — the class that supported it — were its major foes, because they sought to transform the temporary power given them into an object of private ownership. The flaw was not that officials became owners, but that privatisation took place in areas which, in the West, remain under state control: the army, law and taxation.

Contemporary Russia displays many symptoms of the free market. It has entrepreneurs, stock exchanges and banks; but the Russian businessman is as far from his Western counterpart as Zhirinovsky's Liberal Democratic Party is from genuine liberal democracy. Because of the indolence of the state police, he is forced to deploy a private army. And of course he wouldn't be silly enough to use it only for the purposes of self-defence. Because of the lack of coherent laws he is forced to bribe officials. The officials like it so much that they are in no hurry to establish a consistent legal system. They know that while there is contradiction, the law will be determined by the official who interprets it.

A Russian entrepreneur is legally bound to pay 70 per cent of his profits to the state treasury, and the percentage may rise or fall depending on the goodwill of individual officials. Additional taxes payable to the mafia are unavoidable, so the businessman has no alternative but to offer the official a sweetener for interpreting the law in his favour. Consequently the Russian entrepreneur finds himself scratching his head and musing: Yeltsin accepts my bribes and Zhirinovsky will doubtless do the same. Is there really any difference between them?

Against the backdrop of an urge to order, so characteristic of the mafia, Russian politicians have demonstrated an astonishing capacity for disorder. The political party, in the sense of a non-governmental organisation with its own rules and regulations acting as a mediator between an authoritarian state and an irresponsible politician, does not exist in Russia. Consequently, the concept of lawful opposition — which imposes equal rules on the parliamentary majority and the opposition — does not exist either. Zhirinovsky's success is symptomatic. Zhirinovsky is not a party; he is (like Yeltsin) a charismatic leader. Zhirinovsky does not hold a position equivalent to that of the leader of the opposition in a democratic state, but a position like that of an official conspirator against the existing regime.

Western democracy today is based less on the rule of the majority than on the latter's respect for the minority — the opposition. Russia's December elections gave rise not to an official opposition, but to the emergence of a set of official conspirators: the release of Rutskoi and his collaborators from prison is evidence enough of that. The notion of 'democracy' is becoming as meaningless in Russian politics as the notion of the 'free market' is in the Russian economy. When coups or elections take place every six months; when the difference between the results of these elections and those of the coups are barely discernible; when every party that comes to power feels insecure until it has dealt with its opponents; and when decisions on ways of dealing with these opponents are deferred because of squabbles between comrades-in-arms, then the only solution is the creation of a non-party authoritarian power.

Before 12 December 1993 Russia had a choice between democracy and authoritarianism. Now there is only the choice between the mad dictatorship of a Zhirinovsky and the more reasonable kind under a Yeltsin. The question is no longer is democracy possible in Russia but, rather, is authoritarianism still a feasible proposition?

One of the most serious problems facing Russia is how to shift the mafia from control of the business community to its protector. In mediaeval Europe, this was resolved when unruly barons understood that annual taxation was more lucrative than armed robbery on the highway. The same process is now under way in Russia. A small businessman who is just starting out will tell you the following story. 'I've got the money and the equipment. What I need now is protection.' 'You mean the mafia?' 'All I have to do is go to them and say: I'll pay you 15 per cent to protect me from robbery. If I don't, they'll come anyway.' 'What if another lot appears?' 'Not my problem. I present them with a telephone number and let them sort it out among themselves.'

During the night, shots ring out on the Altufesky Road; next morning our entrepreneur may have another set of visitors: 'The matter's been settled and you'll be paying your 15 per cent to us'. You might try to cancel the payments of course; but then you'll find yourself lifting your shirt to show a visiting journalist the iron marks on your skin, and saying bitterly: 'I was a bit late paying the shareholders.'

But there is progress. The mafia have crossed the boundary between robbery and taxation. In the past it nullified the state. Now it replaces it.

V KHRISTOFOROV: CAMERA PRESS

Moscow 1994: capitalism strikes lucky

It takes its tax; but it also offers protection.

The swift development and transformation of the mafia into the state, in the former Soviet Union, is as salutary as the transformation of the Vikings into civilised rulers in the eleventh century, after they had spent 200 years plundering Europe. You can't defeat the mafia, any more than you could the Vikings. But they might be persuaded to move into a more profitable position, in other words — into the free market.

In the early years of perestroika, the Russian press viewed the fall of the planned economy and the establishment of the market as two sides of a single coin. The fall of the Soviet Union was perhaps a historical necessity, forced by the economic superiority of the West. But the transformation of an unstable, embittered country which directs disproportionately large amounts of money to its officials and 'protectors' is by no means inevitable. In the modern world, European and American democratic capitalism is the exception rather than the rule. There is no reason to suppose that Russia will be numbered among these exceptions in the foreseeable future.

*Translated by Irena Maryniak*

# Between two fires

Algerian voices make
themselves heard
above the silence of
censorship and the
sound of gunfire

# LYES SI ZOUBIR

# Journey through fear

Algiers, the Agha Station, 7.30am. The train to Oran, crammed and dusty, starts to move slowly out of the station. Faces are tired and anxious. The journey ahead is far from safe: Blida, Chlef, Oued-Rhiou, the stops on the way are places to be feared. In the capital rumours abound. The Islamists have forbidden travel by train because there are no separate sections for men and women. A few days ago, the night train between Bejaia and Algiers was attacked and set alight. The travellers escaped unharmed, but army conscripts were taken off. 'I'm taking a bus or a taxi back,' says a young smuggler. 'I don't want everything we bring back from there to be confiscated by the terrorists.' 'There' means Morocco, the blessed border through which everything comes, trendy clothes and domestic appliances, but also arms, *kif* (hashish) or the synthetic drugs young Algerians favour.

The carriage reeks of tobacco and most of the windows are down despite the chill of the morning... 'We'd better finish our cigarettes now,' jokes the smuggler, 'we're entering the territory of the "one-armed".' Another rumour, already a legend, in which the 'one-armed' is an Afghan veteran who has lost an arm in the Holy War against the Soviets. Without having ever seen him, the Algerians from the centre of the country claim he reigns supreme on the section of the route between Blida and Chlef. 'He has an accomplice who boards the train at Algiers', recounts a man from Oran. 'At a pre-arranged time, he pulls the alarm and the band attacks the train. It's said he's executed people who were smoking in front of him.' Another swears the 'one-armed' never uses fire-arms, but is content with a sword, hence his title 'Emir'...

Algiers 1991: municipality won by FIS in local elections

On the streets of Chlef the tension is palpable. Yesterday the town council and the municipal park were set alight. Leaflets call for strict observance of the curfew which Islamic groups are trying to impose. 'Read this leaflet and go on your way. Tear it up and you'll be dead. Work is banned after 15.00. By continuing to work, you are helping the Pharaoh [the secular government]. Do not bring the wrath of the *mujahedin* down on your head.' No-one knows how these little duplicated sheets get pasted up, but the majority choose not to linger longer than necessary at work.

But the shops stay open and police patrols are constant. 'As soon as the police presence lessens,' says a newspaper vendor, 'the Islamists emerge and are vigilant again. As for me, I've decided not to sell French-language newspapers anymore. Why should I endanger my life?'

...'The earthquake of 1980 pulverised the city and insecurity was total. Today, the terrorists have no difficulty in filling the void,' explains Abdelkader, a young university lecturer. Town of heat and *zemla* (earthquake), Chlef is also the smugglers' town: drugs, hunting rifles, stolen European cars. Everything is on sale, anything can be bought.

The station at Boukadir is burned out. Its attendant nearly died in the attack.

People begin to relax. We still have to get past Oued-Rhiou, but as the smuggler says, 'They've never attacked a train around this area.'

Again, the acrid smell of local tobacco, the wailing of a poor impersonator of Khaled, the *rai* singer, and the inevitable food vendors.

There are no signs of a ticket inspector — the job has become too dangerous — the fare-dodgers profit and most first-class compartments are full of them. Should an inspector appear, some will not hesitate to claim that they belong to the *Jamaat el moussalaha* (the armed groups), and no-one will risk a confrontation.

Oran is a bleak place. The killing of the playwright, Abdelkader Alloula, on 10 March 1994 is still fresh in everyone's mind. The authorities have divulged the name and address of the alleged killer without scruple. 'Some people came a few days ago in a black car,' says a local shop-keeper. 'They asked questions about the man who was shown on TV. I didn't know him, but it looks like he was a student. They nearly beat to death a chap who belonged to FIS. They didn't look like policemen or army people and were almost certainly members of OJAL.'

The *Organisation des Jeunes Algériens Libres* (OJAL), is still relatively unknown. It first came to public attention after kidnapping a well known professor of mathematics, a member of the FIS. 'It suits the government to let OJAL do its dirty work,' comments a sociologist. 'We are the victims of massive manipulation. The security forces are in retreat, and attacks are on the increase. The democrats who are in fear of their lives are demanding weapons to protect themselves. As a result, the system stays in place.'...

Despite the deaths, despite its dreariness, Oran is far more pleasant than Algiers. There are no curfews, no shots fired in the night, no tank-fire; but life for the young is as bad as in the capital. 'There's nothing to do,' says an illegal street vendor. 'We do a few deals [in drugs], we steal, and the money we make goes towards buying *chira* (cannabis resin) or *cachiyattes* (narcotics, etc).' The addicts are potential recruits for the armed groups, most of whose funds come from drug trafficking. Entire networks have been established or been absorbed by existing criminal structures now converted to protagonists in the 'holy war'.

'New drugs keep coming,' warns Kamal, organiser of a youth club. 'The kids are discovering the 'white powder'. Cocaine is having devastating effects and people are ready to kill to get their hands on it.' French-language newspapers are demanding the border with Morocco be closed, or at least better monitored. 'It's impossible,' explains a customs officer. 'Everything filters through this border, same as the one in the south. I'm not talking about the smugglers, but of the big fish, those who are in bed with government officials and who export truck-loads of foodstuff which the country then re-imports wasting valuable hard currency.'

In some Algerian circles, rumour has it that President Mohammed Boudiaf's determination to put an end to the scandal of customs clearance forms, the D-15s, which have allowed the formation of powerful smuggling networks, was behind his assassination. 'This is what this regime is all about,' comments a tea-shop owner. 'It wants to fight against terrorism without giving up any of its privileges and perks.'...

The taxi driver is happy. He hasn't had to wait long before filling his car, a family Peugeot seating seven. Before setting off he warns his passengers: 'I hope there are no terrorists among you. The road to Tiaret is long and there are at least 10 checkpoints. So we're going to be searched and I don't want problems. If anyone has something illegal, throw it out or get off.'

The inevitable discussion on the country's situation gets going as the taxi moves out of Oran. None of the passengers lowers their guard or reveals their political preferences, but all are agreed that too much blood has already been shed.

The Ouarsenis Massif in the distance reminds us that a civil war is being waged daily. Since the end of March, the air force has been bombing the mountain camps of the Islamists. The losses in the *Mouvement Islamique Armé* (MIA), that claims allegiance to FIS, are believed to be heavy, enough, anyway, to force the *mujahedin* to take refuge in the cities in the highlands. Roads are heavily guarded and checkpoint succeeds checkpoint.

The discussion in the taxi turns to the notorious 'false checkpoints' which have cost the lives of many army and police officers. Believing they were dealing with colleagues, they had shown their identity badges, only to be decapitated and have their heads put in plastic bags before being set alight.

Tiaret is an angry town, Here, the actions of the *Groupe Islamique Armé* (GIA), more radical than the MIA, is the constant object of debate, even though the papers in the capital focus on attacks on Blida or Medea. 'There are deaths every day,' sighs a tobacconist. 'Anonymous bodies, mutilated corpses by the dam on Bakhadda lake. No-one knows why they have been executed.'

In Blida conversation dwells obsessively on military reprisals. A copy of *Le Monde* circulates covertly. The inhabitants state confidentially that the parachutists have been given carte blanche. 'The escape of several hundred Islamists from the labour camp of Lambeze (near Blida), has irritated the military intensely. They do not hide their mistrust of the employees of the ministry of justice...'

They stop at nothing to get information. A few days before the visit of the interior minister, Selim Saadi, on 23 March, the police decided to take the initiative. Soon after the curfew at 23.30, officers knocked at the doors of houses in the Islamist areas of the city, and asked for asylum, pretending to be from the Islamist groups; a number of Blida inhabitants who showed their sympathies have since lost their lives.

Other 'unfortunate mistakes' have been reported: some young smugglers, suspected of being sympathetic towards the Islamists, have been abducted and not been seen again. 'It's war,' says an ex-army officer. 'Without trying to justify anything, we must understand. Army and police officers are being killed every day. Some officers resent the population's passive attitude, which they equate with support for the armed groups.'

In town, the *hijab* (Islamic veil) remains an important feature for women. However, the police have put pressure on hairdressers and public baths to re-open. Despite everything, people remain cautious and, in some inner-city areas, the satellite cable has been cut off.

On the return journey to Algiers. The train is slower than the 'express'; Karim has a ravaged look. He hasn't been able to regularise his military service documents. The officer behind the counter had not even looked at his medical file, and had given him his travel warrant. Karim has a difficult choice: follow orders, leave, and put his life and that of his family in danger as a soldier, or desert. 'The *ikhwans* (the Muslim Brotherhoods) have forbidden young men to do their compulsory military service. Without a deferment, I can't do anything. The only solution is to go back to my village, making sure all the neighbours know I'm there. I don't want them to think I've gone to do my military service.'

Like the rest of the population, Karim is caught between the two sides. He hopes better days lie ahead, but is not optimistic.

The train has just gone through Boufarik, another stronghold of the armed groups. People light their cigarettes again and a bad *rai* starts to crackle out of a radio. 'Can one even grow accustomed to the worst?' asks Karim, fatalistically.

*Translated from* Le Monde Diplomatique, May 1994 *by Nathalie Vartanpour-Naalbandian*

## SAÏD ESSOULAMI

# Attacks on the press and journalists

Since the cancellation of the second round of Algeria's first democratic elections for a National Assembly in January 1992, the country has been plunged into a cycle of violence which has claimed the lives of more than 4,000 people. Even before the *Front Islamique du Salut* (FIS) was deprived of an outright victory in the second round, the government had launched its onslaught on FIS by arresting its leaders and conducting a campaign against them in the media. With the end of the democratic process, followed by a military coup, FIS became the immediate target of the army and the various government factions that made up the ruling High Council of State.

The party was banned and thousands of suspected members or sympathisers arrested and imprisoned. The majority are still held under harsh conditions in special detention centres. The state of emergency ushered in further violence and arbitrary arrests.

The FIS press was the first target of a renewed campaign to muzzle opposition to the authorities. In January 1992, the Algerian authorities arrested a number of its journalists and several newspapers were banned or seized.

Under the state of emergency, the lively independent press which had been given its head by the introduction of the February 1989 Constitution after 30 years of censorship under the ruling FLN, came into the army net: its short-lived — and highly relative — freedom was severely curtailed. Journalists on both sides of the Islamic/secular divide were arrested and detained for varying periods of time; many newspapers have been banned, suspended or placed under constant surveillance since 1992. All FIS publications, or those suspected of sympathy with their views because they published FIS statements calling for army desertion and public disobedience, were closed down.

Since its banning and the loss of its own media voice, FIS too has been implicated in attacks on the press. Islamic armed groups have assassinated many journalists and writers who oppose FIS and the establishment of an Islamic state in Algeria.

The death of the FIS press, much of it created with the foundation of the party in 1989, was total.

● *Al-Mounqid*, an Arabic-language weekly newspaper was the first FIS publication to be banned on 28 January 1992. Its director-general, Salah Gouami, was arrested for publishing a statement by imprisoned FIS leader Abdelkader Hachani, calling for the army to disobey orders to shoot at demonstrators.

● *Al-Forqan*, an Islamist French-language newspaper, was banned in February after the police had raided its premises and arrested some of its journalists, including the editor-in-chief, Fouad Delleci. *L'Eveil*, another French-language weekly, was banned in the same month for an article on a violent clash between FIS militants and the police in the Casbah in Algiers. *Al-Sahwa*, another French-language weekly, met the same fate for publishing articles the authorities alleged were dangerous for national security.

● *Al-Hidaya*, an Arabic-language weekly, was closed down on the grounds that it posed a threat to national security. The weekly *Al-Balagh*, also Arabic-language, was closed down on January after the police arrested its editor-in-chief, Abdelaziz Layoun, and director, Mohammed Denideni.

Denideni was an outright FIS winner in Sidi Aissa constituency in the first round of the legislative elections. The 22 January issue of *Al-Balagh* carried the front-page headline 'army has betrayed Muslims and supported the Communists' along with several other highly critical articles denouncing the army's intervention. The two journalists were charged with 'undermining a constitutional institution (the Higher State Council), national unity and state security'; 'attacking the army's leadership'; calling for 'civil disobedience'; and 'publishing false information'.

Denideni was detained for four days and was reportedly ill-treated. He was released temporarily to allow him to defend his case in court, but police harassment forced him to go into hiding and later to leave the country clandestinely. He is now seeking asylum in the UK.

During these months, the secular press continued to enjoy considerable freedom. Following the assassination of President Mohammed Boudiaf, the secular press, too, found its newspapers closed down or suspended and a number of its journalists arrested on defamation charges, or for 'diffusing erroneous information'.

The French-language daily *al-Watan* was in the frontline. Under its editor Omar Belhouchet, it has maintained its independent line throughout the conflict, criticising the army and virulently attacking the FIS and its political agenda. The paper has been suspended many times for publishing information deemed sensitive by the army, and its journalists have been sentenced to several months' imprisonment as well as being attacked by armed Islamic groups.

Armed groups have assassinated journalists and writers known for their opposition to the activities of the Islamist movement or for their support of the coup d'etat or simply for working in the state media. More than 20 journalists and writers have been assassinated and a number of others injured or narrowly escaped attacks. A climate of fear amongst Algerian intellectuals has been instilled and is furthered by repeated threats in the form of anonymous letters, telephone calls and abduction attempts. By August this year, after what appeared to be a respite, the killings were renewed: four journalist were killed or kidnapped in July and August.

There is thought to be an assassination 'hit list' with the names of 140 journalists circulating in mosques around the country. Underground

cassettes containing explicit calls by Muslim radical leaders to execute anyone collaborating with the authorities have also been making the same round. Many journalists have received letters and telephone calls threatening them with assassination. For example, *al-Watan* newspaper has received several hundred threatening letters and innumerable telephone threats. Most of the letters are anonymous and generally contain accusations such as 'enemy of Islam and the Quran', 'traitor', 'extremist of the francophony', and 'Communist'.

Suspected assassins have visited the homes of several intellectuals and journalists and have threatened their families. Many journalists now sign their articles with pen-names to protect their real identity or resort to self-censorship as a method of survival. Many have already left the country to seek asylum and work in France or other European and North African countries. Those who cannot leave the country have left the profession. Others are moving house frequently, altering their working patterns and lifestyles; others again have started a new life in hiding.

Armed groups rarely claim responsibility for these killings, but at least two Islamic opposition groups, the *Mouvement Islamique Armé* (MIA) and the *Groupe Islamique Armé* (GIA), are accused by the authorities of carrying out some of the assassinations. One letter signed by the MIA and sent to Omar Belhouchet, reads: 'You are going to die, if not today, be sure it will be tomorrow! And your death will be registered in the glorious pages of the Islamic movement.'

Anwar Haddam, leader of the FIS parliamentary delegation in the United States, described the killing on 15 June 1993 of Mahfoud

Boucebsi, as 'a sentence and not a crime'. In an underground communique released shortly after a series of assassinations, the FIS justified the killings thus: 'What is happening is not bloodthirsty terrorism, but a holy war... it is a legitimate fight against those who denied the choice of the people.'

# The state of emergency

The state of emergency decreed on 9 February 1992 empowers the minister of the interior to 'order the internment of any person whose activity endangers public order'. The minister is empowered to:

● restrict or forbid people's movement in certain areas and at precise periods of time;
● institute zones where movement of non-residents is controlled;
● impose restraint orders or confine to house arrest any adult whose activities are deemed harmful to public order and to the normal functioning of public services;
● to order staff of public as well as private enterprises to work during unauthorised or illegal strikes.

The minister has the power to 'order a temporary closure of public galleries and meeting venues, whatever their nature, and ban any demonstration deemed troublesome to peace and law and order. Military tribunals can deal with criminal cases and cases of serious offences against state security.'

New and even more restrictive measures were introduced in a presidential decree on 11 August 1992. It authorises the suspension or closure of any 'company, organ, institution or body whose activities endanger public order and security, the normal functioning of the institutions or the supreme interests of the country'. The decree sanctions anything that may constitute a destabilising factor, be it in the press or in sermons in the mosque.

In response to the increasingly violent attacks by Muslim militants on police officers, the security forces and public buildings, the Algerian authorities extended the emergency measures on 1 October 1992. They decreed a new anti-terrorist law increasing the number of capital offences, doubling all other penalties for 'terrorist acts', reducing the legal age of punishment to 18 and instituting special courts to try 'terrorist offences'. The law provides for life imprisonment for anyone convicted of organising a 'terrorist' association; members or sympathisers of such associations are liable to receive a 10- to 20-year sentence. Defending or reproducing the documents of such an association can result in five or 10 years' imprisonment.(*Décret législatif No 92-03 Septembre 1992 relatif à la lutte contre la subversion et le terrorisme*).

On 28 November 1992, the prime minister announced the dissolution of all institutions and movements on which the authorities believe FIS depends for its clandestine activities. These included local and regional authorities, business companies, charitable and cultural groups and labour unions controlled by the FIS. All these, the minister said, 'have become like a spider's web spreading across the country... and I gave special instructions that necessary measures should be taken regarding everything relating to propaganda and publications. Everything published containing subversive ideas should be confiscated and those who write, print or publish such material should be brought before the law.'

Algiers 1990: voters give FIS a resounding victory in local elections

# AÏCHA LEMSINE

# Death or exile

**'I'm 17 and I don't want to die. I dream of becoming an Olympic champion like Hassiba Boulmerka. I also dream of taking flying lessons and becoming a captain... Today, they ban even our dreams'**

This excerpt from an open letter to the head of state from a schoolgirl encapsulates the agony and uncertainty in Algeria. Here, as in Sarajevo, death comes daily: there, mortars rain down on the community because they are Muslims; here, we are shot at, have our throats slit or are imprisoned. Rival concepts of Islam have divided us and thrust us into a barbaric fratricidal conflict.

In Bosnia, rape became a tactical weapon of war in pursuit of ethnic cleansing; here the final solution against women has become a terrorist strategy for cleansing a religion.

Between 1988 and 1994, secret armed groups have killed more than 4,000 — soldiers, policemen, bureaucrats, farmers, workers, journalists, writers, women, children, old men and women, known and unknown — in the name of political Islam. The list of the dead takes no account of the Islamists, their families and supporters imprisoned or executed by the state forces of law and order.

The present situation is the result of political drift and incompetence under the four preceding governments: a history of wasted opportunities and human folly.

After the October 1988 riots which brought crowds onto the streets and in which many lost their lives at the hands of the army, the initial plan was to transform Algeria into a democracy, complete with a new constitution and multiparty system. By allowing the formation of parties based on ethnicity and religion, former President Chadli Benjedid was the first to violate his new constitution. While the ruling FLN attempted to wipe out the memory of its brutal repression of the riots by consolidating its control over the press, bestowing cars and office premises on the opposition parties and new organisations, the newly formed FIS quietly set about enlisting and organising its grassroots support.

While other opposition parties wrangled over their share of the government largesse, the FIS addressed the problems of the poor in language they could understand. The lack of any government initiatives or moves by the women's organisations in those areas most severely in need, allowed the Islamist parties to grow and consolidate their power.

Running against the discredited FLN and the badly divided democratic opposition, FIS's well disciplined party machine won the municipal elections of June 1990 and the first round of the parliamentary elections in December 1991. Fearing an overwhelming FIS majority in Parliament, it was the opposition parties and women's organisations that encouraged the army to take power and call off the second round of the elections. Thousands of Islamists were arrested and became, in the eyes of their supporters, martyrs to the law. Deprived of their legitimate victory, banned and badly affected by the arrest of its leaders, FIS responded with violence and gradually took control of the country through terror.

In the first instance, their campaign was directed against those who represented the state — police, army, bureaucrats, journalists and writers who had either joined in the appeal to ban their party or written against them. Intellectuals who had been selected by the government to make up the new Consultative Council in place of the former Parliament, now suspended, were officially condemned to death by the secret armed groups attached to FIS. Their campaign was later widened to include anyone, women as well as men, who collaborated with the government that took over after the coup d'état of February 1992 which FIS considered illegitimate. On 21 June 1992 the new president, Mohammed Boudiaf, was assassinated; no arrests were made and his death remains a mystery.

Terrorism mounted in direct proportion to state repression: as successive governments increased their attacks on the Islamists and the press grew increasingly hostile, the latter responded with further violence. Civilians were murdered, often in front of their children; finally women and children became the target of the armed Islamic movements. At first, schoolgirls were killed for not wearing the *hijab* (veil); then, on 30 March 1994, 18-year-old Meloudjemi Rasika and 19-year-old Ali Naïma, both wearing the *hijab*, were killed just outside their school on the outskirts of the capital, Algiers.

It was the first time that girls wearing Islamic dress had been killed. Suddenly it was not only women journalists and writers — 'modern' women — who were being targeted; simply to be a woman was enough. Caught between the 'democratic fundamentalists' and the 'religious fundamentalists', regardless of age, Algerian women became a human shield, the animal brought to slaughter, marked down for the final solution by madmen.

But Algerian women, who have been in the forefront of Algeria's fight for freedom since the French invasions in the nineteenth century, have gone on the offensive. Refusing to accept the fate of women in Iran, Sudan or Afghanistan, women's organisations have initiated a campaign of peaceful resistance. On 22 March this year, joined by several political parties, mainly from the left, they mounted a huge demonstration against the violence in the country.

Algeria's post-independence constitution gave women equality with men. In practise, they were no more than token figureheads socially and culturally as well as politically. In 1984, a new family code relegated women to the status of minors. The unprecedented level of physical violence against women of all ages between 1989 and 1994 forced women to organise and to demand human rights and democracy. Faced with the women's demonstrations, the mosque became the focus of a vicious onslaught on women who found themselves alone and bearing the brunt of deals and concessions struck behind their backs by the men of both sides.

The mounting confrontation between terrorism and repression is characterised by words like 'hatred' and 'extermination'. They have become common currency among 'democrats' and 'religious fundamentalists' alike. No-one is safe from their murderous confrontation, not even in their own homes. Delinquency is spreading; there is no longer any distinction between sordid everyday villainy and that of the fundamentalists or others. Algerians with the means are leaving as fast as they can — mainly for France; those who must remain live their lives under constant threat.

As well as the physical danger there is the worsening economic situation. Over the past five years something like 300,000-400,000 jobs have been lost annually; the country only produces 10 per cent of what it consumes; the only state revenue is from oil, most of which goes to service the national debt — and is no longer sufficient even for that. Given the instability and lack of security, any hope of an economic recovery, despite the goodwill of foreign investors, remains still-born. Foreigners are also leaving and foreign embassies have reduced their staff to a skeleton. Having first paralysed the population by fear, terrorism is now starving it to death in isolation from the rest of the world.

Algeria remains split in two — half Islamist, half modernist. Both sides continue to count their dead. Even the women are a long way from forming the united front that could be the force for change needed to restore peace and prevent Algeria being carved up like Bosnia or Somalia.

Some of the women's organisations, particularly those allied to the radical democrat parties, seem unable to grasp the wisdom of the strategy proposed by President Lamine Zeroual: only dialogue with the Islamists has any hope of leading the country out of the spiral of violence into which previous governments have plunged it.

The Algerian people are, at heart, deeply Muslim, including those who favour a more modern society. The problem lies in getting each side to talk to and accept the other. The answer is neither the form of federation proposed by the more radical modernists, nor an Islamic society based on the Iranian or Sudanese model. The blinkered intransigence of the warring clans that refuse to treat with the enemy and refuse to countenance the presence of the other, offers only death or exile and the certainty of further bloodshed.

Both sides must be exposed. In the name of freedom the so-called democrats refuse it to others by playing on the fear and vulnerability of women: the chief victims of intransigent political parties are widows, orphans and martyrs destroyed by terrorist attacks. Angered by their own losses, the women of these parties refuse to recognise that the women of the Islamists also mourn their dead.

The Islamists are equally blinkered and intransigent. They see themselves as the true representatives of Islam but are nothing more than the grave-diggers of those who have hijacked a religion founded on tolerance, forgiveness and compassion. They have already been denounced by Islamists outside Algeria — 'The Algerian Islamists kill women and we are ashamed' — and must be exposed in their own country. The vast majority of Algerian women, ignored by the government and by the media, know they have nothing to fear from Islam itself, only what is being done in its name.

Hassiba Boulmerka: champion of the world

## MOHAMMED HARBI

# Clans against factions

**The roots of the Algerian situation go back at least to the early days of independence. Nurtured by the 30-year rule of the FLN, old divisions and rivalries have resurfaced with a vengeance**

More than any other factor, FIS's appeal is founded on the hatred most Algerians feel for the incumbent system and its former ruler, the *Front du Libération National* (FLN). Even the cruelty and bigotry demonstrated by the Islamic armed groups has not changed this, as the growing number of those joining the groups testifies.

' By its own account, the army has drawn into its orbit the secular middle class that is also, to varying degrees, the main beneficiary of state handouts from a centrally planned economy. However, this class is deeply divided on many issues — the role of the public sector, methods of transition to a market economy, the official status of the Arabic, Berber and French languages, and equality between the sexes. Their support hardly gives the army a stable base. The senior ranks of the army are themselves divided into various factions: former officers in the French army like Larbi Belkheir, Khaled Nezzar, Abbas Gheziel, Mohammed Lamari, Mohammed Touati; Algerian army officers sidelined by President Chadli and called back in an attempt to heal the rifts and deal with the deepening problems in the country. These are represented by men like Liamine Zeroual — now President — and Mohammed Betchine. Another group is the 'Class of 1962', and so on.

The common agendas and regional links, without ever being exclusive in the way one imagines, are reflected in the factions and clans, but do not always conform to relationships within the formal hierarchy.

The balance of power between the various groups shifts regularly and results in a lack of any decisive, longer term action. This in turn results in stagnation or ad hoc decisions. However, the Belkheir, Nezzar, Mediene faction suffered a severe setback when their candidate for the presidency, Ahmed Bouteflika, was first opposed and finally sidelined.

In addition to the above problems, maintaining control over a vast territory in the throes of an acute social crisis is impossible. Here and there the smouldering grievances from the time of the war of independence are breaking out again in rural areas where there are old scores to settle. Many in the countryside are supporting the Islamists for this reason. To speak of a return of the *harkis* (Algerian troops loyal to the French at the time of the war of independence) would, however, be a gross caricature of the actual situation.

But the confrontation between the army and the Islamists has all the ingredients of a dirty war: regular and deadly attacks by the navy and air force; the use of napalm; torture; psychological warfare; an endless spiral of blood and tears. There is no news in the so-called 'independent' press; press freedom generally is curtailed by government threats and warnings. The weeklies *La Nation* and *al Hadeth*, to name only two, no longer appear. Everyone is resigned to civil war, saying in effect: 'If we have to risk our lives, better risk them with guns in our hands.' Driven by fear and hatred, whole regions are switching their loyalties from the government and its chaos to the Islamist opposition.

Even if, with hindsight, the roots of the present situation can be seen to go back a long way, Algeria has, nevertheless, been taken by surprise by the turn of events. What does the future hold? Civil war? The break up of the country into fiefdoms?

The tragedy appears intractable. The political scene appears to be locked into two false options, neither of which has any legitimacy nor mandate throughout the country. On the government side which, having held power for so many decades, bears the greatest responsibility for the present situation, democracy and dialogue have nothing more than a facade. Today that facade purports to be seeking, at best, a broad consensus, a two-way split of the booty. However, there is no solution other than a thorough and radical overhaul of the entire system. Failing this, one group will drive the other out; the wrenching apart and the causes of disintegration will continue.

Whatever the misadventures have been, there is only one way of coming together and ending this fratricide: by giving the people a say. But doing this implies conditions guaranteeing that there can be no manipulation or fraud. The minority must be assured of their rights and have confidence that they too could one day become the majority. If there is to be another election, it must also ensure that all views and opinions are reflected; there are many more views and voices than are reflected in the two poles of the army and the Islamists. An election based on proportional voting could give the country a new start.

Room for manoeuvre gets less every day. There is little time left to halt the march to the abyss.

*Translated from* Le Monde Diplomatique, *May 1994, by Judith Vidal-Hall*

Dessin de Maz - *El Watan* - 22 février 1993

# HUGH ROBERTS

# Meddling while Algeria burns

## French intervention prolongs the agony

'R ound up the usual suspects,' says the engagingly cynical French
police chief at the end of the film *Casablanca*. French interior
minister Charles Pasqua's rough populist appeal may be a far cry from the
subtle charm of Claude Rains, but the essence of their respective
manoeuvres is the same. 'The usual suspects', of course, are those whom
the police do *not* suspect of committing whatever crime has been
committed, and who are rounded up precisely in order that the real
suspects may be allowed to go free, for one reason or another.

Since the killing of three French paramilitary gendarmes and two
French consular officials in Algiers on 3 August, over 25,000 north
Africans resident in France, many of them French citizens (in theory),
have been subject to humiliating identity checks and worse at the hands
of Pasqua's police, and 26 of them have been incarcerated in dubious legal
conditions in the detention centre at Folembray. Not one of those
detained has been shown to be connected, or even accused of being
connected, in any way with the perpetrators of the killings of Frenchmen
on 3 August. This attack was the work of the *Groupe Islamique Armé*
(GIA), which publicly claimed responsibility for it. Those detained in
Folembray were arrested on the grounds that they have links with the
*Front Islamique du Salut* (FIS), which has had nothing to do with the
killings of Frenchmen in Algeria and is well known to be fiercely at odds
with the GIA.

This is not the first time this has happened. Last October three French consular officials were abducted in Algiers and held for a week by the GIA before being released unharmed. Immediately afterwards, Pasqua organised a nationwide clampdown on Islamists in France, arresting some 85 individuals.

There is thus a pattern, and it is this: the GIA does something spectacular in Algeria, the French government reacts with extremely heavy-handed and almost entirely unwarranted police measures against 'the usual suspects' in France, the 'usual suspects' turn out to be the FIS or its sympathisers, the FIS is accordingly tarnished in the eyes of Algerian public opinion as the whole story is given headline treatment by the Algerian French-language media, and those politicians and parties in Algeria that advocate the admission of the banned FIS to the 'dialogue' process in Algeria as a way to end the violence there are, once again, put rudely on the defensive and held up to public obloquy as 'soft on terrorism'.

**In war the first casualty is truth. Since the crisis of the Algerian state began, with the riots of October six years ago, truth has been assassinated daily**

Why? Whereas the Claude Rains character had decent personal reasons for his behaviour, the motive in Pasqua's case is *raison d'état,* whether we recognise it or not and whether we understand it or not. It is no purpose of the French media to help the rest of us to understand it.

In war the first casualty is truth. Since the crisis of the Algerian state began, with the riots of October six years ago, truth has been assassinated daily.

Ever since October 1988, the French view of the Algerian crisis has dominated Western perceptions in general. Initially, the Islamists did not figure in the picture, which was presented as being a struggle between liberal 'reformers' and socialist 'hardliners' as in the USSR and other Communist countries, with Chadli as the Algerian Gorbachev whom the West should follow France's lead in backing to the hilt. With the rise of the FIS, the terms of the dualism changed into 'Islamists' versus 'modernists', with Chadli presented as the defender of a secular state menaced by the Iranian scenario. When it turned out that Chadli was perfectly willing to do a deal with the victorious FIS in order to stay in power, he was unceremoniously dumped, and thereafter we have been invited to interpret events in Algeria as an uncomplicated duel between revolutionary Islamists on the one hand and the Algerian army on the other.

It is the latter picture which is now being vigorously touted in Paris. It is admitted that the present military regime in Algiers leaves something to be desired but it is far better than the only possible alternative, the sanguinary Islamic theocracy which is bound to be set up if the other side wins.

The function of this view of things is to justify France's support for the policy of massive repression being followed by the Algerian army, and to mobilise the panic factor on an international scale in order to put on the defensive all those countries — the USA, Italy, Spain and Germany to look no further — that have well-founded doubts about the repressive strategy Paris favours and an interest in distancing themselves from it. The picture thus promoted is rubbish.

First, it is not the case that the situation in Algeria is one of a simple confrontation between two equally monolithic antagonists, the revolutionary Islamists on one side and the state on the other. The Islamists, even those engaged in violence, are profoundly divided between the AIS which proclaims its allegiance to the FIS, and wants to negotiate with the regime, and the GIA, which is opposed to any and all dialogue. Similarly, the politico-military elite which staffs the Algerian state is equally divided between hardline opponents of dialogue with the FIS (the so-called 'eradicators') and those who argue for re-admitting the FIS to the constitutional political process (the so-called 'conciliators').

Second, it is not the case that the alternative to the present regime would be an Islamic theocracy. Neither the AIS nor the GIA are seriously capable of overthrowing the state and neither of them is seriously trying to do this. Whatever their rhetoric may suggest, they are both following strategies of applying pressure, with a view to influencing the policy and orientation of the state, not overthrowing it. It may be thought that the more extreme GIA nourishes a revolutionary vision, but it is widely admitted that the GIA is the smaller movement, largely confined to the Algiers region, even if better placed to grab the headlines. It is absurd to suggest that it can realistically aspire to establishing a revolutionary Islamic state. As for the more broadly based AIS, which appears to be dominant in the east and west of the country, it is precisely the less extreme of the two movements, and has made clear its allegiance to the FIS and thus its

Algiers 1991

LAHCENE ABIB: CAMERA PRESS

support for the negotiated compromise solution which the FIS leaders, both those in jail and those abroad, have repeatedly made clear they seek.

Thus it is quite misleading to suggest that the violence in Algeria is the product of a gratuitous revolutionary onslaught on the status quo. On the contrary, it is first and foremost a *reaction* to the behaviour of the state.

The violence in Algeria stems from the decision of the Algerian army leadership to ban the FIS in February-March 1992. It does not stem directly from the fall of Chadli and the interruption of the electoral process in January 1992, since the FIS leadership called repeatedly for calm in the wake of these developments and did all it could to keep within the law. The fateful decision to place it outside the law destroyed the position of those Islamists, previously in a comfortable majority, who had argued successfully up until then for a constitutional strategy, and the initiative passed immediately to those who argued for guerrilla warfare. But there can be little doubt that if the constitutional option was made available again, and the FIS relegalised, the greater part of the violence would come to an end.

**There is a lot for people to be angry about, and politically and ideologically radical about**

Nor does it follow that relegalising the FIS would simply be the prelude to another FIS landslide victory at the polls and thus an Islamic theocracy via the ballot box. What is almost invariably forgotten is that the FIS's landslide victory in the legislative elections in December 1991 was a freak result; polling only 3.26 million votes, that is less than 25 per cent of the total electorate of over 13 million, the FIS won 188 seats outright on the first ballot and were heading for a final tally of over 75 per cent of the seats in the second round. This freak result was largely due to the extraordinarily low turnout, the even more remarkable collapse (or defection) of the FLN vote in many areas, and the particular electoral system being employed. There is every reason to think that the FLN would poll far better in a fresh election than it polled in 1991, and that this alone would deny many seats to the FIS. But even if the FLN vote remained the same, the simple expedient of proportional representation would be sufficient to ensure that the FIS could never capture more than a narrow majority of seats at best. There would be enough of a balance in the resulting national assembly to block any moves to replace the pluralist constitution with a totalitarian theocratic one.

It is this possible outcome that Paris refuses to envisage, and is trying to eliminate. The French government, in the shape of M Pasqua, even says there is no such thing as a moderate Islamist, and that if they do exist, it is up to them to manifest themselves. Let us remember, then, that the extremely moderate Abdelkader Hachani, who took over the leadership of the FIS following the army's arrest of Abassi Madani and Ali Ben Hadj in June 1991, who led it into the 1991 elections, and who called repeatedly for calm in the critical days of January 1992, was arrested soon afterwards on the flimsiest of pretexts. He has been held without charge in prison ever since, along with many of his equally reasonable colleagues. How does M Pasqua propose that Abdelkader Hachani manifest himself?

Let us also remind ourselves that all the other smaller Islamist parties which remain legal in Algeria have called for the FIS to be re-admitted to the political process. No doubt this makes them extremists in Paris's eyes.

But the argument about 'moderates' and 'extremists' is beside the point; its function is precisely to confuse the issue in the Western mind. Of course there is a case for saying that all Islamists are 'extremists' in some sense, in that they adhere to a radical doctrine. But conditions in Algeria are extreme. There is a lot for people to be angry about, and politically and ideologically radical about. What is at issue is not whether Algeria's Islamists are 'moderate' or not, but whether they are prepared to play the constitutional political game or not. Between February 1989 and February 1992, the vast majority of Algeria's Islamists demonstrated comprehensively their willingness to operate within the framework of the pluralist constitution. They have only resorted to guerrilla violence since this option was abruptly and brutally denied them, on no good grounds whatever, with the lunatic decision to ban FIS in spring 1992.

There is thus a strong case for the view that the only way to end the increasingly terrible violence in Algeria, and halt the catastrophic disintegration of the Algerian body politic which is taking place, is to reverse that mistaken decision of February-March 1992 and admit the Islamist mainstream, whether doctrinally 'moderate' or not, to the constitutional political process. Short of relegalising the FIS, another way might be found to resolve the political crisis. If President Zeroual can find such another way, he deserves support. But it is clear that repression alone is not working, and that repression is the only policy that France will support for as long as Zeroual is president.

And this brings us to the realisation that France is a major player in the drama in Algeria, and that it is the French *veto* on a political settlement that is prolonging Algeria's agony. Repeated statements by prime minister Éduard Balladur and foreign minister Alain Juppé to the effect that 'it is up to the Algerians to solve their problems' and that 'France will not and cannot interfere', are humbug. France is not only interfering systematically in the internal affairs of Algeria, it no longer recognises Algeria as a sovereign state separate from France itself. Why is it the French minister of the *interior* who is making the running on France's policy towards Algeria? And what were French paramilitary gendarmes doing in Algeria in the first place?

Along with the truth, the other great casualty of the events of the last six years in Algeria has been Algeria's own existence as a sovereign state. Algeria is no longer independent. The Algerian army is functioning more and more as a dependent appendage of the French defence establishment. France, having systematically stymied all Algeria's attempts to solve her debt problem without rescheduling, has now assumed the role of orchestrator of international financial aid for the country and also of international 'acceptance' of the discredited military regime.

As for the Algerian people, they can reflect, as all routes to democracy are relentlessly blocked off in the name of combatting 'theocratic totalitarianism', that it is all their own fault for wanting to liberate themselves from France in the first place and for voting in such numbers for the FIS in the second place. They can console themselves with the knowledge that, despite the manifest errors of their ways, they still enjoy what M Juppé calls France's 'solidarity'.

Meanwhile, M Pasqua is only too happy to do business with those nice, non-violent, moderate, pro-Western, un-theocratic Islamists in Khartoum.

● *On 9 August, the French interior ministry banned five Algerian emigré papers. Al-Ansar, published in Warsaw by 'the partisans of djihad in Algeria and elsewhere', al-Ribat and al-Fath-al-Moubine (all in Arabic) and el-Djihad and Front Islamique du Salut, Armée Islamique du Salut (both in French) were removed from sale because of 'the violent anti-Western, anti-French tone, and their incitement to violence', said the official banning order*

# TAHAR DJAOUT

*Tahar Djaout, 39-year-old journalist, poet and novelist, was struck by three bullets on 26 May 1993. He died on 2 June. He was the founder and editor of the weekly* Ruptures, *an openly anti-Islamist publication. He is the author of several novels including* Les chercheurs d'os *(1984),* L'invention du désert *(1987) and* Les vigiles *(1991) for which he won the Prix Méditerranée. The following piece is the last he wrote. What can be expected from a dialogue between parties whose social programmes are light years apart? he asks, and attacks the High State Committee for its failure to determine a direction for Algeria*

# The family that's moving ahead and the family that's going backward

Impossible to figure this one out. When the president of the HCE [High State Council] addressed the nation not long ago in a speech that was, among other things, supposed to sum up the dialogue between itself and various parties and associations, an unexpected extension [of the dialogue] was announced. Does this mean that at the end of the time formally allotted to the dialogue there was a tie? Undoubtedly. How could it be otherwise when people continue to believe that visions of society separated by 10 centuries can co-exist, when they continue to take seriously a party leader who proclaims that Algeria has no need for any law since the Quran already contains all that is needed?

Given the profound crisis Algeria is undergoing, one that confounds any predictions on the future, wouldn't salvation lie rather in a determined choice (even if this means stirring up discontent)? A choice that would snatch Algeria out of the claws of darkness and propel it toward the light? This choice is so late in emerging that we are beginning to ask ourselves anxiously whether it is really toward the light of day that those charged with the destiny of the country want to lead us.

The second original aspect of this political dialogue is that it is supposed to group together the different formations in 'families' of ideas. And this throws us right back into the great Algerian dilemma: except for a few minor points of detail, there *are* only two families: the family that is moving ahead and the family that is going backward.

Among the five political formations accepted by the HCE we can count two fundamentalist parties, two parties that support fundamentalism, and a single party that is working for a modern, republican Algeria.

What law is to be applied in such a case: quantity or quality? Which party should we listen to: the one that pleads for a democratic, fully developed, modern society, or the four that want to take Algeria back to a period that is worse than the one it is enduring today? Let's hope that the government, which admitted in January 1992 that the law of numbers is not always omnipotent, will lend a good ear and make the right choice. Otherwise, wouldn't it seem as though the government, which has been self-perpetuating since 1962, only interrupted the absurd electoral process of a year and a half ago to preserve its own continuous succession and not, as many believe, to save Algeria?

...We are starting to lose our footing, getting dizzy from the hesitation waltz and the balancing act that we are being lured into. An example: on the one hand, the *adhan* [call to prayer] is introduced on the television (something we have done without for 30 years without losing our Islamic identity); on the other hand, public servants are required to come to work in neutral dress that does not impose the display of their devotion on other citizens. We shall not dwell on the first point, but let us say that the second is entirely to the government's credit. It indicates that the executive branch is preoccupied with reimposing order and giving a bit of authority back to a state that has been trampled underfoot for so long. It is thus agreeable for us to think that in the future we shall no longer be welcomed by employees in *djelbab*, clappers, or *gandura*, or whose cheeks have not experienced a razor for 20 days.

But wait, the one time that the government has taken a decent initiative, the reaction will probably come from those from whom we should least expect it — though we should by now be accustomed to them. We can bet that the starving human rights advocates, who are looking for the slightest cause to appease their hunger, will soon be calling it a violation of I don't know what. Unfortunately, populism is not the monopoly of one camp, and the least expected people have been known to contaminate a well, even if they have then had to transform themselves into professional mourners before the writhing victims of a fatal poisoning.

*Published in* **Ruptures** *issue 20 (25-31 May 1993)*

In The Name of Allah Most Gracious Most Merciful

# ECHOES
## Of Truth

## ABDELKRIM ZEROUALI

# The people's choice

Since Algeria's military-backed regime decided, on 11 January 1992, to annul the second round of a general election which the FIS was poised to win, the country has been plunged into an undeclared civil war. In the words of a US Congressman at the time: 'Algeria is a clear-cut case of how a people's will which was expressed at the ballot box was thwarted through the barrel of a gun.'

The gun of an oppressive oligarchy has, for the last two and a half years done more than merely thwart elections. Concentration camps still hold thousands of people without due process of law; institutionalised torture has brought back vivid memories of Algeria in 1958 under French occupation, when Algerians were systematically subjected to torture by the French Parachute Battalion. Used in conjunction with the provisions of the state of emergency, 'special courts' are used to expedite cases, hand down capital sentences and execute people in phoney trials. Human rights organisations have reported close to 400 death penalties carried out in Algeria. A number of independent organisations have given the death toll as over 4,000 since the declaration of the state of emergency.

Even up to 11 January 1992, Algeria was a country based on well founded institutions. Since that date, and amid widespread corruption, total lack of security and the absence of law and order, it has decayed to the point of total chaos — civil war.

By ignoring the results of free parliamentary elections, by destroying all the institutions that are necessary for the proper running of the state and by eliminating all forms of free expression, the regime has blocked all avenues for political activity. The Algerian people, with FIS at the forefront, were left with no option but to resort to armed struggle with the aim of ridding the nation of the corrupt and unpopular regime whose conduct has led the country to ruin.

The armed action has been subjected to a ferocious media campaign, inside and outside the country, that resorts to falsification and fabrication with the intention of deceiving the masses into believing the Islamists are the root cause of their problems.

The FIS leadership in exile complained that foreign reporting on Algeria's civil strife, largely dependent on heavily censored state media and newspapers, is one-sided and ignores mass killings of Algerian civilians by the security forces. 'Ample publicity is usually given to specific incidents involving foreigners or so-called intellectuals while repeated kidnappings and mass executions inflicted on civilians go unreported,' said Anwar Haddam, US-based leader of the FIS parliamentary delegation.

'Who are these so-called intellectuals?' Haddam asked in October 1993 in an interview with the Paris-based French newsagency Agence France-Presse. 'Among them are members of the National Consultative Council, which has usurped the place of the people's elected representatives, persons who wrote murderous editorials, and those who, as psychiatrists, advised torturers on how to obtain confessions. The Algerian people has chosen as targets only those individuals upon whom the military-security system in Algeria relies. We know them one by one, and they are far from being innocent.'

In other words, intellectuals who use their intellectual capacities to co-operate with the regime are considered as 'Intellec-tueurs', accomplices in the crimes against the Algerian people.

As for the killing of foreigners in Algeria by armed opposition groups, Rabeh Kebir, the official spokesman of FIS in Europe, told Radio France International (RFI) in a radio interview on 22 October 1993: 'It is not the policy of FIS to kill foreigners, but it is very difficult to control actions by the mass of the people.' In its report on Algeria, Human Rights Watch/Middle East (*Index* May/June 1994), quotes Kebir further: 'People are never targeted for their ideas. As long as a journalist's opposition to the Islamist's programme is merely intellectual, and his/her criticism is along these lines, there is no problem.... But some journalists have been used to inform on our young men. If a journalist is associated with the process of informing (the authorities), he/she ceases to become a journalist and becomes, in effect, a combatant.'

As for freedom of expression, its scope has narrowed for both Islamists and others. Scores of preachers have been tried and sentenced for sermons deemed to be inciting or defamatory toward state institutions; thousands of FIS sympathisers have been convicted for attending 'illegal' gatherings, or distributing or possessing 'subversive' tracts. Simply calling the regime a 'junta' or 'illegitimate' has led to the prosecution of many.

Algeria's independent press has also lost much ground. With continued government control of the major printing presses, distribution networks, and advertising budgets, editors cannot afford to ignore repeated threats from ministers to punish newspapers that 'destabilise' the country. The press has also been intimidated by the arrest of some 20 journalists during 1992 for reporting deemed 'objectionable', and by the suspension of a number of weeklies and national dailies.

As the world scrambles over Bosnia, Rwanda and Yemen the Algerian crisis looms ever larger across the Mediterranean. Unless this crisis is looked at within its proper dimensions, the situation can only get worse. It may be that the West needs to invest more thought into how this particular situation can be healed. The West must realise that it cannot continue to support the Algerian regime nor ignore the people's right to choose its leadership. At the last G7 meeting in Naples, the Italian foreign minister, Antonio Martino, said: 'I am convinced that the Algerian government has a problem of legitimacy: it has lost the elections and "stolen" the ballot results.' He added: 'A government that is not legitimate cannot survive on foreign aid. It needs, one way or another, to re-establish at least part of its legitimacy.' Italy, he says, is in favour of a dialogue between the regime and the 'non-extremist' elements of society, noting that his French counterpart, Alain Juppé, does not believe there are such elements in Algerian society. Martino believes the situation could have been avoided had FIS been 'allowed' to win the first free elections in 30 years.

Let us hope that, slowly and gradually, the West will come to realise that the alternative to the people's choice — the military regime — is far worse than predicted, and that a legitimate and representative government can achieve better results than a dictatorship, even when the former is blindly considered by many as the enemy to fear.

CHEB
KHALED

MANGO RECORDS

*Cheb Khaled, known throughout the Mahgreb and in its exile communities as the 'King of Rai', and hero of a disaffected generation, is unwelcome at home. The Algerian government has banned his lyrics for infringing social taboos and stirring its youth to rebellion; the Islamists who took over several local councils in Algiers in the municipal elections of 1990, have closed discos and nightclubs where his music reigns supreme.*

# Serbi serbi

One drink after another
And yet another
I drink to my lost love
And the life we'll never know
I drink to the empty glass around me
The barman knows my sorrow
And fills another glass
As I drink to one more broken promise
One more sad twist of fate

# Attack on justice

**Lawyers are a prime target for those who hold human rights in contempt**

Around 9am on Saturday 18 June this year, armed men shot **Youssef Fathallah**, a lawyer and president of the Algerian League for Human Rights (ALHR). According to witnesses in the area at the time, a group of men stormed into his office in central Algiers, shot him in the head and made their escape. No group has claimed responsibility for the crime and there have been no arrests.

After his election to the presidency of the ALHR in 1991, Fathallah was an outspoken critic of political violence, the assassinations by armed groups as well as the widespread extrajudicial killings by government security forces; his organisation has criticised abuses by both sides in the civil conflict.

Sixty-four-year-old Fathallah was also a member of the commission set up to investigate the death of President Mohammed Boudiaf in June 1992. As a member of the commission, he called for the closure of special internment camps set up in the desert for the thousands of Islamists swept up in the mass arrests after the cancellation of elections in January 1992. He had accused the government of using torture in the camps and of holding prisoners without charge.

Fathallah is not the first lawyer to be killed in Algeria in the last couple of years. Since last February, a number of lawyers have received death threats from Islamic groups warning them not to plead in the special courts set up under the 1992 anti-terrorist decree to try Islamists accused of terrorist attacks. Several have been killed in the last few months: Brahim Benghanem on 17 April; **Laïd Grine** on 14 May; and **Saadi Benghoul** on 21 May.

The authorities have also harassed, suspended and imprisoned lawyers for criticising procedures in the special courts, defending Islamists or appealing their sentences in higher courts.

# Cases in court

Numerous reports of **police harassment of lawyers** and subsequent judicial acquiescence in police behaviour:

● **Deputy prosecutor** for the Tribunal of Algiers assassinated leaving his home.
● **Eleven lawyers** sanctioned by the Algiers Special Court. They had complained of irregular and unfair procedures in the Special Courts and called for a general boycott. They were given a three-month suspension under the April 1993 amendment to the anti-terrorism law. Suspensions cancelled after objections from the Algerian Bar Association.
● **Bekai Mahfoud,** judge and president of the Kolea Court and the Blida Military Court assassinated on 15 June 1993 allegedly by FIS.
● **Brahim Taouti,** lawyer, arrested on 2 February 1993 for violating Article 96 of the Algerian Penal Code outlawing the dissemination of 'subversive tracts.' Taouti was accused of carrying a document out of prison at the request of his client, Ali Belhadj, deputy chief of FIS, and distributing it to FIS leaders and human rights organisations. The authorities claimed that in the document Belhadj advocated armed struggle against the Algerian government. Taouti claimed the Belhadj document was for use in preparing his client's defence. He was held in preventive detention from the date of his arrest. On 3 May 1993, the Blida Military Court sentenced him to three years, the maximum allowed by law. Taouti had been active in defending human rights since the government began its crack down on FIS in June 1991. At the time of his arrest, he was preparing to appeal the convictions of FIS leaders.
● **Ali Zouita,** lawyer, detained without formal charge and held incommunicado since 1 February 1993 for 'disseminating subversive documents' given to him by his client, Abdelkader Hachani, a leader of FIS. Also accused of incitement to murder and subversion, belonging to an armed movement, and possessing weapons. Before his arrest, Zouita had been defending members of FIS, and was preparing their appeal before the Algerian Supreme Court.

# Camera obscura

● The Algerian legal system includes Military Courts which are controlled by the Directorate of Military Justice within the National Defence Ministry. Article 25 of the Military Justice Code gives these courts jurisdiction over crimes committed by civilians against the security of the state as well as those committed by military personnel. In contrast to the Special Courts, the names of Military Court judges are made public.

● The Military Courts relinquished their competence in 1989, but were reactivated in 1992 and given discretionary power to hear certain cases considered to be politically sensitive. The decision to bring the leaders of the FIS for trial in the Blida Military Court is a typical example. The trial was conducted in camera.

● The Military Courts' discretionary jurisdiction and subordination to the executive contravene the UN Basic Principles on the Independence of the Judiciary.

● The anti-terrorism decree of 30 September 1992 further undermined the independence of the judiciary and the ability of lawyers to provide adequate defences for their clients by introducing a system of Special Courts in flagrant violation of the UN Basic Principles. The anti-terrorism law not only suppresses freedom of speech, it has also resulted in a lawyer being held liable for the contents of a client's documents (see the case of Brahim Taouti above). The new law also extends the legal length of incommunicado detention from 48 hours to 12 days, with no access to counsel.

● There are three Special Courts presided over by civil judges appointed by the president of the republic. Hundreds of government opponents have been summarily tried in Special Courts, often without benefit of counsel; at least 19 defendants have been sentenced to death by the Special Courts. Six of those condemned by the State Security Courts were executed earlier this year. On 2 August 1993, a Special Court sentenced seven more members of the FIS to death, raising the total of death sentences to about 165. Six defendants in this case were tried *in absentia* for crimes 'linked to acts of terrorism.'

● In April 1993, an amendment to the anti-terrorism law to 're-inforce the efficiency and the effectiveness' of the Special Courts gave them even greater powers. They may now expel from court any lawyer who uses 'dilatory and obstructionist manoeuvres,' suspend the lawyer's professional activity for a period of three months to one year and deny the defence access to documents. Lawyers may not appear in either Military or Special Courts without prior permission from the legal authorities.

*Compiled from* **Attacks on Justice: the harassment and persecution of judges and lawyers** *(International Commission of Jurists, 1993)*

Algiers 1991: peace in the Rue Didouche

LAHCENE ABIB: CAMERA PRESS

# REVIEWS

JULIAN PETLEY

# Little devils

*Censored: What they didn't allow you to see and why: the story of film censorship in Britain.* Tom Dewe Mathews, Chatto and Windus, London 1994. £14.99.

*Freedom, the Individual and the Law.* Geoffrey Robertson, Penguin, London 1993 (seventh edition). £12.00.

*Men, Women and Chain Saws: Gender in the modern horror film.* Carol Clover, British Film Institute, London 1992. £11.95

*Managing Monsters: Six myths of our time.* Marina Warner, Vintage, London 1994. £5.99.

*Sex and Sensibility: Reflections on forbidden mirrors and the will to censor.* Marcia Pally, The Ecco Press, Hopewell, New Jersey 1994.

*Video Violence and Young Offenders.* Home Affairs Committee, HMSO, London 1994. £14.40.

'It is not for me to pass judgement on their upbringing but I suspect that exposure to violent video films may be in part an explanation.' Thus Mr Justice Morland in his summing up of the James Bulger murder trial last November, setting off, by these exceedingly ill-informed and uncalled-for speculations, a train of events which would culminate, last April, in an amendment to the Criminal Justice Bill which threatens further to tighten film and video censorship in this country.

Crucial to this sequence was a veritable Niagara of 'video nasty' stories in the press. If you believe them, Britain is awash with 'video nasties' which are freely available to young children, there is a direct link between the video *Child's Play 3* and the murders of James Bulger and Suzanne Capper, and the British Board of Film Classification is irresponsibly liberal in its decisions. In fact, 'video nasties' were outlawed by police action under the Obscene Publications Act even before the Video Recordings Act came into force in 1984; there are no causal links whatsoever between *Child's Play 3* and the Bulger and Capper murders, as the police involved in the cases readily agree; and Britain has one of the strictest regimes of film and video censorship in the Western world.

Just how strict can be gauged from Tom Dewe Mathews' *Censored* and the chapters devoted to censorship and regulation in the latest edition of Geoffrey Robertson's indispensable *Freedom, the Individual and the Law.* What both books make abundantly clear is that a good deal of the rationale for film censorship in the UK lies in the fact that local authorities have the power to cut and ban films. This stems from the Cinematograph Act of 1909 which, in the wake of various cinema fires, required cinemas to be licensed by their local councils. Inevitably, the new medium had already attracted the attentions of the moral busybodies, and many councils were quick to use the granting (or withholding) of licences as a means of exercising control over the content of the films shown. Thus local censorship was born, and the industry was soon faced

MILEN RADEV

with a bewildering array of differing standards of acceptability across the country. Its response, in 1912, was to set up the British Board of Film Censors and to win the councils' faith in its judgements. In this the industry succeeded, but unfortunately the powers which the councils had abrogated to themselves were never abolished, and the industry still lives in terror of an uncontrollable hydra of local censorship systems. Hence, as

Mathews points out, the depressing spectacle of the industry baying for the sacking of BBFC's Secretary Stephen Murphy in 1972 for being too liberal in passing *Straw Dogs* and *A Clockwork Orange*. As Robertson notes, such powers are archaic, a waste of councillors' time and taxpayers' money and mean that 'the cinema, alone of art forms, is subject to moral judgement by local councillors'. Their abolition would be a notable step in the struggle to establish a less restrictive form of film censorship.

The BBFC also exists to ensure that the films which it classifies do not break the law, especially the Obscene Publications Act. As Robertson reveals, there exists a 'gentlemen's agreement' between the BBFC and the DPP going back to 1957 when the latter admitted to the Select Committee on Obscenity that 'as long as I rely on the judgement of the British Board of Film Censors as to the suitability, under the various categories, of films for public showing, which I do, I do not prosecute'. This is all very cosy, of course, but it does raise the question of why the 'publish and be damned' rule cannot apply to film and video as it does to every other art form. There are two answers to this question. First, film and video are essentially popular art forms and, as Mathews points out, there is an unspoken rubric in this country that 'the larger the audience, the lower moral mass resistance to suggestion'.

Secondly, of course, the industry benefits from such a protective system. As the abovementioned case of Stephen Murphy all too clearly demonstrates, when it comes to choosing between protecting freedom of expression and its own pockets, the industry will always unerringly choose the latter. Similarly, the industry's desire to appease

those who shout 'video nasty' at the slightest chance, as opposed to telling them to put up or shut up, simply bears out the remark by Steve Woolley, the independent distributor of the much-demonised *Evil Dead*, that all that the majors want is 'a sanitised environment for them to make a profit in'. So the sad fact is that it's difficult to get the film industry on board the anti-censorship struggle.

Both Robertson and Mathews reveal that the BBFC, under its present Director James Ferman, sees its duty as going well beyond ensuring that the films which it passes don't break the law. When it comes to the depiction of violence, the Board feels it necessary to take into account 'the moral position of the film-maker towards his own material'. In assessing the film's moral stance (and thus the Board's own stance towards the film) the Report reveals that the following questions are taken into consideration: '(1) Is the sympathy of the film-maker on the side of the victim or the aggressor? (2) Is the process of the violence indulged in for its own sake, rather than to tell us anything significant about the motives or state of mind of the persons involved? (3) Does the camerawork or editing belie the ostensible moral stance of the film by seeking to enlist or encourage our vicarious enjoyment of the atrocities portrayed?' Thus for example we find

**Like Miss Prism's view of fiction, the BBFC's view of feature films is that the good should end happily and the bad unhappily**

cuts in the video of *Lethal Weapon II* (over and above the cinema cuts) because 'the hero indulged his vengeful instincts far beyond the needs of the narrative', and Ferman not only cutting but re-editing a scene in the video of *Henry: Portrait of a Serial Killer* because he wanted the audience 'to take a properly moral view about the violence that's shown on screen'. Clearly we're dealing here with a latterday Dr Bowdler or Charles Lamb. Or as Robertson acidly puts it: 'Like Miss Prism's view of fiction, the BBFC's view of feature films is that the good should end happily and the bad unhappily'.

Given the criteria by which the Board appears to exercise its judgements it's not surprising that so many films and videos are subject to cuts, some of them as short as one second. The Board's latest Annual Report, that for 1992, reveals that 11.1 per cent of all '18' films and 18 per cent of all '18' videos were passed only after cuts had been made, and it's important to remember that some of the video cuts will be in addition to the cinema cuts. Since the Video Recordings Act was first implemented by the Board in September 1985, 25.1 per cent of '18' videos have been cut. It's impossible to know how many films and videos have been in effect banned, since distributors know the Board's standards and don't bother to go to the expense of submitting a product which they know full well won't be passed at all.

There's now a considerable and sophisticated literature on the horror film, which frequently features on university film and media courses. One of the best recent additions is Carol Clover's *Men, Women, and Chain Saws*. This book should be required reading for anybody who takes seriously press descriptions of horror films as 'video nasties'. Unlike the journalists who write this hysterical, ill-informed rubbish, Clover has actually seen the films and come to the conclusion that 'there are in horror moments and works of great humour, formal brilliance, political intelligence, psychological depth, and above all a kinky creativity that is simply not available in any other stripe of film-making.' She also understands that, more than any other film genre, horror is distinguished by its 'engagement of repressed fears and desires and its re-enactment of the residual conflict surrounding these feelings', and she brings into play a formidable (though by no means daunting) array of psychoanalytic theory in order to prove her point. Particularly striking is her analysis of that most despised subgenre of horror, the stalk 'n' slash film (*Halloween, Friday the 13th* etc.), which is usually regarded as the ne plus ultra of sadistic voyeurism and misogyny. Clover, on the other hand, discerns in its threatened but ultimately triumphant heroines 'the use of the woman as a kind of feint, a front through which the boy [that is, the male spectator] can simultaneously experience forbidden desires and disavow them on grounds that the visible actor is, after all, a girl', concluding that 'by any measure, horror is far more victim-identified than the standard view would have it.' Through close attention not only to movies, but also to their audiences, Clover captures brilliantly the

LUBOMIR MIHAILOV

way in which, whilst watching this kind of movie, our sympathies and identifications ceaselessly shift this way and that but always and inevitably come round in the end to what she evocatively calls the Final Girl. And she understands, too, that watching horror movies is a highly ritualised social activity involving an

active and discerning fan culture with high levels of visual literacy and competence. What a refreshing change from the British press's snobbish denigration of the horror fan as a mentally defective incipient criminal.

A less dubious motive for censorship is the desire to protect children from scenes which might upset and disturb them. The problem here, however, is that the notion of childhood has itself become increasingly mythologised, as Marina Warner has pointed out in her Reith Lecture *Little Angels, Little Devils: Keeping Childhood Innocent*. As she notes, though, the mythology is distinctly Janus-faced. On the one hand, 'the nostalgic worship of childhood innocence is more marked today than it ever has been' but, on the other, 'in the very midst of consecrating innocence, the modern mythology of childhood ascribes to children a specially rampant natural appetite for all sorts of transgressive pleasures — including above all the sado-masochistic thrills of fear... the Child has never been seen as such a menacing enemy as it is today. Never before have children been so saturated with all the power of projected monstrousness to excite repulsion — and even terror.' Nothing, but nothing, could illustrate this schizophrenic mythology more clearly than the press representations of James Bulger and his killers. The relevance of this kind of thinking to the will to censor is obvious: on the one hand 'innocent' children must be protected from visions which might shatter that 'innocence'; on the other, the 'little devils' must not be allowed to see anything which might trigger the demonic within them. And where did the image of the demonic child first appear in post-war culture? Why, in the despised horror genre, in movies such as *Rosemary's Baby* (1968), *The Exorcist* (1973), *It's Alive* (1974) and *The Omen* (1976). The fact that *The Exorcist* is effectively banned on video in the UK today is as good an example of shooting the messenger as I've come across.

But, of course, the biggest impetus to the will to censor is the idea that the media have 'effects' upon us, and negative ones at that. This is an extremely vexed subject, both within academic circles and without, and looks like becoming even more so.

The academic debate suddenly shot to wider prominence on 31 March this year when, in the run-up to David Alton's largely successful attempt further to tighten film and video censorship by tacking on an amendment to the already much discredited Criminal Justice Bill, the *Evening Standard* announced its lead story with the headline 'U-Turn Over Video Nasties', informing its readers that 'Britain's top psychologists today confessed that they had got it wrong in denying a link between video nasties and real life violence.' What the paper was referring to was a document signed by Professor Elizabeth Newson of Not-

tingham University, and 32 others. However, these included psychiatrists and paediatricians, and only three of the signatories had ever spoken publicly on the topic before. The story omitted the rather important fact that the document was actually commissioned by David Alton specifically to be used as evidence in support of his amendment! The *Standard* article set the tone for most of the subsequent reporting, which featured on the front pages of numerous papers. In all the hullabaloo a Policy Studies Institute paper on the viewing habits of young offenders was largely ignored by the press. Commissioned by the BBFC, BBC, Independent Television Commission and Broadcasting Standards Council, the findings are summarised in *Video Violence and Young Offenders*, and the most crucial one states that 'in general terms, offenders do not watch more television or select more violent programmes or films than schoolchildren. Indeed, offenders had less access to television, video or other equipment than other children.' Still, the PSI report got more coverage than a paper signed by 23 media academics which questioned the whole basis of the Newson document and forcefully stated that her conclusions were completely out of kilter with most recent UK academic research on the media. This was sent to all the same places as the Newson document — and totally ignored.

The 'effects' theory is nothing like as cut and dried as the press would have us believe. Here, for example, is the conclusion of the

Association of Chief Police Officers in *Video Violence and Young Offenders*: 'The accumulated evidence does not warrant the conclusion that viewing violent/pornographic films and videos is directly linked to violent criminal behaviour in the vast majority of cases. Although there is evidence that the viewing of such material can lead to aggressive and dehumanised behaviour in some cases, hardly, if at all, can these influences be disentangled from a mass of other psychological and social factors which together explain actual human behaviour in specific instances of violent crime.'

A different view was expressed by Ann Nelson's 'Colours of Violence' in the May/June issue of *Index* , in which she argued that 'there is a growing body of evidence establishing the link between films and violent behaviour, particularly in the case of children watching without adult supervision.' By the end of the same page 'growing' has swollen to 'overwhelming'. But in Marcia Pally's *Sex and Sensibility*, at least one of the sources quoted by Nelson is challenged at some length in a chapter entitled 'Minors and Media Minotaurs'. This survey of growing censoriousness in the USA is a disturbing book for anybody who has ever looked to the First Amendment as a means of protecting freedom of expression, and it also takes an extremely critical view of the way in which those of the Dworkin/MacKinnon persuasion have at times allied themselves with the forces of the

Right in their various campaigns against material which they believe to be harmful to women.

As these various examples, taken in toto, clearly imply, there is a great deal of controversy over the notion of 'media effects', a notion which, nonetheless, is crucial to the whole censorship project. There are disagreements within as well as between disciplines, and also between US and UK approaches to the subject. In the end there may be very little point in comparing and contrasting studies from quite different standpoints since, in a very real sense, they aren't really talking about the same things. This doesn't mean, however, that we simply shrug our shoulders and fall back on 'common sense' explanations.

This point is forcefully driven home by Ian Vine, a member of the Department of Interdisciplinary Studies at Bradford University, in one of the most interesting contributions to *Video Violence and Young Offenders*: 'Establishing causation within the psychological realm is massively more difficult than lay-persons, medical practitioners, and too many American psychologists trained within the 'behaviourist' paradigm will normally suppose. That is why it is so easy to find different 'experts', and differing empirical enquiries, flatly contradicting one another's conclusions. It may be frustrating for the public to be told that more evidence has to be gathered, when so many reports have already appeared. But the reason is simple. Too many researchers have repeatedly asked the wrong questions in the wrong ways — using quick and cheap methods to get almost worthless answers.' And as Vine points out, the reasons for this are largely economic rather than stemming from any ideological bias in favour of behaviourist analyses: 'Funding and support are rarely adequate for the painstaking, intensive, long-term studies which could hope to settle the relative importance of various causal contributions to anti-social dispositions and actions. Pressures within the social scientific professions actively militate against research with substantial but only long-term payoffs.'

*Video Violence and Young Offenders* contains cogent statements both of the pro- and anti-censorship posi- tions, and gives a valuable insight into the controversies currently surrounding 'effects' research. However, notwithstanding the deeply conflicting opinions laid bare in its pages, the British government seems determined to press ahead with an amendment which, with its talk of videos causing 'harm' to 'potential viewers' appears to endorse the crassest, most crude kind of behaviourist dogma. Still, since in every other aspect of the Criminal Justice Bill the Government has clearly demonstrated that it would rather pander to the *Mail* and the *Sun* than act on research which it had commissioned itself (but which, unfortunately, came up with the 'wrong' answers) I suppose we shouldn't be too surprised.

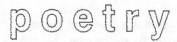

# DIARY

## RADHA KUMAR

# Dying in Sarajevo

Sarajevo 1994

**4 April 1994**
Arrived here two days ago. The Washington agreement of last month is
widely heralded as ushering the transition to peace and the UN and
UNHCR people are all talking about their headquarters moving here.
They seem to think a settlement is imminent — or at any rate, act as if
they think so.

Local opinions of the Washington agreement differ. The optimists see
it as a genuine Bosnian-Croat rapprochement achieved by US pressure,
and they expect equally successful pressure on the Serbs to join a
confederation. The pessimists see the agreement as a decisive step towards
the acceptance of partition, but the question is whether partition will be
achieved through fairly cynical land swaps (and ethnic cleansing) or
whether there will be more war. The 10pm curfew continues, and I am
told all telephones are routinely tapped and all of us have our own
personal minders.

## 7 April

The Serbs have begun an attack on Gorazde. UN commander General Rose went on CNN to announce that everything was under control — while the Serbs captured key strategic positions around the city. President Izetbegovic is issuing appeals to NATO to bomb the Serbs.

Saw Ademir (Kenovic)'s film [*Umrijeti u Sarajevu* — 'Dying in Sarajevo'] yesterday — the sequences with the young Serb paramilitary who confessed to a series of gruesome murders are spine-chilling.

We went out to dinner afterwards, a popular black market restaurant full of people. The streets were full of soldiers — everyone was commemorating the 'Bosnian day of independence', when the European Community recognised Bosnia-Hercegovina as a sovereign state. Several people were arrested for violating the curfew, including the editor of *BH Days*, who spent the night in the lock-up and the next day writing a wry piece on the combined ironies of the commemoration and the curfew.

It is cold and wet. Everyone is very tired. While they were being shelled survival was a triumph and, to keep the spirit of Sarajevo alive, a defiance. Now there is no shelling, but the city is still surrounded and there is no way for people to get on with their lives. There is very little food, electricity every three days and water every two. A lot of ugly petty feelings are surfacing. Tomorrow I go to Split to buy food.

## 14 April

The Serbs have arrested all the UNPROFOR monitors and a number of soldiers in the 20 kilometre zone around Sarajevo. Serb TV broadcast that 200 UNPROFOR soldiers were withdrawing from Mount Igman and giving the positions to Bosnian troops. UNPROFOR has denied both the arrests and the accusation. Meanwhile the Serbs are pushing on to fulfil their historic goal of crossing the Drina.

Zdravko (Grebo) is back from Mostar. He feels the radicalisation process has advanced quite far. Neither of us can quite envisage the re-integration of the city. He says that during the shelling by Croats there were many messages from Croats on the left bank to Muslims on the right saying they did not want the war, but they were not disseminated.

## 15 April

The Serbs have taken the right bank of Gorazde. One UN monitor has been killed, and there are reportedly thousands of Bosnians killed and wounded. One NATO plane has been shot down. Lord Owen, Mr Stoltenberg and most of the senior UN officials are in Pale negotiating for the release of their personnel, and asking the Serbs to withdraw three miles from Gorazde by 8am on the 17th. As far as we could see from Serb TV, the Serbs are not averse to this...

But the lines in Mostar seem to be hardening. Today television covered a Muslim delegation to Mostar west, led by the muftis, and a Catholic Croat mass in Mostar east. The Zenica mufti was on television opening a sports event.

## 18 April
The Serbs did not withdraw and the deadline has been extended... The news from Gorazde is terrible. The hospital has been repeatedly shelled. There was an attack on the UNHCR building and now they are all holed up in a basement. UNPROFOR has taken its troops and monitors out and left UNHCR, Médicins sans Frontières, etc behind. There was a UN monitor's report warning of an impending Serb attack on Gorazde, but it was ignored.

## 21 April
Serb television shows gloating sequences of the NATO plane falling through the air, dead soldiers, and the brave Serb defiance of Western imperialism. Bosnian television shows endless sequences of Muslim victims interspersed with lacrimonious songs against a melting backdrop of rain-hazed minarets. The other day, they repeated sequences of the wounded and dead in Gorazde and then moved straight on to shots of anti-UN demonstrations in Iran.

## 24 April
A young UN soldier attached to the UNHCR was shot a few days ago while violating the curfew. It seems he was wearing civilian clothes and the guards panicked. Apparently the Bosnian government are considering loosening the curfew but not lifting it.

I went with Mr Hiko to the black market today. There isn't very much to buy: a few tins of UN food, some bars of soap, a bottle or two of cooking oil, all very expensive. A bottle of whisky is 150 DM and a bottle of Loza 100 DM. And the average wage is 2-4 DM — that is, when people are not paid in cigarettes.

Sarajevo 1994: not a lot to buy, cooking difficult

There are a lot more women in head scarves than before. We are told that an Islamic charity called Igasa, funded by Iran, pays them 50 DM a day to do so. And that Saudi Arabia has offered to pay for rebuilding the schools and university, but on condition that courses on Islam and Islamic education be introduced.

### 30 April

Went to see Mr Eagleton, the UN co-ordinator for Sarajevo, today. The UN's approach is to concentrate on rebuilding utilities according to the pre-war integrated system in the hope of keeping routes open between Sarajevo and the Serb-controlled districts of Grbavica, Illidja, Rajlovac. Rebuilding the utilities is going to cost US$500 million... There is already brisk competition between the different Western nations on whose companies will get a share of the pie... Mr Eagleton's brief is very narrow. It doesn't include policing and even justice, which was at one time included, has now been excluded...

I am growing more and more convinced that it will be a very long time indeed before Sarajevo will have openings to reintegrate. Here everyone says that the Serbs will never give up their little pieces of Sarajevo — these are their claims to culture. But this city too has changed. It is being progressively radicalised, and one senses considerable hostility, even on this side, to the minor UN forays at normalisation and reintegration. A couple of weeks ago four people died in sniper fire on a tram. Yesterday, a man who had been to Grbavica and back was shot. The chief of the Grbavica *opstina* [municipality] has been killed: four men with machine guns just burst in and opened fire. A bystander — a man from Sarajevo who had gone to collect a food parcel waiting for him in Grbavica — was also killed. People shrug their shoulders and snigger a bit when talking about his death. Nobody bothers to talk about the *opstina* chief's death at all: the general consensus is that it was some kind of minor mafia war.

### 7 May

Yesterday we had our one-day meeting on refugees and the right to return. Eighty-six people turned up! Even Vlado, who is often so superior, smiled and said it was the best meeting that Sarajevo had seen since the war began. This is the first time that representatives of international institutions, the Bosnian government, and independent intellectuals have discussed anything together in a public forum. The 'internationals' tend to keep apart from the 'locals', and this breeds both suspicions of colonialism and colonial attitudes. The UN is the worst.

I learned an enormous amount from what people said. The dominant view is that the Bosnian government wants refugees back because population is a good bargaining counter at the negotiating table. But they are still not ready to grant a general amnesty so returning refugees are in danger of facing trials for desertion or draft-dodging and there is also the danger of conscription. An even bigger problem is that everyone wants a return to the pre-war 'original native' population... There were rather pointed references to the 'men from Sandzak'. Ganic comes from Sandzak, which has a reputation for being more Islamic than other areas. We caught a hint of territorial claims to Sandzak by the new Bosniaks.

## 16 May

UNPROFOR is madly spreading stories about how Gorazde has been exaggerated and the Bosnian government figures on wounded and dead are blown up. They say no more than 200 were killed, but they have no evidence either way and the UN, UNHCR et al have always used Bosnian government figures since they had none of their own. I think UNPROFOR ignored the reports of an impending attack on Gorazde because subconsciously they all assumed that a partition agreement was imminent, and Gorazde seemed just one more losing battle between the Bosnian and Serb armies. And now they are trying to cover up by accusing the Bosnians of playing up the whole thing.

The other story going the whispering round is that the Bosnians themselves set up the killing of an SAS man in Gorazde in order to provoke NATO air attacks... Everybody suspects everybody's motives, even amongst us. I am becoming aware of a great silence under which a thousand assumptions seethe.

## 17 May

A man phoned Radio Zid a few days ago saying the US Senate had voted to lift the arms embargo. So we had a great kerfuffle telephoning around to find out what had really happened. The UNPROFOR press officer told us to keep our hats on, this was only the first stage in a very long process. Then we called David (Rieff) in New York, and he said pretty much the same. We rather hastily concluded it was more of a PR exercise than anything, because the British and the French would never agree to it, and the US would risk challenging the UN if they were to press on with it.

We had a party for Radio Zid last night. I decided to use up all my food and drink as I am leaving for a couple of weeks. Trisha, who is only 17, took me shopping to the black market and we bought lots of beer. We all played a delightfully silly game while the young sophisticates of the radio wandered gaily through the room looking super-cool and filming the party. They really are a bunch — Adi who wears his green baseball cap backwards and has a politely ironic wit, Aida the sixties kid who does a show on people's dreams and desires, handsome Vedran in his dark glasses who is so very kind to everybody, Trisha the baby who is also the rock, Egon from Grbavica who cannot go home. We had spinach from Mr Hiko's garden. Everyone has been growing vegetables in boxes on their balconies, and most of the parks have been transformed into vegetable patches. I actually had salad at Zlata's the other day.

The UN man who was with me on the flight out of Sarajevo says that all the negotiations have broken down and they are back where they started two years ago.

## 4 June

The markets are full of vegetables, and there is even fruit. Prices have come crashing down: tomatoes are 5 DM a kilo, whisky is down to 50 DM, but wages (when it's money and not coupons or kind) are still 3-4 DM. Cafés have sprung up everywhere and are a terrible temptation to abandon work and sun oneself over a beer. The Bosnian government has just passed a law forbidding the sale or consumption of liquor in cafés. They say it is because there are too many young men with arms who might shoot while tipsy. The Brekin Potok front line, near our house, has suddenly become active. There has been some shelling as well as gunfire.

## 15 June

Have just gone through an English version of the federation constitution. There is ethnically based political representation at every level, even in the courts. It is very difficult to see how political cleansing can be avoided.

We were wrong to take the initiative to lift the embargo so lightly. In the last week, the Germans, Austrians, Turks and US have stepped up pressure; Senator Dole has been in Sarajevo to talk about his campaign for lifting the embargo, and it is becoming more and more likely that this might be the easiest way out for the international community if the Serbs reject the new maps which the Contact Group is supposed to come up with. [They did, in early August, despite pressure from the Milosevic's government in Belgrade.]

Iran has had an embassy here for three months. The Iranian ambassador spoke of Iran's humanitarian aid and willingness to supply both arms and soldiers in one breath — and bitterly of the international community's refusal of the latter, when they were accepting a large contingent of Turkish and Pakistani troops.

## 29 June

We held a two-day workshop on human, minority and collective rights this weekend. It was even better attended than the last one. Prime Minister Haris Silajdzic came and the UN and UNPROFOR were well represented. The atmosphere was electric — it was as if the just-concluded assembly elections of the government have more or less closed the Washington agreement and there was nothing left to say but a great deal to fear. Government representatives made clear that the agreement is an interim war-time arrangement.

The key political issue was that the agreement and constitution name two constituent nations of the federation, Bosniaks and Croats, but put the Serbs into the category of 'Others'. The official defence for this is that the Bosnian Serb nation has already carved out a territory for itself and so the Serbs who remain in the federation cannot be called a nation. The Serb Civic Forum argues that this is to give up pluralism and integrity and accept ethnic nationalism, which is pretty much what the agreement and constitution actually do. The proportion of Serbs in federation territories is only marginally lower than the proportion of Croats. Everyone thinks there will be more war.

## 31 June

Zdravko says the latest issue of *Lilian,* a nationalist magazine, has a full-page interview with US Ambassador Jakovic saying that the US is committed to the integrity of Bosnia — and that they believe that Sandzak belongs to Bosnia! From start to finish this war will be solely about forcing Bosnia into a Muslim identity. The irony is that the West did as little as they could because the Bosnians were categorised as Muslims — by them — and the thrust of their actions has been to create a Muslim state.

# LETTER FROM LAGOS

## ADEWALE MAJA-PEARCE

# Battle for Nigeria

In a speech delivered in Lagos in 1988, Wole Soyinka, the Nobel laureate, called upon the Nigerian military to 'stop this denigration of the popular will' and disengage from politics once and for all. Five years later, in June 1993, the military government of General Ibrahim Babangida inexplicably annulled the results of the democratic election which he himself had organised, thus paving the way for his second-in-command, General Sani Abacha, to take his turn as the country's new 'strongman'. The presumed winner of the elections, Chief Moshood Abiola, initially acquiesced in this new-style coup, but exactly one year later, on 12 June this year, he suddenly rediscovered his mandate and announced himself President at a rally in Lagos. The Chief was promptly arrested and charged with treason, precipitating a political crisis that many fear will lead to a second civil war in 34 years of independence.

Hatred of military rule goes deep. Accountable only to itself and the narrow political interests which it serves, the military is held directly responsible for the impoverishment of a wealthy nation by enthroning corruption, thereby destroying every institution in the country: there are no books in the schools nor drugs in the hospitals; electricity is rationed, water is in short supply and the phones don't work. But it goes far deeper

VOL. 11 NO. 6,168       AUGUST 14, 1994       TWENTY NAIRA

than that, beyond even Abiola himself, who is only a symbol of what has come to be widely regarded as 'the struggle'. There is also the deep sense of humiliation that the most populous nation in the continent has become pariah in the international community, unfit to compete with newly liberated South Africa for the coveted African seat in the United Nations Security Council. A US senator was recently heard to tell an official Nigerian delegation on a begging mission that their country was 'a disgrace'. Few Nigerians demurred. The foreigner had only spoken the truth.

The military itself is aware of all this, but is adamant that it will not be 'disgraced out of power', a phrase it never tires of repeating, but which only confirms what the populace already knows: that the Nigerian army is an army of occupation, and that the civilian population, all 100 million souls, have been reduced to what Soyinka called, in the same speech, 'a second-class breed of humanity'. To make matters worse, military intransigence is gradually destroying what is left of the economy.

No sooner was Abiola thrown into a police cell than the National Union of Petroleum and Natural Gas Workers (NUPENG) downed tools. Six weeks later, the government is still refusing to negotiate with a union which effectively controls 90 per cent of the country's foreign exchange earnings on the grounds that their demands — the unconditional release of Abiola and his inauguration as President — are 'political' and therefore unacceptable. To which the secretary-general of NUPENG, Frank Kokori, retorted that the government itself was 'illegal' and in no position to lecture anybody about politics.

In the meantime, the populace is suffering terribly. Prices of basic foodstuffs are rising daily, transport fares make nonsense of the weekly wage packet (when it's paid), and a new stove has been invented, called the 'Abacha stove', which is capable of burning sawdust in the absence of kerosene and bottled gas. But there is no evidence that ordinary people are disgruntled with NUPENG's action. On the contrary, most are irritated at the feeble stance of the Nigerian Labour Congress and its president, Comrade Pascal Bafyua, who has spent the last two months trying to disprove charges of corruption. But when even he realised that something had to be done, he summoned the courage to call a strike, only to call it off the next day because, he said, he was giving the government 'one last chance' to engage in 'fruitful negotiations'.

For its part, the military has given no indication whatsoever that it is prepared to vacate power of its own volition. Quite the reverse: its growing hostility to dissent of any kind led to the closure of all five titles of Guardian Newspapers Ltd on Monday, 15 August, following an article in the previous day's edition of the daily *Guardian*. The article: 'Inside Aso Rock: the raging battle to rule Nigeria', claimed that the cabinet was divided between the 'old, conservative order' and the 'progressives', insofar as these terms mean anything in a military administration. Considering that most papers have written much worse, and that the *Guardian* is the most widely-respected newspaper in the country because of its responsible

Lagos 1994: Abiola makes his appearance

reporting throughout this crisis, as well as its commitment to liberal values, the closure of the paper indicates that the old order is currently prevailing. And so it happened when, on 16 August, Abiola was brought before the Federal High Court in Abuja for the fifth time since his incarceration, only to watch the judge withdraw from the case, while he, Abiola, was returned to his cell.

The judge, Justice Abdullahi Mustapha, acknowledged his 'accidental utterances and actions' at the previous sitting when he had said that he had needed to consult with some of his colleagues on certain aspects of the case, and that this had shaken Abiola's confidence in his impartiality. In a radio interview shortly afterwards, the Attorney-General, Dr Olu Onaforuwa, hinted that the government might not want to continue with the case after all. This seems unlikely. How to free Abiola without triggering more instability is as tricky as how to try him without risking the same. The NUPENG strike is now in its seventh week, making life even harder for the ordinary people, who must struggle to find bread to eat and water to drink.

# BABEL

## JUDITH ADLER HELLMAN

# Mexican lives: on the border

**Continuing our series focusing on the voices of those silenced by poverty, prejudice and exclusion**

*Rosario Valdez, secondhand clothes dealer from Mexico City, Adelita Sandoval, domestic worker, and Pedro P, pollero or 'coyote', both of Tijuana, are fronteristas — people who haunt the Mexican-US frontier. All depend on it to make a better living than they could anywhere else in the country, particularly in the rural Mexico from which all have come in search of a better life.*

*Rosario makes the 15-16 hour journey in each direction once a week from Mexico City to her mecca — Los Tres Hermanos, a huge wholesale warehouse, or* bodega, *for secondhand clothing in Laredo, Texas. She has all the correct papers for a temporary visit to the USA and crossing presents no problems. Coming back is a different matter.*

When we cross [back] to the Mexican side in the *camioneta* that we hire to go from the *bodega* to the bus station, they stop us at the *aduana* and ask, 'What are you bringing in?' When we say what we've got in the bundles, they tell us how much money we have to pay them to be allowed to cross with our clothing. It's very simple. They just cite us a figure.

Sometimes we say: 'Oh, I don't have the money, I spent it all in Laredo,' but this generally doesn't work. They just tell us: 'Good, then go back to Texas with your stuff.' At that point we begin to bargain a little, saying: 'Oh, you're asking so much, you didn't charge us so much last time,' or 'the other customs guy, the nice one, he doesn't charge us so much.' But in the end they don't come down more than a few pesos from their original price.

Can you imagine how many people cross the border in the space of an hour? Every one of them pays *mordidas* many times the price of the goods they are carrying. No one escapes.

On four different occasions they impounded my merchandise. When they do this they give you a little piece of paper that's supposed to be some kind of receipt to retrieve the goods when you have paid your duties. Then they send you running back and forth to this office and to that

Mexican wetbacks: on the look out

office to report to this comandante and that comandante. They send you chasing all over the place while all the time it's costing you money to stay over at the border. In the end, you don't get your stuff back anyway. I've never known anyone who actually managed to retrieve the goods.

You have to understand, thousands of people at the border live from collecting bribes. The entire economy of cities like Nuevo Laredo rests on the money people extort from others. It's a way of life. One thing you can be sure of is that these guys are not going to stand around with their arms folded while their main source of income disappears. If free trade comes, they'll find another way to shake us down, or maybe they won't let us cross at all. The NAFTA treaty isn't meant to rescue people like us, it's meant to help the rich.

Anyone who is willing to make the sacrifices that we make travelling all the way to Laredo to buy goods can do all right with used clothing. You can't get rich, but you can get by.

*But Doña Anita, who runs the taco stand adjacent to Rosario's stall, has another theory.*

The weekly trip to the border grinds people down. But for the women it offers a break from the drudgery of their lives at home. Market people work every day of the week, but the market women work every day and every night, because they leave their stalls only to go home to face the cooking, cleaning, and child care. For the women, the trip to Laredo is gruelling but, in a certain sense, it gives them two days of relief from housework, husbands, children and in-laws. And in that respect it is appealing.

I tell my old man: '*Viejo*, watch your step or I'm going to switch from tacos to used clothing and leave you every week to go to the border.' The truth is that life on the border moves faster than here. People feel different, more alive when they go to the border, even if they go every week, and have to sit up 16 hours on a second-class bus to get there.

*For three eight-hour workdays as a domestic cleaner in San Diego, California, and after splitting travel expenses with her sister-in-law Graciela, Adelita is left with just under US$200, three-and-a-half times the take-home pay she earned working a 48-hour week in the maquilas that have grown up on the border to furnish cheap Mexican labour for the finishing and assembly of goods for re-export to the USA. The flour, salt and lard that Adelita uses in her cooking, the sugar, coffee, rice, beans, and all the staples with which she stocks her kitchen, as well as the meat, dairy products or fresh produce when she can afford them, are bought on the 'other side'.*

I don't notice it [the strange things that go on on the border] now as much as I once did, because I've lived here for 12 years and I guess I've gotten used to it. But, believe me, life at the border is really crazy

First, we're all running to the other side to buy manufactured things we can't get here, or that cost too much here. If you want a hair dryer, or a radio, or clothing for your kids, or somebody steals your gas cap or breaks off your windshield wiper, you've got to find a way to get to the other side, or you give money to a friend who can cross to buy you these things in Chula Vista.

And then the *americanos* come over here to buy huge sacks of rice and beans and flour. Or at least they used to, when prices on these goods were still set by the government. Now that the politicians have taken away all the price controls, we're running over there to buy even the most basic things. That's because, strange as it seems, it's cheaper to buy a bag of rice in the US, which is a rich country, than in Mexico, which is poor. And this is true even when something comes from Mexico, like oranges or tomatoes, or gasoline.

It seems like half my life has been spent trying to get to the other side. The funny thing is that I didn't come here thinking I would work in the United States. I came to Tijuana to find a job in the assembly plants. I came because I had a cousin who was already working here in a factory. But after I'd lived and worked in Tijuana a few years I got the picture: you can work hard and get paid in pesos, or you can work hard and get paid in dollars. You can work here and get paid by the day, or work there and get paid by the hour. And even someone like me who comes straight from a little village in Michoacán can figure out which is better.

It wasn't difficult to find that first job [as a seamstress in a *maquila*]. Dolores [my sister-in-law] recommended me and all I needed to show was a birth certificate. They didn't even ask to see my primary school certificate. I started work that same morning.

What was difficult was the work itself, or at least the conditions in which we had to work. I had always liked to sew, and we were very proud of the Singer we had in our home in the village — the kind you crank with your feet. But this work was nothing like the sewing I knew. In the *maquila,* you sewed the same piece over and over. For months I did nothing but zippers. Hundreds of thousands of zippers. Later I did nothing but pockets. At night when I lay down to sleep I would close my eyes and, I swear, I would see pockets.

We couldn't go to the bathroom when we needed to, and we could only eat lunch in the 20 minutes when the supervisor said we could take a lunch break. It was like being a little kid in school. In fact, we used to joke that this is why the *maquila* owners always want to know if you completed primary school. It's not because you need to know how to read or write in order to sew zippers. You just need to know how to sit still in your chair when, in reality, you have to leave the room to pee.

*Adelita had worked only five months in this* maquila *when the plant closed down. Within three days she was seated at a microscope in another factory soldering micro circuits at a rate of one thousand per day.*

When I was sewing all day, my back ached, my kidneys ached, and my feet swelled up for lack of circulation. But with the micro-assembly what started to go was my eyesight. I had all the other aches and pains, but now my vision started to go blurry. At that point I just said no. I have to feed my kids and I've got to have a job that gives me the right to go to the Social Security hospital. But I was only 27-years-old and, I thought, I've got to hang onto my eyesight. I'm going to need it later in life!

*Adelita worked at this job for four months before quitting and moving on to a Mexican-owned factory making rattan furniture. The pay was lower but the conditions better than in the US factories.*

More than half the workers in any factory are likely to leave in the course of a year, and in some *maquilas* the *rotación* is a lot higher. Each time I left a job, I'd just find a friend or neighbour who was working in a *maquila* and I'd get her to recommend me at that plant. Mostly the people who hire you just want to examine you to make sure you're not pregnant, and they want to see your birth certificate to make sure that you're not under-age or over-age. If you're too young to work, they may have to pay a fine or they may have to pay a bribe in order to avoid paying the fine. If you're too old, they don't want you either, because they figure you're not going to put up with bad conditions.

**It seems like half my life has been spent trying to get to the other side**

I didn't stay long enough in one place to get involved [with the union]. That's the way it is in this industry: the *maquilas* come and go, and we also come and go. I can't even tell you if the unions in the plants where I worked — the ones that were unionised — were good or bad. I wasn't around long enough to find out...You have to remember that I was never fired from any of these jobs. I just left, or they shut down the line and had no more work for me. I wasn't fired. No one's going to fire someone like me. I just sat there quietly stitching, soldering, wiring, sticking eyes in dolls' heads — whatever they asked of me. I'm not the kind of person who gets fired.

It's basically the same work no matter which *maquila* hires you. You're going to arrive at the factory, punch in, put on your apron — on top of your overcoat, if it's winter — clean your machine and start cranking away. Unless you get 'promoted' where you work for the same base pay, but in the quality control or packing department, you're going to sit all day at an assembly line or a module doing the same thing over and over again. You're going to work ten hours a day, Monday through Thursday, and eight on Friday, and get paid by the piece or by an hourly rate based on piecework standards. The plant is going to be cold in winter and hot in summer. The supervisors can be men or women, they can be *norte americanos* or Mexicans. But, whoever the supervisors may be, it's always the *güeritos*, the 'blondies', who have the last word.

Sure, there are a few differences [between *maquilas*]. Some of the plants have cafeterias. Some take you on excursions to the beach in Ensenada. Some give you a little present on Mother's Day. Some have beauty contests and prizes for the fastest workers. Some give you masks to wear, but it's often too hot to put them on. Others give you gloves to protect your hands, but then they give you assembly tasks that you can't do or that take too long if you're wearing gloves. Some of the supervisors let you talk to the other girls. But usually there's too much noise in any case, and when the machines aren't deafening, they play loud music to speed you up.

*After six years, Adelita determined to leave the* maquilas *to find work on the other side. By 1986, Héctor had come into her life. Héctor had come to the border straight from the countryside of Colima, and had worked his way up from dishwasher to busboy to his present position as waiter in a seafood restaurant in Rosarito on the coast south of Tijuana..*

*Héctor's base pay was negligible but he did very well in tips and his benefits included social security. Inclusion under Héctor's coverage freed Adelita to look for a better-paying job, even one that did not provide social security. Thus, when Héctor's cousin, Graciela, proposed that she could get work for Adelita cleaning houses in San Diego, Adelita jumped at the opportunity. Adelita held a border-crossing card that she had been granted during her two-year stint of steady employment in the furniture factory.*

The pass allows you to cross to the other side in order to spend money, but they don't want you to come over to earn money. So you have to convince them that you're doing one when you're really doing the other. Fortunately, Graciela figured out how to do this.

Graciela guided me through every step. First she found me two jobs with friends of her *señoras,* and then she lent me the clothing I would need to cross. I worked my hands with lotion for a week until all the redness was gone. I polished my nails and I bought a ring for each hand: one looked like a ruby and the other looked like a sapphire.

At first I felt nervous, but now the border crossing is routine for me. On the mornings we go to work, the *migra* [the agents of the US Immigration and Naturalization Service — INS] almost never even ask to see our papers. 'They look at our hands, the way we're dressed, and they figure us for the kind of middle-class ladies who have maids in their homes in Tijuana, and plenty of time to spend in the shopping malls on Avenue H in Chula Vista.'

*Pedro P, pollero, a 'coyote's coyote' with a near perfect record of success, lives in a working class district in the centre of Tijuana with his wife and four children. But most of his life is spent at the border, leading his* pollos, *'chickens' — would-be immigrants — into the USA. He can leapfrog the fence back and forth as many as three times in a night with different groups, evading the 800 INS agents who guard this most popular section of the 14-mile-long, 12-foot-high barrier that separates Mexico and the USA. More than half all illegal immigrants cross at this point. Illegal immigrants in the 1960s and '70s were packed by recruiting agents into crates and carried in poultry trucks across the border — hence the terms.*

*Rates vary from US$250 to US$350 per* pollo, *but the exact price depends on age and distance. More money takes immigrants to any destination throughout the West. Pedro can earn over US$1,000 in a busy night, but expenses come high. Pedro is 32, tall and dressed in the sort of clothes — windbreaker, cotton shirt, jeans and a baseball cap — that make the* pollero *indistinguishable from his chickens. Should they all get caught, better he is taken for one of them; that way the penalties are a lot less serious.*

The *migra* is going to catch you from time to time. It's inevitable. It happens to everyone — to me, perhaps, less than to others because I've been very lucky and I don't take too many chances. Once, however, I was caught with my *pollos* and the *gringos* decided — I don't know why — that I had to be the coyote for the whole group. I think one of the agents recognised me as someone he'd picked up before. My clients were sent back to Mexico, but I was put in the San Diego city jail.

The next day I was transferred to the Federal Penitentiary in Pecos, Texas. This is the place where they take coyotes, drug-smugglers, and *contrabandistas*. But I can tell you one kind of person you don't find serving time in Pecos. That's the Americans who employ the illegals. These guys are smart, and they pass along the risk to 'labour contractors' who vouch for the workers, saying that their papers are all 'in order.' It's the contractors who end up in Pecos charged with falsification of documents and transport of illegal aliens.

To tell you the truth, I would rather spend a month with the *gringos* in Pecos than one day in a Mexican jail. Other coyotes have told me some bad stories about beatings and other stuff that went on when they were in custody in the US. But, in my case, the only thing I suffered was worry for my wife and my kids, who didn't know what had become of me and had nothing to live on while I was gone.

In the ten years I've worked as a *pollero,* I've brought thousands of people across — men, women, and children. And in all those years, no one has ever ratted on me. Mexicans are good people in this way. Besides, no one has any reason to finger a coyote who deals honestly with his customers.

Mexican wetbacks: waiting to cross

LOURDES GROBET: CAMERA PRESS

The stories you hear about coyotes who rob the *pollos* who collude with *asaltapollos,* the bandits who assault the *pollos* while they're in no-man's-land — all these things really do happen. You hear about coyotes who rape the women they have promised to deliver safely to the other side, or who abandon people who have broken a leg or twisted an ankle jumping over the fence. These stories are true. But it is only a few *polleros* who do these things. This is a business like any other; you're going to find all kinds of people, good and bad, doing this work.

My business is based on trust, on the recommendations of people I have passed to the other side. Folks come to me because I have a reputation for skill and reliability. I work with very competent people in San Ysidro — guys in whom the *pollos* can have confidence. People think of me as someone who is serious, who doesn't take stupid chances. I would never do anything that would put my name at risk.

With the *migra*, it's always a game of cat and mouse. You study their moves, you figure out how many men and what kind of equipment they're using that night. And you rely on the fact that you know that they know that they can't stop everyone who decides to cross on a given day. The trick is not to be one of the people they catch that day.

> Of course I'm afraid...
>
> I'm scared of the police
>
> on this side and the
>
> *migra* on the other, and
>
> the bandits who attack
>
> you in between

The *migra* knows all the regular overland routes that we can use, and they patrol these with horses and helicopters. So we just have to invent new routes. To do this work, you have to believe that there's got to be one last way the *migra* hasn't thought of yet. The other thing to remember is that the people we guide are very needy. They're very desperate. So they'll put up with a lot to reach Los Angeles.

Once past San Clemente, we can relax, especially as we get closer to East Los Angeles, where everyone speaks Spanish and looks like us. My job is to deliver the client safe and sound to an address in East LA. Then I collect my $300 and leave. If, three minutes later, the guy I just dropped off sticks his head out the door to put out the garbage and is grabbed by the *migra,* that's not my problem. I just bring him there. Staying out of the way of the *migra* afterwards — that's his problem.

At the end of the day, I make a lot of money, but I have some very big hidden costs. The federal judicial police, the state judicial police, the municipal police — you name it — they come around as often as once a week to shake me down. They know more or less what I make, so they want as much as a thousand dollars a pop. And, believe me, they get a lot more than that from the drug runners.

*Pedro says that even members of the Grupo Beta — the elite corp of federal police formed to co-ordinate with the INS to halt the worst abuses that occur on the border, the rapes, armed robbery and murders — are now 'on the take.'*
It's logical, isn't it? These guys are supposed to protect the *pollos* from the *polleros*. Thus, they are in a perfect position to extort bribes from the coyotes because they have all kinds of information on us: where we live, where we cross, where we recruit our customers. The Grupo Beta is supposed to be especially honest and upright. But the temptation to shake us down is too great for some of these guys. They come around to your house and either you pay up or they expose you to their buddies, the *migra*.

Of course, I'm often afraid. Everyone who does this kind of work is afraid. I'm scared of the police on this side and the *migra* on the other, and the bandits who attack you in between. The worst thing is the bandits, because they carry knives and guns, and they go after you when you're on your way back from San Ysidro and you have all the money you earned that night in your shoe.

I continue to work as a *pollero* because it is the only job I can get in Mexico where I can make really good money. My problem is that I don't want to live on the other side. I don't want to bring up my kids in the United States. I want them to live here, in their own country, where they can feel proud of who they are.

But, I'll tell you what my dream is. My dream is to get papers: to get a real green card, not a fake. Then I could work in construction on the other side, and live here in Tijuana with my family. I'd like to operate the heavy equipment. I know how, and you make great money doing that in the US. I'd just go across every day to work, and then I'd come home to Tijuana at night. I could be really happy with that kind of life. Not just economically OK, but really happy, really content.

© *Judith Adler Hellman. Excerpted from 'The Border', Mexican Lives with permission of The New Press, New York, 1994*

# SARA WHYATT

# Taslima Nasrin

Taslima Nasrin, the Bangladeshi author and feminist, has been living in fear of assassination since September 1993, when death threats were issued against her by Muslim extremists who accuse her of blasphemy and 'conspiracy against Islam'. The threats followed the banning in July 1993 by the Bangladesh authorities of Nasrin's book *Lajja* (Shame), on the grounds that it had 'created misunderstanding among communities'. Written shortly after the December 1992 destruction of the Ayodhya Mosque by Hindu militants, the novel describes the plight of a Hindu family under attack by Muslim extremists. Apart from posting two police officers outside Nasrin's home in response to international pressure, the Bangladesh government made no move to guarantee her safety despite threats from extremist groups.

After over a year fighting for the return of her passport, withheld by the government on a technicality, Nasrin travelled to France where she spoke at a meeting marking International Press Freedom Day. She returned to Bangladesh through India where she gave an interview to the *Calcutta Statesman* which quotes her as calling for changes to the Quran. This revived calls in Bangladesh for her death.

Nasrin says she was misquoted. In letters to the *Statesman* and elsewhere she acknowledges that the Quran cannot be changed and that she had in fact called for changes to *sharia* law that would improve women's rights. Far from placating those calling for her death, this clarification fuelled calls for her arrest. On 4 June, the Bangladesh government issued an arrest warrant against Nasrin for 'insulting religious sentiments', an offence which carries a maximum two-year prison term. Nasrin went into hiding for two months. Demonstrations in the capital, Dhaka, saw tens of thousands on the streets demanding her death.

On 3 August Nasrin appeared briefly before a court in Dhaka where she was bailed and ordered to appear for trial at a later, unspecified, date. On 9 August she arrived in Stockholm where she is staying as a guest of the Swedish PEN Centre.

# The forces of darkness

*Four days before going into hiding, Taslima Nasrin explained the reasons for her struggle against religion and against the oppression of women*

*Muslim fanatics have sentenced you to death for blasphemy. There is a price of US$1,250 on your head. Do you often think about death?*
I am careful, but not frightened. When I hear them shouting through their megaphones in front of my house, whipping up passers-by, when they demand my death with slogans such as 'If you wish to protect Islam, hang Taslima!', I am sad for my country, not for myself. So many injustices are carried out here in the name of Allah. I cannot stop writing against all these simply to save my own skin.

*For five years now, you have been publishing articles against the discrimination to which women are subjected.*
And it's since that time that they have been demanding my death. In my view, the Quran is wrong on several accounts. They rely on it to oppress women in our society. I have to denounce this situation: for example, why does a girl inherit less than a boy? Why does the *sharia* forbid women to divorce? Why can a man have up to four wives, whereas a women cannot even choose her only husband?

*Other women who defend the rights of their sisters in Islamic countries pose the same questions. But they don't go as far as questioning the Quran. According to Islamic law this carries the death penalty. Where do you find the courage to question the Quran?*

I must have been 11 or 12 when I first understood: even the Quran can be wrong. We were learning at school that the Earth revolves round the Sun. The Quran, however, says the Earth is stationary, and supported on a mountain. My mother was incapable of explaining this contradiction. She used to say: 'The Quran is the book of Truth. You must believe what is written.'

*Your father was a doctor. As a scientist, how did he react to your doubts?*

My father used to say: 'Religion is not logic; you must not engage in a debate with it.' From that time I stopped believing in the infallibility of the Quran.

*Do you really want to rewrite and modernise the Quran as people have alleged?*

The Quran can no longer serve as the basis of our law. Four thousand years ago it may have been useful for fending off barbarism. But we live in modern times, the era of science and technology. The Quran has become superfluous. It stands in the way of progress and in the way of women's emancipation.

**The problem is the intolerance of the fundamentalists. I fight with my pen and they want to fight with a sword**

*Are you arguing that the Quran simply be abandoned?*

In a modern, civilised society, religious books are no longer the most useful. They have alway served to strengthen men's domination over women. In our country, a woman has no right to self determination. She must control her sexual desires, remain silent about the rape and abuse she endures. She doesn't even have the right to give her opinion on the number of children she will bear. She is the slave of her husband — who uses her uterus for his own satisfaction and to produce male infants. Women must have power over their wombs and be able to express their ideas freely.

*Muslim feminists such as the Moroccan sociologist Fatima Mernissi think it is not*

*the Quran that opposes emancipation, but more those who 'want to return to the past to hold women in contempt'.*
The problem is Islam's intolerance: it refuses any modern interpretation of the Quran. The problem is the intolerance of the fundamentalists. I fight with my pen, and they want to fight with a sword. I say what I think, and they want to kill me. I will never let them intimidate me, I will never accept any compromise with a government that guarantees Islam as the state religion. Progressive forces and the Islamists are at war.

*Do you still consider yourself a Muslim?*
No. I am an atheist. All forms of religion are anachronistic to me. I dream of a world without religion. Religion gives birth to fundamentalism as surely as the seed gives birth to the tree. We can tear the tree down, but if the seed remains it will produce another tree. While the seed remains, we cannot root out fundamentalism.

*Things like this offend even moderate believers.*
All believers have narrow minds.

*Many men would say the same of feminists.*
I am not a feminist. I am a human being who writes against discrimination and racism.

*Salman Rushdie says the most dangerous people are those who claim to know what is good for the world.*
It seems to me that Rushdie is afraid of the fundamentalists. I'm absolutely convinced that a system based on religion is no good. In any case, my concerns are not the same as his; I have gone further than he. Rushdie has tackled the private life of the Prophet; my aim is to change this society and improve life for women.

*And you believe that only a head-on confrontation with extremism can achieve this?*
We live in darkness. We must use extreme methods to be heard. Every attempt to change this society gradually, softly-softly, has failed. Twenty-three years ago, this country became independent from Pakistan. The women of Bangladesh are still waiting for their liberation. Family laws, deeply marked by the *sharia*, have not been modified. On the contrary,

six years ago, Islam was made the state religion. For the last three years fundamentalists have been the fourth political force in parliament. Their influence is growing and because the government fears alienating the deeply religious masses, it does nothing.

*In one of your poems, you write: 'I could well buy myself a young boy... A tasty young boy, a virgin with a hairy chest. I could well buy myself a young boy, and I would ill-treat him at will.' Do you want to reverse existing relationships?*
No. This poem should be read as an allegory, as a rebellion against a male-dominated social order, where it is natural for men to purchase women and ill-treat them. The opposite would be equally shocking...

I don't hate men, I hate macho societies. When I was 18, on my way home from the movies, a young man came up to my rickshaw and stubbed out his cigarette on my arm. It wasn't just my flesh that was scarred, it was my soul too. Other men who were standing around did nothing to help me: I had the impression they were enjoying my helplessness. And it came to me so clearly that if a woman did not envisage the destruction of the entire system of oppression, her personal rebellion would come to nothing.

*Your family is not overly religious: you have been able to choose your successive husbands, your father allowed you to study. What are you referring to when you write in your collected essays: 'Low writing from a woman fallen low', of 'the unbearable pain and suffering' of your childhood?*
From the age of 11, I could not leave the house to go to school, I could not play in the fields, nor in the playing field, nor could I go to the shops. Yet my brothers could do as they pleased. What kind of society is it that needs to lock up women to protect them?

*To escape being shut away, you have cut yourself off. To what extent have Western feminists inspired you?*
I have read several chapters of Simone de Beauvoir's *Second Sex* and parts of Virginia Woolf's *A Room of One's Own*, nothing else. I write from my own experience. As a doctor, I have seen so many women cry after having given birth to a girl. They were afraid that their husbands would leave them. I have seen the torn vaginas of women raped by their husbands. I have cared for little girls of six, raped by neighbours. It is this collective suffering that I write about. I write about things I cannot bear.

*Who has been your biggest disappointment in life?*
Men.

*Even your father?*
Yes, because he adapted himself to this society while teaching me to
break the chains.

*Who hasn't disappointed you?*
Only myself. I often dream that I am running in a field beside a river.
The field is vast. Endless. I run alone. I want to see others running with
me. At that point I shall have achieved my aim.

*First published in* Der Spiegel. *Translated by Nathalie Vartanpour-Naalbandian*

# Poems

## Border

I'm going to move ahead.
Behind me my whole family is calling,
my child is pulling at my sari-end.
my husband stands blocking the door.
but I will go.
There's nothing ahead but a river
I will cross.
I know how to swim but they
won't let me swim, won't let me cross

There's nothing on the other side of the river
                              but a vast expanse of fields
but I'll touch this emptiness once
and run against the wind, whose whooshing sound
makes me want to dance. I'll dance someday
and then return.

I've not played 'keep-away' for years
        as I did in childhood.
I'll raise a great commotion playing 'keep-away' someday
and then return.

For years I haven't cried with my head
        in the lap of solitude.
I'll cry to my heart's content someday
and then return.
There's nothing ahead but a river
and I know how to swim.
Why shouldn't I go? I'll go.

**Taslima Nasrin**

*Note:*
*The children's game in the third*
*stanza, played by the writer*
*during her childhood, was played*
*mainly by girls in rural areas. It*
*is one of the few games in which*
*running, shouting, and being*
*part of a team — activities*
*usually reserved for boys — is*
*permitted for girls*

*Translated by Farida Sarkar and*
*Carolyne Wright*

ANWAR HOSSAIN: CAMERA PRESS

# Female Product

Would you like a woman, a woman?
Various kinds of women are in stock
White, tall, knee-length hair,
Slim waist, well-endowed body,
No fat, no salt,
There's no crease in her skin.
She has the right perfection
In the nose in the ear
Also in her digestive system,
Check for yourself with your own fingers
That there are no other holes
She is a virgin, still unbroken.
She is unsmelt,
Would you like such a woman, a woman?
Give her meals three times a day,
Give her sari, jewelry and a good soap,
For her face and body
She won't look up, she won't raise her voice.
She is indeed a shy person,
She can cook seven times in one noon.
This product can be used in any way you like.
If you like you can chain her feet,
Her hands or her mind.
If you like, you can divorce her:
Just say, 'I divorce thee,'
And get rid of her.

**Taslima Nasrin**

*Translated by Farida Sarkar and Carolyne Wright*

# LINDSEY COLLEN

# The rape of fiction

On 7 December 1993, four days after *The Rape of Sita* was published in Mauritius, it was plunged into a strange limbo: driven from circulation by Hindu fundamentalists, banned by the government, and temporarily withdrawn by me and my publishers

My novel is still in this limbo. Hindu fundamentalists whipped up hysteria within some 72 hours of publication, and I started to get anonymous rape and death threats. Slogans were painted on walls saying 'The Rape of Lindsey Collen, scandal soon!' My publishers and I heard that some hysteria had been whipped up within a section of the police force (the Special Mobile Force), and that my arrest and the confiscation of all copies of the novel were imminent.

As no-one had read the book — though 250 people had already paid for their copies — we withdrew the novel from the bookstands to create time and space for an open debate. We would then decide whether or not to change the title.

Some hours after the withdrawal, but apparently without knowing about it, prime minister Aneerood Jugnauth stopped proceedings in parliament and made an unprecedented statement against an author. He attacked me saying I may have committed 'an outrage against public and religious morality' under Section 206 of the Criminal Code; adding that I might be a blasphemer — an odd thing to say in a secular state with no anti-blasphemy laws. He referred to his own decree to ban Salman Rushdie's novel, and gave direct instructions for the police to act against me. Obviously the prime minister had acted under direct pressure from what we call 'communal' lobbies. I am known not only as a writer, but also as a feminist; feminists generally annoy fundamentalists of all ilk, and

I have been no exception. I am also a known political opponent of government, member of a party called Lalit, active in trade unions, in an adult literacy organisation, and in the 'housing movement'; opponents of government often get more summary treatment than others.

Despite withdrawing the book, the police came around the next day with orders to confiscate all books and take a statement from me as part of an inquiry. My publishers and I informed the police that they had no right to confiscate the books, as they were not exhibited for sale, as the law says they must be, if they are to be confiscated. I refused to give a statement. So we kept the books and distributed them. *The Rape of Sita* has been widely reviewed in the press and has caused literary and social debate on a fairly national scale. I have had massive support from women of all political views, and also from journalists and writers. All those against the book — from prime minister to authors of threatening articles — made it clear that they have not read the book.

Now, over six months later, the novel is still 'in limbo'. On 19 May and again on 28 July I wrote to the commissioner of police to demand to know the results of their inquiry. On 5 August a letter from the police informed me that they had referred my case to the director of public prosecutions on 5 January 1994.

At present I am working out what to do now. I am advised by my lawyers, publishers, the political party and the women's organisation of which I am a member, and the group set up in Mauritius to fight for free expression called Readers & Writers for Freedom of Expression. I believe that both the government and even some of the less irrational fundamentalists in Mauritius have been influenced by the national and international support given to me, and by those who have stood up against the repression and against the threats of violence. But we have certainly not won yet. We have to be prepared for difficult times ahead.

# Excerpt from *The Rape of Sita*

And then she met something.

She drove into it with her whole self. Something large and dense and hard and terrifying and real and unknown.

She bumped into an illusive heavy, dense, *presence*. Like the big hole in the universe. The presence of an absence. The hole.

It was Anger. It was Rage. It was Fury.

That is what the hole was.

It changed its texture as she studied it. Its substance changed, or her perception of the matter it was made of changed. Like after eating psychedelic mushrooms.

Mainly it was a dense hole. With a heavy gravity around it. So that as you approached it, new things could fall in, and get lost in it.

But as her courage grew and she got closer, it would change. First she felt she had bumped into a great *ball* of anger. Wound up tight like fine single-ply wool, having been worked out of a loose skein and wound into an immense, fraughtly tight ball of fury. As if you couldn't knit from it. The wool wouldn't get unwound. It was stuck.

And then it turned back into a hole again. She got vertigo at the edge of it. It wasn't just a hole below you, like a mineshaft. It was a hole on every side of you, vastly wide and vastly deep and as if you got a premonition of falling down it, so that it was above you as well as below and on the sides.

Now it takes on the form of a knot, a gnarled knot of sinew. Slippery sinew tied into endless knots, like nylon fishing line. How will I ever undo that, Sita thought. There isn't even a loose end to start with. Knots of rage.

And now it turns into a great wall of anger. Up against it. Iron and steel anger. You couldn't dent it. Or move it. It was heavy and inert and unresponsive anger. It was absolute.

And then it was a hole again. Always becoming a hole again. Dizzy edges. A hole of lost thoughts, that more thoughts would fall into. Or would she herself fall into it. She stepped back.

And then, as she calmed herself, controlled the vertigo, and studied the hole. It turned from a hole into a *hall* a great hall of anger, with walls on all sides. Infinitely large and long and concrete. The main feeling of this manifestation of what was lost was that it was of concrete. But it hung, like curtains, only they were concrete. Concrete anger. Rage of reinforced concrete. How could she open concrete curtains and look behind them?

Whose anger was it? She wondered, looking at it. She looked at it. She went up to it and touched it.

And then she knew. She recognized it. Like it was her own hand, only seen under water with goggles, all big and frightening. She knew at once. It was *her own* anger.

©*Lindsey Collen*

# HUMAN RIGHTS

## CAROLINE MOOREHEAD

# Spotlight on India

Like China until Tiananmen Square, India has got off lightly when it comes to violations of human rights. Whether because of its history and political and economic ties, its status as a democracy, or because the government has been so adept at fending off visits from human rights monitors, India has retained a certain moral superiority over countries like Sri Lanka and Burma. Though stories of torture, rape in custody and summary executions have been reported, they have received little publicity, not least because they have proved hard to corroborate.

All this may now be changing. Human rights organisations have at last decided to force through investigations into the atrocities being reported from Jammu and Kashmir and from the Punjab in the drawn-out conflicts between government forces and armed opposition groups. Though indignantly denied by the Indian government — an Amnesty International report on 208 recent disappearances has been denounced as 'substantially incorrect... and totally objectionable...' — the evidence mounting up is extremely damning. Disappearance and torture, as a recent Human Rights Watch report shows, are apparently now seen not just as an acceptable means of combating political violence, but as a possible model for successful counter-insurgency.

When Amnesty International launched its campaign against disappearances last October, India was only listed as one among 24 guilty countries, and not a particularly grave offender at that. Indeed, up until the late 1980s, the disappearing of dissidents and troublemakers was not a tactic used by the Indian police forces. But the numbers of the disappeared are growing, and the problem with disappearance is that once it becomes tolerated it proves very hard to eradicate. One of the worst aspects of disappearance — that no-one knows what is happening and families fear that interference may jeopardise the life of the person who has gone — is precisely what makes it a useful weapon for a country and a government trying to avoid accountability. And when corpses do turn up, their identity is often masked by burning.

In their war against the militants in Kashmir and the Punjab, the Indian police and security forces have come to treat disappearances with a combination of lethargy, obfuscation and threats, connived at by the judiciary. Court orders are ignored, relatives warned to stop making enquiries, and the case is shifted from place to place while documents are mislaid and those responsible posted to other places. But the case of Harjit Singh now under investigation promises not only to expose the brutality of the police in a way that has not been possible before, but to provide a precedent for other victims. Harjit Singh, now missing for over two years, has a determined family, friends and relations in the United Kingdom, and the full backing of a number of human rights groups. In his case, calls for accountability are not likely to go away.

Harjit Singh was 22, and the father of two small children, aged two and four. On 29 April 1992, the bus in which he was travelling was stopped by the police. He had been on his way to the Punjab State Electricity Board, where he had once worked, in search of a new job, having spent the previous months working on a dam far away to avoid the very danger that had now caught up with him. He was arrested and driven away. A friend travelling with him hurried to find his family. Harjit Singh's father, Kashmir Singh, immediately set off to make enquiries. After several frustrating visits to different police stations he was told that if he could produce 30,000 rupees — approximately £600 — his son would be returned within three days.

This was the start of a nightmare that is still continuing. The money was found but Harjit Singh did not reappear. For a while the police denied that they were holding him at all. Then information reached his family that he had been taken to the Mal Mandi interrogation centre in Amritsar and that he had been so badly tortured that he could not walk; both his arms and his legs may have been broken. His father hurried to Amritsar where a sympathetic policeman admitted that Harjit was being held on suspicion of being involved with a terrorist killing. Later came the news that he had died in crossfire during an ambush. The police produced ashes said to be his.

Five months later Harjit Singh was again spotted, this time in a police van in the Beas area near Amritsar. His father was able to persuade the High Court to appoint a warrant officer to search for him but by the

Indian High Commission, London 1991: pressure from afar

time they reached the detention centre where he was said to be the young man had vanished, though not before he had been glimpsed, apparently naked and chained to a wall. When the cell was searched, all that was found were some handcuffs. Two villagers, who accompanied the warrant officer, swore affidavits that they recognised Harjit. In the last 20 months, court dates for a hearing have been set — and at the last minute cancelled — 27 times. The expense of the legal process in India is such that few relations have the money to pursue it.

One of the most depressing aspects of Harjit Singh's case is its ordinariness. He is just one of hundreds of innocent people falling victim to one or other side in a war that grows constantly more violent. In

Kashmir, India's only predominantly Muslim province, the conflict is further confused not just by the presence of foreign fighters, particularly from Afghanistan, but by growing discord between the militant groups, some of whom call for union with Pakistan, others for the setting up of an independent state. Internecine battles are leading to attempts on the lives of several of the prominent protagonists, a number of whom have died. In the Punjab, where 60 per cent of the 20 million inhabitants are Sikh, the call for greater autonomy has been met by total opposition from the government, which sees any concession as likely to encourage similar demands in other parts of India. It fears, too, that any changes would cause further trouble in the long-running border security battles with Pakistan. Violence in the Punjab has grown steadily worse since some 3,000 Sikhs died after Prime Minister Indira Gandhi was assassinated by her two Sikh bodyguards in 1984.

**The distinction between police and army is unimportant, since the result is much the same: arrest followed almost certainly by torture, then almost as surely by death**

In the Punjab, the crackdown on the militants remains in the hands of 60,000 police and the director general of the force, KPS Gill, having been given a free hand in his tactics, is known to reward his men generously for their performance. Between January 1991 and March 1993, over 41,000 special payments were made to members of the Punjab police force. Not long ago, Gill was quoted as saying that the special police would never leave the Punjab 'until the last terrorist was killed'. In Jammu and Kashmir the fight is led by paramilitary troops.

For the victims, the distinction between police and army is unimportant, since the result is much the same: arrest or kidnapping, followed almost certainly by torture, then almost as surely by death. 'Renal failure' is the reason for the deaths of many detainees, caused by rolling heavy objects up and down the body, thereby releasing toxins with which the blood stream cannot cope. In a period of 33 days early last year, 132 people died while in custody in Kashmir, where over 13,000 people have lost their lives in the last four years. The figures for dead and disappeared are similar for the Punjab.

The victims are all those suspected of belonging to, or feeling sympathy towards, the secessionists, their relations, and, increasingly, lawyers and human rights activists. On 16 August 1993, a human rights lawyer from the Punjab called Kulwant Singh Saini was travelling in his car with his wife and baby son on his way to collect a woman client from a detention centre. They disappeared. A few days later, their bodies were found in a canal. No investigation has been made. In the cases where the police do admit to having made an arrest, families are often informed that the detainee has committed suicide, was shot 'while trying to escape' or 'killed in the crossfire', even when the person in question was known to be too ill or injured to move at the time.

One rare survivor, 19-year-old Masroof Sultan, was left for dead after being shot five times in the chest. Later, he told how he had been repeatedly tortured, and his legs broken, to make him confess to being a terrorist. As one policeman told Reuters not long ago: 'Anyone who utters the word 'independence' can be arrested. That means everyone.'

In both Kashmir and the Punjab, those who carry out the disappearances tend to come in plain white clothes, driving unmarked cars with no number plates and darkened windows. While the right to habeas corpus is guaranteed under Indian law, in practice it is rarely exercised. Legal safeguards are simply being ignored. No police officer has been convicted of any violation of human rights and there are some 70,000 people in detention in the Punjab at any one time, under special measures that blatantly flout the major international treaties.

Not, of course, that the violence is all one way. In both regions, the armed militants are also kidnapping, torturing, and often murdering, as well as resorting to a tactic that became infamous at the time of partition, namely the stopping of buses in order to separate and shoot those whose religion or political allegiance is wrong. Police as well as civilians suspected of supporting them are regular targets. In Jammu and Kashmir, the security forces lost 499 dead and 1,558 injured in 1992 alone.

The part played by international pressure in human rights is both delicate and interesting. Harjit Singh's father, who visited the United Kingdom and the human rights centres in Geneva and New York last month, believes that only continued publicity will keep his son alive, just as it may be the only way to deflect the security forces from attacking himself and the rest of the family — a brave decision when police encourage families to believe silence is the best policy. But in a country where to disappear means almost certainly to die, he may well be right.

## MOVEMENT FOR THE SURVIVAL OF THE OGONI PEOPLE (MOSOP)

# No minor matter

'I can only hope that by the time you read this, I will not be dead. My health has deteriorated badly and I have been denied access to my doctor, lawyer, family, newspapers etc these seven weeks of my detention. When the crunch came, a doctor from the military hospital in Port Harcourt was allowed to see me — just once. He made a recommendation which Lt Col Komo [Military administrator for Rivers State, which includes Ogoniland] refused to accept. In short, my murder is being officially planned and executed.

'The writ of Habeas Corpus we filed has come up four times. We have not been produced in court, so nothing can be done. After seven weeks, the police are yet to charge us to court which is what I need to clear my name. And the courts are going on recess soon.'

Ken Saro-Wiwa, Nigerian human rights worker and founder of the Movement for the Survival of the Ogoni People (MOSOP), was arrested on 22 May 1994 accused by Komo of inciting members of MOSOP's youth wing to kill four Ogoni leaders. No charges have been brought against Saro-Wiwa ,who has always advocated non-violence.

The latest arrest follows four earlier detentions in 1993 on charges of sedition and unlawful assembly in relation to a MOSOP meeting in June 1993. Saro-Wiwa has made many enemies within the Nigerian military by publicising the situation of the Ogoni people at home and abroad. Growing international support for the Ogoni appears to have fuelled the military's attempts to break MOSOP and, says Saro-Wiwa, silence him once and for all.

Ogoniland in southern Nigeria is rich in oil. Saro-Wiwa complains that this wealth is being 'looted' from Ogoni people by the Nigerian government in alliance with Shell. The Nigerian government seem more interested in defending the rights of Shell to pollute the countryside, an action for which the authorities are amply rewarded, than in listening to Ogoni demands for a clean up of pollution, a share of the profits and adequate compensation for land ruined by oil leaks. Despite international standards to which, as a UK-affiliated company Shell, should subscribe, its ecological standards in Ogoniland are much lower than elsewhere. Oil leaks, for instance, occur on average four times a week, and Saro-Wiwa accuses Shell of racism. 'Shell,... having successfully waged an ecological war against the Ogoni people since 1958, has been paying protection money to the Nigerian security agencies to complete the genocide which it began. ... Of the 126 Ogoni villages, the military regime have burnt around 30 and they have visited every single village or hamlet... No business can go on in Ogoniland, the farms have been destroyed, there are no schools functioning, the markets are regularly raided, there is no hospital to heal the wounded and the raped.'

Following Saro-Wiwa's arrest violence against the Ogoni by the security forces has increased. According to one MOSOP member 'the place is under a terrible form of martial law... The soldiers have been given an order to do what ever they like.'

'When, following the recent brutal murders, Komo, in less than 24 hours, laid the crime at the door of MOSOP, he knew precisely what he was doing,' states Saro-Wiwa in an open letter to the Nigerian weekly, *The News* on 8 August. 'Misleading the public and the police from the criminals and ensuring that MOSOP members, the only protectors of the Ogoni people are not available to organise them to resist the mayhem he was about to unleash on them.'

Many Ogonis see their struggle as one more aspect of a continuing conflict between northern and southern Nigeria, most recently demonstrated, they claim, by the refusal of the northern-dominated military government to respect the results of last year's elections, widely believed to have been won by Moshood Abiola, a businessman from the south.

'I appeal to all Nigerians not to think that what is happening in Ogoniland is some minor event. It lies at the root of the Nigerian malaise and must be rooted out if coming generations are to find peace and progress,' continues Saro-Wiwa's letter. He concludes: 'I appeal to the international community to send help to Ogoniland now and to intervene and set up an international tribunal to try all these, men and company alike, who have organised the genocide of the Ogoni people. Should anything happen to me.. ensure that justice is done to my memory as a man of peace and fighter for social justice and right.'
*Jason Garner*


## Ogoni ! Ogoni !

Ogoni is the land
The people, Ogoni
The agony of trees dying
In ancestral farmlands
Streams polluted weeping
Filth into murky rivers
It is the poisoned air
Coursing the luckless lungs
Of dying children
Ogoni is the dream
Breaking the looping chain
Around the drooping neck
      of a shell-shocked land.

**Ken Saro-Wiwa**
*Written in prison*

## HUMAN RIGHTS WATCH/AFRICA

# Doing time

When Nelson Mandela invited his ex-jailer to his inauguration, it was an act of forgiveness unlikely to be shared by many former prisoners. Human Rights Watch/Africa's report, *Prison Conditions in South Africa*, compiled after visits to over 20 jails in 1992-93, reveals how little daily life in South Africa has been touched by that country's recent tumultuous changes.

South Africa still has one of the highest prisoner-to-population ratios in the world, despite the release of 1,600 political detainees and over 50,000 ordinary prisoners. Of the present 110,000 inmates, around a quarter have been awaiting trial for up to three months in overcrowded and insanitary jails. Pollsmoor high security jail holds twice its capacity; one communal cell seen by Africa Watch, eight-by-eight metres, contained 35 men. Segregated facilities were abolished four years ago: the few whites who were moved to formerly black prisons were so shocked at sleeping on the floor of crowded cells with only lice-ridden blankets for comfort that they attempted to sue the government. Only the most privileged prisoners are allowed to receive newspapers or write poetry — an 'indulgence' system that arouses huge resentment. Most

defendants are convicted without receiving legal aid, despite the right of access to lawyers being established in a case brought by Mandela against the minister of prisons in 1983.

Assaults by staff on prisoners are commonplace in spite of prohibitive regulations. Physical restraints and solitary confinement are considered by warders and inmates to be routine methods of punishment. Africa Watch has called for an independent investigation into the deaths of six prisoners following a violent protest in Barberton jail in 1991. Torture in police cells also continues and, by

South Africa 1994: still to be set free

the Minister of Law and Order's own admission, 114 people died in police custody in 1992.

Gangs originating in the mining compounds are now entrenched in prisons. One gang is known to collaborate with the warders by informing on and attacking fellow prisoners. The practice of forcing younger prisoners to become 'wyfies' — homosexual partners — has also been inherited from the mining compounds.

One of the most distinctive features of apartheid was the brutalisation of children. Over 2,000 were detained under the State of Emergency and Africa Watch was concerned to find very young prisoners still incarcerated with adults, at a maximum security prison.

Much of the evidence given against warders came from concerned members of the Police and Prisons Civil Rights Union, founded in 1989 by 'coloured' and black police and prison staff. Media coverage of prisons was suppressed until last year and the taking of photographs is still restricted.

This timely report shows how far the 'new South Africa' has to go in order to overcome years of apartheid's practices. Among those most keenly awaiting change will be the nearly 400 people on death row, hoping that the new government will keep to the ANC's promise to abolish the death penalty.
**Oren Gruenbaum**

*Prison Conditions In South Africa: Africa Watch Prison Project* (Human Rights Watch/Africa, February 1994, 116pp) Available from Human Rights Watch, 485 Fifth Avenue, New York, NY 10017

## HUMAN RIGHTS WATCH/HELSINKI

# Under siege

The non-Serb peoples of Kosovo province in the Republic of Serbia are a population under siege by a police state. In the name of the Kosovo Serbs, a tiny minority of the province's population, Serbian authorities 'rule with an iron fist', violently silencing all dissenting voices. By publishing the previously unheard testimonies of victims and witnesses in *Open Wounds: Human Rights Abuses in Kosovo*, Human Rights Watch/Helsinki reveals that the Serbian fist is tightening its brutal grip on the people of Kosovo.

Since 1990, Kosovo, previously an autonomous province in the former Yugoslavia, has been ruled directly from Belgrade, part of Serbia's self-proclaimed Federal Republic of Yugoslavia (FRY). Regarded by Serbian nationalists as the historical cradle of their national consciousness, Kosovo has equal historical importance as the centre of Albanian national revival: up to 90 per cent of the population are ethnic Albanians. A Turkish minority are also victims of Serbian abuse. Most Albanians, refusing to recognise the legitimacy of Belgrade's rule, look to the 'illegal' Albanian government, headed by Ibrahim Rugova, for leadership. The Albanian Kosovar Parliament, elected in May 1992, has been unable to meet because of harassment by the Serbian authorities.

The Serbian fist is always evident in Kosovo: heavily armed police and army patrols maintain a visible presence; raids on homes and businesses take place as a matter of course; and campaigns of terror and intimidation, apparently aimed at driving Albanians from their homes, are on the increase. Arrests, beatings and torture of Albanian activists, intellectuals and men with military experience have become commonplace and victims have little chance of legal redress.

Discrimination against non-Serbs is central to the Serbian state's attempts to dominate all spheres of society in Kosovo. From 1990, non-Serbs were dismissed en masse from their jobs. In response, ethnic Albanian teachers, doctors, police, judges and lawyers set up parallel health, education and welfare services which, though operating on a shoestring, offer reasonably effective alternative structures. However, *Open Wounds* shows that the lack of resources in the parallel health service has had serious consequences for public health standards and deaths due to malnutrition or to formerly treatable diseases are increasing. Those who participate in these insti-

**The Albanian-language media have been systematically silenced: of 40 or so papers existing in 1990, most were forced to close**

tutions risk beatings and detention for 'informative discussions.'

The Serbian authorities regard Albanian aspirations for autonomy as evidence of planned violent revolution and play on the fears of the Serb minority. *Open Wounds* cites evidence of house searches, detentions, police violence, and even killings justified on the grounds that Albanians are stockpiling weapons. However, according to Human Rights Watch and other sources, few Albanians are armed. It has, however, been alleged that weapons distributed to Serb civilians have been used to harass their Albanian neighbours. Police and paramilitary forces have collaborated to terrify Albanians living in Serb-populated areas into flight. Civilian authorities have used pseudo-legal methods backed up by threats or brute force to order Albanians from land that they legally own.

The period between August and November 1993 saw the arrest of several Albanian politicians and former soldiers. In most cases they were charged with organising an armed uprising and reportedly beaten and deprived of food and sleep. Access to lawyers and family was denied, an abuse of legal procedure tolerated or condoned by the courts, despite complaints being filed by the defendants' lawyers. The report cites cases where convictions were based solely on confessions extracted under torture. Furthermore, administrative courts are used to pass judgements without trial.

The Albanian-language media have been systematically silenced: in 1992 a Serbian publishing house, Panorama, took control of all Kosovo newspapers and of the forty or so Albanian-language newspapers existing in 1990, most were forced to close. One Turkish-language newspaper exists but is hampered by a lack of funds. Albanian broadcasting consists of direct translations of Serbian programming. There are instances of Albanian journalists' harassment by the authorities who accuse them of spreading false information, inciting national hatred or campaigning for Kosovo's secession from FRY. Recently, donations from charitable organisations have helped to resurrect some Albanian-language publications.

Foreign human rights monitors find it increasingly difficult to operate in Kosovo while local human rights activists who meet or assist foreign delegations are routinely persecuted. The Council for the Defence of Human Rights and Freedoms, a legally registered organisation, says it is only tolerated to convince the world that all in Kosovo is well.

This 148-page report gives the lie to that claim. By no means an exhaustive list of rights violations, it seeks to bring the most recent alarming developments to the world's attention. While the West is preoccupied elsewhere, Serbia has a free hand in Kosovo.

*Laura Bruni*

*Open Wounds: Human Rights Abuses in Kosovo* (Human Rights Watch/Helsinki, March 1994, 148pp). Available from Human Rights Watch/Helsinki

## ARTICLE 19

# Rushdie alert

After two years of travel to 17 countries, culminating in a meeting with the American President and a visit to the European Parliament in Brussels, the International Rushdie Defence Committee has now received firm promises of political support. National Rushdie Defence Committees have been formed in Denmark, France, The Netherlands, Norway, Sweden, USA, and most recently in Germany to maintain pressure on their governments and help keep the Rushdie case high on the international political agenda.

The campaign has also launched *RushdieAlert*, a newsletter which will keep the committees and the wider world regularly informed of actions and developments and let those who are less familiar with the details of the Rushdie affair know what has and can be done. For subscriptions to *RushdieAlert*, please contact The International Rushdie Defence Committee, 33 Islington High Street, London N1 9LH Tel (+44) 71 713 1355, fax: (+44) 71 713 1356

# LEGAL: MEDIA OWNERSHIP

**A legal column dedicated to the memory of Bernie Simons (1941-1993), radical lawyer and defender of human rights**

ERIC BARENDT

# Never mind the ownership, what about the quality

*Strong measures against concentration of ownership go some way to guaranteeing freedom of expression, but they do nothing for programme standards or public access to the media*

Historically there has been much to justify that view that governments pose the greatest threat to freedom of speech and freedom of the press. Though newspapers in the United Kingdom have not been controlled in this way since the end of the seventeenth century, in almost all countries the press and other media have at one time or another been subject to a system of official licencing. In addition, there are of course the restrictions imposed by the criminal laws of blasphemy, sedition, obscene publications, by contempt proceedings and other restraints on the publication of trials, and by the civil (and criminal) libel laws.

Perhaps we should consider whether the threat to freedom of speech does not now come as much from private sources, in particular where there is a concentration of media ownership. Consider for a start the position in the United Kingdom. The News International Group, which owns five newspapers, enjoys over 30 per cent of national daily circulation and about 35-36 per cent of Sunday circulation. The Mirror Group is not far behind. Indeed, virtually 85 per cent of both daily and Sunday newspaper circulation is under the control of four companies, the two already mentioned, United Newspapers and Associated Newspapers. Three large groups dominate the regional newspapers, and it is rare now for there to be more than one local paper serving a particular town or county.

At the end of last year the Secretary of state for national heritage liberalised the rules on ownership of television channels, which led to a flurry of take-overs. The four large groups which each hold two regional licences control over 80 per cent of Channel 3 advertising revenue.

It is the same story in other

European countries. The German press industry is dominated by the Hamburg Axel Springer group, which also now has substantial interests in former Eastern European countries, particularly Hungary. The French press and magazine sector has been dominated by the Hachette group, which also had a controlling interest in the fifth television channel, La Cinq, which went bankrupt in 1991. Hachette was in partnership with the Italian media magnate, now prime minister, Silvio Berlusconi. His company Fininvest controls three national channels, as well as a number of journals and magazines; its associated advertising company, Publitalia, influences the whole media market by its selective placing of advertising. The position in the United States and other countries is similar: television is dominated by a handful of private networks, few cities have more than one newspaper and there are increasing links between the press and broadcasting — the phenomenon of cross-media ownership.

PETER CLARKE

These developments pose enormous problems for freedom of speech and for the working of effective democracies. A handful of media magnates, men such as Rupert Murdoch, Conrad Black, Silvio Berlusconi and Leo Kirch, are able to set the political and cultural agenda, not only for particular countries, but for whole continents, for media oligopolies are increasingly continental and, in one or two cases, world-wide. Murdoch, for example, has substantial media interests in Britain, the United States, Australia and the Far East. Some magnates may not exploit their ability to dominate political debate, but others do. The most notable example this year has been the use by Berlusconi of his three national television channels and his control of influential weekly reviews to launch a new Italian political party, Forza Italia, which went on to win the spring general election.

How can these dangers be met? Traditionally, governments in Europe have controlled private broadcasters by tight programme restrictions that stop them editorialising and require them to show a balanced range of impartial programmes. But these rules are difficult to enforce, as the USA Federal Communications Commission found, and they are unpopular with advertisers — the financiers of private broadcasting — as well as the licensees themselves. Moreover, they have never been applied to the press. Indeed, restraints on newspaper editorialising and a requirement, say, to present a balanced range of letters and features, would be regarded as contrary to our traditional understanding of freedom of the press. Editors and proprietors, whether of the print or electronic media, might equally object to the introduction of strong right of reply and access laws, the use of which would give the man and woman in the street greater opportunity to use the media. More reliance now is placed on anti-concentration rules, or to use the US term, anti-trust law. There is every reason why conventional anti-trust law should apply to the media. Its object is to stop groups abusing their dominant position in a particular market. Rules which apply, say, to the car or petroleum industries should equally apply to the newspaper and broadcasting industries. There are, however, some problems of application: what, for instance, is the relevant 'market'? Do newspapers, magazines, and the broadcasting media reach three different markets, or is there in substance one media market, comprising all actual and potential readers, listeners and viewers? Moreover, it is surely more important that we have access to a rich variety of newspapers and broadcasting channels than that we have a wide range of cars and petroleum products to choose from.

For these reasons there are in most countries special controls on press and broadcasting concentra-

PETER CLARKE

tions, and on the increasing phenomenon of cross-media ownership, that is, participation by newspaper groups in broadcasting companies or vice versa. In the United Kingdom, for instance, there are specific rules in the Fair Trading Act 1973 to control press mergers, under which they may, or in some cases must, be referred to the Monopolies and Mergers Commission. That body must consider the impact of a merger on freedom of expression in deciding whether it is against the public interest. The Broadcasting Act 1990 introduced restrictions on the accumulation of radio and television licences, together with new rules on cross-media ownership, though, as already mentioned, some of the former have now been relaxed by the Secretary of State. Other countries have comparable rules. Interestingly, in both France and Italy the constitutional courts have compelled their parliaments to introduce anti-trust laws to counter the risks of media concentration; in 1986 the French Conseil Constitutionnel refused to approve the Chirac bill deregulating broadcasting, until it contained tougher cross media ownership rules.

Are these measures likely to be more effective than general anti-trust laws? There must be some doubt about the enthusiasm of national governments to tackle this job properly. Understandably they want their own media companies to compete effectively on the international stage, an argument for allowing greater concentration at the national level. Moreover, for political reasons they may be sympathetic to the ambitions of particular conglomerates; this was obviously the case when the Conservative government refused to apply the cross-media ownership rules to the link — via Murdoch — between BSkyB and News International. The greatest opposition to effective antitrust rules in Italy came from Berlusconi's Milanese friend, the former Socialist prime minister, Bettino Craxi.

PETER CLARKE

It is conceivable that the European Union might intervene. Two years ago the Brussels Commission issued a Green Paper, which suggested the possible harmonisation of national media competition laws. Its objective was to make more effective the single European broadcasting market, rather than give more adequate protection to the rights of citizens to a plurality of information. No doubt some national governments as well as media interests will do their best to oppose strong Community legislation. Another possibility is intervention by the Strasbourg Human Rights Court. When it held

recently that the Austrian public broadcasting monopoly was incompatible with the freedom of expression clause of the Human Rights Convention, it stressed the responsibility of states to guarantee an effective pluralism of information. If prospective private broadcasters can use this principle to invalidate a public monopoly, perhaps a public interest group could use it to challenge de facto private monopolies and oligopolies?

In any case, control of media concentrations is only part of the battle to achieve an effective plurality of sources of information. It is no use having several independent newspaper titles or television channels if they are all concerned to offer the same mediocre fare. If each of, say, five television networks serves up an endless diet of soaps and game-shows (and avoids investigative journalism) it does not matter much whether they are owned by the same mogul or are genuinely independent of one another. Strong anti-concentration measures are an important step to guarantee freedom of speech in the media, but alone they are not sufficient. They need to be supplemented by programme standards and access rules — measures which market oriented governments would prefer to avoid.

# INDEX INDEX

## Death takes a holiday

*This issue of* Index Index *excerpts from a major new report, by the Committee to Protect Journalists, on the murders of eight journalists who fled to the United States to escape persecution at home, only to find that the death squads had followed them into exile.*

If eight white American reporters had been murdered on US soil over the past 12 years, their deaths would have triggered shock waves across the country and galvanised the media and law enforcement agencies.

Yet the political assassinations from 1981 to 1989 of five Vietnamese-American and three Haitian-American journalists — Duong Trong Lam, Nguyen Dam Phong, Tap Van Phan, Nhan Trong Do, Triet Le, Jean-Claude Olivier, Fritz Dor and Dona St Plite — barely created a ripple in the national press and have yet to be addressed seriously by federal law enforcement authorities.

The Committee to Protect Journalists has appealed repeatedly to the FBI and the Justice Department to launch a co-ordinated investigation of these murders of immigrant journalists. We have spoken about the cases personally to Attorney General Janet Reno. Yet no serious investigation is under way. Instead, understaffed local law enforcement officials are frustrated by the failure of federal authorities to treat the cases seriously.

CPJ has been able to establish new leads and details in many of these cases. But it requires the talents and resources of a professional news organisation to unearth the truth about the murders of these eight journalists. The cases are likely to remain unsolved unless the news media spotlight the apparent unwillingness of law enforcement officials to devote their resources to these attacks on immigrant journalists and the communities they serve.

Between 1981 and 1990, five Vietnamese-American journalists and editors were murdered. Some were targeted because their work was considered to be soft on Communism; others because they criticised corrupt practices of US-based exile groups that collected money in the community, allegedly to finance a resistance army against Vietnam.

In September 1990 a lone gunman murdered Triet Le [*Index* 2/1991], a columnist with the bi-weekly *Tien Phong*, and his wife in front of their Virginia home. A staunch anti-Communist, Le was, however, highly critical of exile groups that raised funds among refugees. His name had appeared on a 1982 hit list signed by a death squad called the Vietnamese Organisation to Exterminate Communists and Restore the Nation.

Status: Unsolved. The FBI investigated the case for six months before turning it back over to Fairfax County police. It remains in the FBI's Violent Criminal Apprehension Program database. Media attention on the murder was spotty and ended after some initial stories.

In addition to the documented murders, there have been three attempted murders, beatings, death threats and countless acts of vandalism against journalists and their property. The violence has frozen dissenting opinions in America's Vietnamese-American communities.

Between 1991 and 1993, three Miami-based Haitian radio hosts, known supporters of deposed President Jean-Bertrand Aristide, were shot dead. Despite arguments from the Haitian community and journalists' pressure groups, law enforcement sources say the three murders are tied to internal business disputes in Miami's Little Haiti.

In Miami, as in Haiti, radio is a lifeline to the community. There are about 40 to 60 radio programmes every week. The Haitian community is highly political, with the majority supporting Aristide. But Duvalierist and army supporters also live in the area, primarily in Fort Lauderdale and south-west Miami. Two radio programmes that were openly supportive of the Haitian paramilitary group FRAPH were recently heard in the area. FRAPH, which carries out summary executions in Haiti, also attempted to open an office in the heart of Little Haiti but backed off after mass demonstrations. Haitian dissidents and journalists, however, say the Haitian army continues to monitor their activities in the US.

Dona St Plite [*Index* 10/1993] had a radio programme on WKAT, a radio station that rents airtime to other Haitians. He was killed last October as he attended a benefit concert in honour of the widow and children of journalist Fritz Dor, murdered in Miami in 1991. St Plite's name had appeared on a death list which circulated in Miami, with a message scribbled in Creole: 'Bravo Americans. Make Aristide pay. Long live the Army. These people must be shot before or on October 30 in Miami and Haiti.' The day St Plite was shot, an anonymous caller warned him that he would be killed if he attended the concert.

Status: Unsolved. Authorities have indicted Francky St Louis Joseph as one of the assassins. Trial pending. Coverage has been sporadic and national media attention has been almost non-existent.

All these journalists had fled repression and turmoil in their native countries only to find death in America for openly expressing their political views. In each case the crimes appear to have been intended to intimidate or silence dissident voices within these communities, which have, as a result, been silenced by fear: Haitian radio commentators in Miami now refrain from openly criticising the de facto regime in Haiti; Vietnamese-language newspapers have avoided taking clear positions on the re-establishment of US trade and diplomatic relations with Vietnam, even after the Clinton administration lifted the embargo; and Latino journalists in Queens do not report on drug trafficking or corruption.

Several questions need answering: were these eight murders considered weak stories? Were the cases simply too hard to crack? Or were they ignored because they involved ethnic journalists from immigrant communities with little political clout?

The non-English press has always been an integral part of the American press, just as immigration itself is the quintessential American experience. For two centuries new arrivals have relied on newspapers — and, today, on radio and television programmes — in their native language as their primary source of information. These news outlets enjoy the same legal protections as English-language media. Thus it is particularly disturbing that, with all of the murders involving immigrant publications, the mainstream press views the incidents as 'exotic' or 'foreign', and not as a direct assault on First Amendment rights.

Once in the US, many immigrant journalists took political positions, or investigated incidents, which they would have avoided in their homelands for fear of retaliation. Many suffered threats in response, or attacks by vandals. Some reported the incidents to the police. Others kept a low profile, still not believing they had much to fear in the US. In the end they were silenced. The same dark forces that would have struck them at home killed them here.

Silenced: The Unsolved Murders of Immigrant Journalists in the United States *is published in September 1994 by the Committee to Protect Journalists, 330 Seventh Ave, 12th Floor, New York, NY 10001, USA*

*A censorship chronicle incorporating information from Agence France-Presse (AFP), the American Association for the Advancement of Science Human Rights Action Network (AAASHRAN), Amnesty International (AI), the Central American Centre for the Protection of Freedom of Expression (CEPEX), the Committee to Protect Journalists (CPJ), the Canadian Committee to Protect Journalists (CCPJ), the Inter-American Press Association (IAPA), the International Federation of Journalists (IFJ/FIP), the International Federation of Newspaper Publishers (FIEJ), the Media Institute of Southern Africa (MISA), International PEN (PEN), Radio Free Europe/Radio Liberty (RFE/RL), Reporters Sans Frontières (RSF), the BBC Monitoring Service Summary of World Broadcasts (SWB), and other sources.*

## AFGHANISTAN

BBC Pashto Service journalist Mirwais Jalil was found murdered on the outskirts of Kabul on 30 July. Jalil was abducted after interviewing the Hizb-i-Islami leader, Gulbuddin Hekmatyar, at the party's headquarters. Jalil's reporting of the conflict in Afghanistan made him unpopular among several factions. The government and Hizb-i-Islami both blame each other for the murder. (BBC, CPJ)

## ALBANIA

The Socialist Party accused the ruling Democratic Party of electoral manipulation and intimidation during local elections on 29 May. In Libofshe,

near Fier in western Albania, six Socialist Party observers were allegedly beaten, requiring hospital treatment. The door of the polling station in Gresihica was reportedly broken down and ballot boxes interfered with. (*East European Newsletter*)

On 28 July Tirana police, some carrying batons, dispersed a crowd rallying outside Tirana's main courtroom in support of opposition Socialist Party leader Fatos Nano's appeal against his 12-year prison sentence for corruption. Between 50 and 60 demonstrators, who refused to disperse, were reportedly detained. *Zeri i Popullit*, the Socialist Party newspaper, reported that Tirana police refused an application to hold a Socialist Party rally on 29 July. (Reuter)

On 2 August opposition papers *Dita Informacion, Koha Jone, Populli Po, Java, Zeri i Popullit,* and *Aleanca* suspended publication for three days in protest at new taxes levied on newspapers, including a 15 per cent tax on distribution, a five per cent tax on imported goods such as newsprint, a 15 per cent tax on advertisements and a 15 per cent income tax. Although pro-government papers are subject to the same taxes, they enjoy regular income from exclusive rights to government advertising and ownership of the Demokracia printing plant, the only modern plant in Albania. (RFE/RL, SWB, Association of Professional Journalists of Albania)

Treason charges against five

leading members of the ethnic-Greek organisation Omonia (*Index* 3/1994) were dropped in August because they were based on the old Stalinist penal code. Charges against the five of spying and possession of weapons remain. On 16 August police broke up a demonstration outside the courthouse and reportedly detained 22 people, many of them Greek journalists. (Reuter)

## ALGERIA

Veronique Thavot, an editor at the French television station France 2, was among several people injured after two bombs exploded during a march in Algiers on 29 June. The marchers were demanding that the findings of the inquiry into the assassination of President Boudiaf in 1992 be published. (*Guardian*, IFJ)

Yasmina Drici, a proofreader at the French-language daily *Le Soir d'Algérie*, was found with her throat cut on 11 July, following her abduction the day before by armed men wearing police uniforms in Algiers. Mohamed Lamine Legoui, a correspondent for the official Algerian Press Service (APS) in the M-Sila region, was shot dead outside his home in Bou-Saada on 21 July by unidentified gunmen. (IFJ, CPJ)

Brahim Taouchichet, director of the monthly magazine *Horoscope*, was abducted by members of the Islamic Salvation Army (AIS) in Algiers on 14 August. The AIS, which claims to be the armed wing of the Islamic Salvation Front (FIS), said it would put Taouchichet 'on trial' but did not specify his supposed offence. (CPJ)

## ANGOLA

Lourenço Adao Agostinho (*Index* 3/1994) of the Angolan Human Rights Association (ADHA) was found guilty of embezzlement in late May. He was arrested together with ADHA president William Tonet after ADHA published a report criticising the conditions in Luanda's prisons. Tonet still faces charges of raping a 16-year-old girl. (MISA, AI)

Atur Gilela, sound engineer for Radio Nacional de Angola, was killed in heavy fighting between the ruling MPLA and the UNITA rebels around the city of Kuito on 16 June. (MISA)

It was reported in June that BBC reporter Gustavo Costa faces a defamation suit brought by the oil minister, Albna Affis, after filing stories about government corruption. It is feared that the action is part of a campaign against Angolan freelance journalists. (MISA)

## ARGENTINA

The Constitutional Assembly is examining a proposal to change the freedom of the press clause in the constitution. If adopted, the revised constitution would give ratified international treaties constitutional status that will override national laws. Consequently, the 'right to reply' provision of the Treaty of San José would compel newspapers to publish replies from readers who are offended by articles. (FIEJ)

## BANGLADESH

Following Taslima Nasrin's court appearance on 3 August (*Index* 10/1993, 3/1994), some 3,000 members of the Islamic Oikya Jote movement held a rally near the National Press Club calling for 'the thwarting of attempts to let Nasrin go unpunished'. On 10 August Nasrin left the country for Sweden, provoking criticism from the Jamaat-e-Islami party that the government had conspired in her flight. Islamic groups believe Nasrin's departure may put pressure on the government to enact a blasphemy law. (Reuter)

Recent publication: *State of Human Rights 1993* (Co-ordinating Council for Human Rights in Bangladesh, March 1994, 168pp)

## BELARUS

Alaksandr Kusnier, a photographer for the paper *Respublika*, was abducted by two men who drove him to a forest and beat and robbed him on 29 June. The two assailants also opened his camera and exposed his film. (SWB)

## BOSNIA-HERCEGOVINA

The remaining newspapers in Sarajevo will be forced to close within weeks if new assistance is not found to buy them newsprint, it was reported on 13 July. (FIEJ)

In late July some 150 civilians, most of them Muslims, were reported being detained and ill-treated in an improvised prison camp outside the town of Velika Kladusa in Bihac. They are being detained by supporters of a local Muslim separatist leader, Fikret Abdic, who believe that they or members of their family support the government of Bosnia-Hercegovina. (AI)

## BOTSWANA

The controversial Corruption and Economic Crime Act, passed by Parliament in August, allows police to search media premises and seize documents without a warrant in the course of corruption investigations. Journalists fear that the Act could be used to force them to reveal sources. (MISA)

## BRAZIL

Lawyer Reinaldo Guedes Miranda and Hemogenes Da Silva Almeida, a poet and historian, were shot dead in their car in Rio de Janeiro on 13 June. Both men were advisors to the Workers' Party and members of the Human Rights Commission of the local council, which is monitoring the investigation into the Candelária and Vigario Geral massacres (*Index* 3/1994, p84). (AI)

## BRITAIN

Government lawyers have conceded that a trade union leader's correspondence was routinely intercepted for the security service MI5. The admission came in a case

LA TÉLÉ CENSURÉE AU BANGLADESH

C'EST QUOI
LA TÉLÉ?

A consortium of British news-papers, including the *Guardian*, *Financial Times* and *Telegraph*, are lobbying for the laws on cross-media ownership to be relaxed. At present, newspa-pers are limited to 20 per cent shareholdings in broadcasting and they fear being unable to compete with media con-glomerates such as Rupert Murdoch's News International. (*Independent*)

brought to the European Commission by the general secretary of the Scottish Trades Union Congress in July, con-tradicting comments by the director-general of MI5, Stella Rimington. She denied that MI5 monitored people with a high public profile and said: 'We do not do it. Such inter-ference would not be justified.' (*Guardian, Times*)

The Press Complaints Commission (PCC) has backed an undercover investigation which exposed two govern-ment MPs for accepting £1,000 to ask a question in Parliament. The 10 July report, in the *Sunday Times* , was in the public interest and this jus-tified the use of subterfuge, the PCC ruled. (*Sunday Times*)

A Northern Ireland judge overruled a coroner's subpoena for the Stalker report on securi-ty force conduct to be released on 11 July. The subpoena would have forced the Royal Ulster Constabulary (RUC) to produce two reports into their alleged shoot-to-kill policy in the 1980s. The judge's ruling

said their release was not in the interests of national security. (*Guardian*)

On 15 July the country's high-est court ruled against the use of public interest immunity (PII) certificates, which allow evidence to be suppressed by the government, in two cases of police misconduct. The decision has narrowed the scope of ministerial use of PII certificates, which was heavily criticised in the Matrix Churchill case earlier this year (*Index* 1&2/1994). (*Guardian*)

Evidence obtained by the police from secretly recorded mobile telephone conversa-tions are admissible in court, according to a unanimous rul-ing by five senior judges on 22 July. A loophole in the law on telephone tapping excludes mobile telephones. (*Guardian*)

The BBC dropped the screen-ing of a documentary on police use of *agents provocateurs* in August after pressure from senior officers who claimed informers would be put at risk. (*Observer*)

The Ministry of Defence (MoD) may be taken to the European Court of Human Rights by gay and lesbian per-sonnel sacked from the armed forces. The MoD admitted in August that 259 people have been dismissed in the last four years. The MoD insisted it was justified and said: 'We dismiss without prejudice.' (*Guardian, Daily Telegraph*)

Recent publications: *Britain's Media: How They Are Related, Media Ownership and Democracy* (Granville Williams, Campaign for Press and Broadcasting Freedom, 1994, 79pp); *Fiction, Fact and the Fatwa: 2,000 Days of Censorship* by Carmel Bedford (Article 19, August 1994, 175pp); *Need for Reform — Muslims and the Law in Multi-Faith Britain* (UK Action Committee on Islamic Affairs, Autumn 1993, 81pp); *Statewatching the New Europe: a Handbook on the European State* (Statewatch, 1993, 207pp)

Customs officers refused to allow Nicolae Gheorghe, vice-president of the International Romani Union, to enter Bulgaria in June. Dr Gheorghe was to have been a keynote speaker at a seminar on police brutality and the legal defence of minorities which took place in Sofia on 10 and 11 June. (*International Helsinki Federation for Human Rights Newsletter*).

On 1 July Parliament rejected a proposal to allow the use of Turkish as an official second language in the armed forces. On 21 July the prosecutor-general's office launched an investigation into remarks allegedly made by Ahmed Dogan, chairman of the mainly-Turkish Movement for Rights and Freedoms, on 2 July, that ethnic Turks should disobey orders if Bulgarian remained the only official language for soldiers carrying out their duties. The investigation aims to gather enough evidence to persuade MPs to lift Dogan's parliamentary immunity so that charges can be raised in court. (RFE/RL)

On 14 July Parliament, over-ruling Presidential objections, approved a controversial law which bars lawyers with less than five years' experience as judges or prosecutors from top positions in the judiciary. The law is retroactive, allowing for those already appointed to be replaced. Opponents of the law say that it will increase the influence of former Communists. (RFE/RL)

### BURMA

Khin Zaw Win, a Burmese student studying in Singapore, was arrested by members of the Military Branch at Rangoon airport as he tried to board a plane bound for Singapore in July. He is closely linked with pro-democracy groups in Burma and is writing a thesis on the political situation there. (AI)

Nobel peace prize laureate Aung San Suu Kyi began her sixth year under house arrest on 20 July. She has been informed that she will not be released before January 1995. Meanwhile, the SLORC military government has agreed to a meeting with the UN secretary-general for discussions on detained dissidents; and the head of military intelligence, Lieutenant General Khin Nyunt, has said that he would accept an invitation to meet Aung San Suu Kyi. He has not, however, arranged any date for the meeting. (*International Herald Tribune, Times*)

Well known writer San San Nwe was arrested in Rangoon on 4 or 5 August, along with her daughter, journalist U Sein Hla, and Khin Maung Swe, a leading member of the National League for Democracy. All three are outspoken opponents of the government. (AI)

### BURUNDI

Opposition parties demanded the closure of the pirate radio station Rutomorangingo on 4 July because of its broadcasts calling on Hutus to kill Tutsis and Hutu opposition activists. The station is believed to be operating from the French-controlled part of Rwanda. (SWB)

### CAMBODIA

The paper *Prum Bayon News* was closed down by order of the information minister on 7 June. No reason for the closure was given. (SWB)

Nguon Nonn, editor of the daily *Dom Ning Pel Prek* (Morning News), was arrested on 9 July and charged with creating disorder, reportedly in connection with articles which implicated the interior minister and other high-ranking officials in the failed coup of 2 July. On 26 July, however, information minister Ieng Mouly said that he expected Nonn to be released 'soon'. (International Human Rights Law Group, Reuter)

Thou Hammangkul, editor-in-chief of the bi-weekly paper *Antarakhum* (Intervention), was attacked in Phnom Penh on 10 June by unknown assailants who hit him on the back of the head. He died the following day. *Antarakhum* has recently published stories accusing military and government officials of corruption. (CPJ)

### CAMEROON

On 30 June Emmanuel Noubissie Ngankam, director of the independent weekly *Dikalo*, was given a six-month suspended sentence for defamation; and the paper's editor-in-chief Thomas Eyoum a'Noth (*Index* 3/1994), who has gone into hiding, was sentenced to six months in prison. On 6 July Ngankam was given a further suspended sentence of one year, fined five million CFA francs (approximately US$8,800) and ordered to pay 15 million CFA francs in damages. The charge related to an article published in early January, which alleged that the former minister of public works and transportation had expropriated property in the capital Yaoundé. (RSF)

Staff at two other newspapers, *La Nouvelle Expression* and *Galaxie*, currently face charges of defamation laid by Augustin Frederick Kodock, state planning and regional development minister. The newspapers published articles alleging that the minister's private secretary had embezzled large sums of money. (RSF)

## CANADA

Unidentified assailants threw a firebomb into the Toronto Spanish-language television station Telelatino on 18 July, apparently in response to the station's recent controversial decision to suspend the programme *Nuestra Visión*. No-one was injured in the attack. (CCPJ)

## CHINA

Dissident Bao Ge was arrested in Shanghai in the run-up to the fifth anniversary of Tiananmen, after he formed a human rights group campaigning for compensation for relatives of those killed during the 1989 crackdown. The group, which has 167 members in China, is also calling for the introduction of free trade unions. (*Observer*)

Li Guiren (*Index* 1&2/1994) was released from prison on 25 June after completing his five-year sentence. He was reported to be in good health and thanked the prison authorities for the 'good care' he had received. (AI)

A major political trial began in Beijing on 14 July to try 14 prisoners — Hu Shigen, Kang Yuchun (*Index* 8/1992), Wang Guoqi, Lu Zhigang, Wang Tiancheng, Wang Peizhong, Chen Qinglin, Chen Wei, Zhang Chunzu, Rui Chaohuai, Xing Hongwei, Xu Dongling, Zhang Guojun, and Liu Jingsheng — who have been detained for over two years on charges of 'counter-revolution'. Most of the defendants were arrested in May and June 1992, after forming or joining three underground dissident groups, writing and printing political leaflets and planning to distribute them before the third anniversary of the Tiananmen massacre. (AI)

Authorities in the northwestern province of Ningxia ordered a curb on the increasing influence of Islamic clerics in local affairs on 17 July. New regulations permit the prior vetting of all religious publications, pictures and videos. Foreigners are also forbidden to form any religious organisation or to proselytise. Around one third of the province's 4.9 million population are Muslims opposed to Chinese rule. (*Times*, SWB)

Freelance correspondent Gao Yu (*Index* 10/1993), who was charged in October 1993 with leaking state secrets, is still in jail two months after a Chinese court said there was inadequate evidence to convict her, it was reported on 21 July. The charge was apparently related to news articles she had written for the Hong Kong publications *Overseas Chinese Daily* and *Mirror Monthly*. After a closed trial on 20 April the Beijing Intermediate People's Court held that the evidence against Gao was incomplete. However, rather than acquitting her, the court ordered the prosecutor's office to find additional evidence for its case, a development described by one Chinese legal scholar as an unprecedented violation of China's criminal procedure.' (CPJ)

Following the renewal of China's Most Favoured Nation trading status by President Clinton in May, China has tightened control on all forms of dissident activity and increased the sentencing of activists, it was reported on 29 July. Police have been given sweeping powers to detain anyone involved with 'spy or enemy organisations', there has been a marked increase in arbitrary incommunicado detention of dissidents and the ability of dissidents to meet and organise, particularly with overseas NGOs, has been severely restricted by a new set of rules to be enforced by the State Security apparatus. (*Guardian*, Human Rights Watch)

Authorities announced on 3 August that, in the first half of 1994, nearly 6 million books and magazines, 200,000 compact discs and 750,000 audio and video tapes had been confiscated. The Press and Publication Administration said 'the crackdown will continue and will create a sound social and cultural environment for reform and opening.' (SWB)

Recent publication: *Pressure Off, China Targets Activists* (Human Rights Watch/Asia, July 1994, 28pp)

COSTA RICA

In July Bosco Valverde, news editor of the daily paper *La Nación*, was sentenced to one year in prison, suspended for three years, and heavily fined for contempt after he wrote an editorial which described three judges as 'pig-headed'. It is a criminal offence to criticise public officials in a way which could be considered insulting or contemptuous. (CEPEX)

COTE D'IVOIRE

Hamed Bakayoko of *Le Patriote* (*Index* 1&2/1994) was conditionally released on 6 July. (SWB)

It was reported in August that Paul Arnaud, director of the Sadea-Editions publishing company which publishes the independent papers *Le Nouvel Horizon* and *La Voie*, was arrested on 29 March and has since been detained in prison. The authorities say he was arrested in relation to financial matters, but some fear that his detention may be politically motivated. Two of his company's papers are closely aligned with the opposition Ivoirian Popular Front. Journalists at *La*

*Voie* have in the past been subjected to harassment and at least two are currently in prison (*Index* 1&2/1994). (FIEJ)

CROATIA

The satirical weekly *Feral Tribune* said in a media release on 13 July that the Ministry of Culture had imposed a 50 per cent sales tax on it from 1 July. The tax, which previously applied only to pornographic magazines, forced the magazine to suspend publication in early August. (*Feral Tribune*)

CUBA

Dissident poet María Elena Cruz Varela (*Index* 10/1992, 7/1993) was given permission to travel abroad for the first time in May. (Reuter)

Human rights activist Elizardo Sánchez Santa Cruz (*Index* 3/1993) was sentenced to six months' restricted liberty on 8 July after being found guilty of hoarding petrol. Sánchez says the charges were fabricated and claims that at least 20 other dissidents have been imprisoned recently on similar charges. (AFP)

It was announced on 14 July that the new UN human rights commissioner, José Ayala Lasso, has been invited to visit the country, thus ending decades of official opposition to human rights investigations. (*Guardian*)

Around 35 people were injured in Havana on 4 August during unprecedented clashes between police and some 400

people who were apparently attempting to leave the island by boat. (Reuter)

CZECH REPUBLIC

On 3 June Tomas Svoboda resigned as head of the Security and Information Service. Svoboda had suffered public criticism over alleged remarks that he would like to meet the former Chilean dictator, General Pinochet, when he visited the Czech Republic. (SWB)

The new citizenship law, which came into force on 1 July, classifies almost all Roma in the Czech republic as Slovaks even if they were born on Czech soil. To qualify for Czech citizenship, Roma must show proof of registered residence and have no criminal record. Roma leaders argue that these rules are deliberately designed to exclude Roma from gaining citizenship since many have never registered with the authorities. Non-citizens may not vote or stand for election. The Ministry of Employment and Social Affairs has told labour offices to withhold social security benefits from those without an official residence permit after 18 July. (RFE/RL)

On 9 July Parliament passed a vote of no confidence in the Radio and Television Broadcasting Board. The Board, which allocates frequencies and awards licences to radio and television stations, has been criticised for its licensing of controversial private broadcasting companies. (RFE/RL)

At the end of July members of the far-right Assembly of the Republic/Czechoslovak Republican Party, including former MP Josef Krejsa, prevented Germans and Czechs from holding a memorial ceremony at the former Nazi concentration camp at Terezin in northern Bohemia. The cemetery's entrance was reportedly blocked, eggs thrown at participants and wreaths destroyed. Police did not intervene. On 3 August Lubos Voboril, head of the Litomerice police external service, and Otra Cermak, chief inspector of the Terezin area, resigned in connection with the incident and disciplinary procedures against 10 policemen were announced. Krejsa was charged on 2 August with causing a disturbance; he was also prevented from taking part in a Czech Radio programme, broadcast on 3 August, on the orders of police chief Stanislav Novotny. (RFE/RL, SWB)

### DOMINICAN REPUBLIC

Narciso González (*Index* 3/1994) was reportedly seen in police custody the day after he disappeared. He was apparently badly injured and has been transferred to a military hospital. The authorities, however, continue to deny any knowledge of his whereabouts. (AI)

### ECUADOR

Radio Emisora Latacunga, an indigenous Quechua-language radio station south of Quito, was raided by armed forces on 22 June. Several employees, including the director, were detained and the station was ordered to limit its broadcasts to music and religious programmes. Two other indigenous-language radio stations, in Riobamba and Canar, were also occupied by soldiers on 21 June. The crack-down on radio stations coincides with a nationwide campaign by indigenous groups against a new agrarian law favourable to large companies and landowners. (CPJ, AMARC)

### EGYPT

At least 10 editions of the English-language weekly *Middle East Times* have been banned or delayed by the government censorship office this year. In May and June five consecutive issues were banned, one edition allegedly for evoking sympathy for terrorists by printing a photograph of a mother and baby attending a trial of Islamic militants. According to managing editor Michael Howard, the censor's office described the paper as 'poison wrapped in honey'. (Egyptian Organisation for Human Rights, Reuter)

Around 30 lawyers were detained in May and June after hundreds publicly protested the death in custody of Abdel-Harith Madani, a lawyer who defended accused Islamic activists and was a member of the Egyptian Organisation of Human Rights (EOHR). Madani, who was arrested on 26 April, is believed to have been tortured to death some time between then and 6 May. (EOHR, Lawyers' Committee for Human Rights, *Guardian*)

A concert by British musician Peter Gabriel and musicians from his organisation WOMAD (World of Music, Arts and Dance), which was to have been held in the Red Sea resort of Taba in June, was cancelled following local government objections. (Reuter, *Guardian*)

In early July a court upheld the 1992 dismissal of novelist Alaa Hamed from his government job for writing a sexually explicit, though still unpublished, book, *El-Firesh* (The Bed). Authorities said the decision was justified in order to protect Hamed's female colleagues from his alleged immorality. (Reuter, *Guardian*)

Recent publications: *Mechanisms of Violence in Egypt: Assiut — A Case Study* (Egyptian Organisation for Human Rights, May 1994, 17pp); *Freedom of Opinion and Belief* (Egyptian Organisation for Human Rights, English/Arabic, June 1994)

### EL SALVADOR

Luis Antonio Méndez, local co-ordinator for the opposition FMLN in Zacacoyo, was shot dead on 12 June. His killing is apparently part of an ongoing campaign of intimidation against opposition and human rights activists. On 10 June the Archibishop of San Salvador, Arturo Rivera y Damas, received death threats from a member of the Comando Domingo Monterrosa death squad, which has recently threatened other members of the Catholic church. (AI)

In July the mayor of San Salvador, Mario Valiente, enacted an ordinance to prohibit demonstrations on work days, reportedly because they obstruct traffic and affect the efficiency of city operations. Opponents believe the law violates their right to free assembly and could be a means of stifling opposition to the government's new economic plan, which calls for further privatisation and raises the price of basic necessities. (*Mesoamerica*)

MILEN RADEV

## ETHIOPIA

Mesfin Shiferaw (*Index* 1&2/1994), who disappeared in February, is reported to have reappeared in early June, and to have written a letter to the pro-government paper *Addis Zemen* in which he claims that he disappeared 'voluntarily'. (PEN)

Mulugetta Lule, the vice-chair of the Ethiopian Free Journalists' Association (EFJA) and editor-in-chief of *Tobia*, was fined 10,000 Birr and given a one-year suspended prison sentence on 1 June. This followed his publication of claims by the armed group Kefagne that it had killed about 600 Ethiopian People's Revolutionary Democratic Front (EPRDF) soldiers. The prosecution is reportedly appealing for a harsher sentence. (AI)

Journalist Daniel Kifle (*Index* 3/1994) was jailed for 18 months on 2 June for publishing 'malicious' articles in the Amharic-language weekly *Fendisha*. The articles alleged that the prime minister, Tamirat Layne, was involved in

illicit trading of mercury and gold. (SWB)

Melaku Tadesse, editor-in-chief of *Lubar*, Habtamu Belete, editor-in-chief of *Ruhama*, and Girma Endrias, editor of *Ruhama*, were arrested around 17 June and sentenced to six months in prison for contempt of court. The sentences are in connection with articles carried by the papers but the specific subjects are unclear. Tesfaye Tadesse, the publisher of *Lubar*, was arrested at the same time and is apparently still in detention. (EFJA)

Tefera Asmare of *Ethiopis* (*Index* 3/1994) was given an 18-month suspended sentence on 29 June for 'disseminating false information', reportedly over an article entitled 'Fascism in Tigray'. An appeal against a two-year sentence

which he is already serving is still pending. (AI, PEN)

## EUROPEAN UNION

On 20 June EU justice ministers took the first steps towards setting up a computerised fingerprint-recognition system to exchange information among all member states about refugees and illegal immigrants. An international consortium has been awarded a contract to study the feasibility of setting up the system. (*Guardian*)

## FRANCE

In early July the Senate approved laws legalising the installation of street cameras and increasing police powers to hinder anti-government protests. The bill will go before the National Assembly this autumn. If passed, the laws will authorise, among other things, video-surveillance of city streets and give police the right to search cars without explanation. (*Guardian*)

On 6 August the Interior Ministry dismissed a demand by the military wing of the Algerian Islamic Salvation Front (FIS) to free 17 Muslims arrested in France following a guerrilla attack on the French embassy compound in Algiers on 3 August. Those detained are accused of 'support for terrorism' while on French soil. The Islamic Salvation Army immediately threatened reprisals. As a result of the killings the Interior Ministry declared a crackdown on suspected fundamentalists within France, including identity checks throughout the capital. By 11 August 10,000 people had been questioned and 149 detained, most of them foreigners without proper residence documents. (*International Herald Tribune*)

### GEORGIA

The Tblisi-based independent paper *Rezonansi* was suspended for one month from 14 July, after it published a cartoon showing the head of state, Eduard Shevardnadze, naked. (SWB)

### GERMANY

On 30 May radio journalist Oliver Ness was severely beaten by plainclothes police officers in Hamburg. There are concerns that the beating may have been in retaliation for Ness's critical reports about the police. (RSF)

A peaceful demonstration held in Berlin on 7 July to protest the state visit of Chinese prime minister Li Peng was broken up by anti-riot police who beat and arrested protesters without warning. The chief of police said the police action was necessary to prevent 'revilement of a foreign head of state'.

### GUATEMALA

The offices of the magazine *Tinamit* (*Index* 10/1993, 1&2/1994) were again bombed on 23 June. *Tinamit* had recently published reports on alleged tax evasion by 98 leading business people and on human rights abuses committed by the Civil Defence Patrols. (CEPEX)

A bomb hit the offices of Radio Progreso in Guatemala City on 1 July, apparently in response to a programme earlier in the day in which well known journalist Hugo Arce (*Index*10/1993, 1&2/1994) said that the procurator general, Acisclo Valladares Molina, should resign because of charges pending against him. On 4 July Cesar Augusto Méndez Auraz, the programme's host, was dismissed and has subsequently been subject to constant surveillance outside his home. (Archbishopric of Guatemala Human Rights Office)

Edwin Miguel Quezada, editor of the daily *Prensa Libre*, reported being abducted and beaten on 16 July by four armed men who interrogated him about his sources for a story on a recent assassination attempt against President de

León. However, the paper's director, José Eduardo Zarco, accused Quezada of falsifying his account of the abduction and dismissed him on 19 July. Quezada maintains that his version of events is correct. (IAPA)

The building of the Guatemalan Journalists' Association (APG) was fired at on 10 August, during a conference on the country's uprooted and marginalised populations. (CEPEX)

### HAITI

Political activist Janne Toussaint disappeared after being abducted by army members from her apartment in Port-au-Prince on 19 June following several interviews given by her husband, Lévius Toussaint, on the US radio station Voice of America. In the interviews, Lévius Toussaint, a journalist resident in the US, condemned the Haitian military and called for a return to democracy. Toussaint's entire family has been active against the military since the coup. (AI)

As a result of the tightening of sanctions by the US in July, two pro-democracy papers printed outside the country — *Haïti-En-Marche* and *Haïti Progrès* — are no longer available. The Creole-language weekly *Libète* has resumed publication again, but is circulating in reduced numbers owing to high production costs and continuing attacks on street vendors. (*Haiti Info*)

The Information Ministry

announced on 14 July that the military government is constitutional and should not be described in the press as 'de facto'. The announcement also called on journalists to be 'more objective' in their reporting. (*Haiti Info*)

A new pro-democracy radio station set up by the US and the government in exile began broadcasting to Haiti on 15 July with an address by President Aristide. The US government reserves the right to vet his addresses before they are broadcast. (*Haiti Info*)

Ernst Ocean, a reporter with Radio Tropic FM, has been missing since 31 July. His last report was on a voodoo ceremony held by army officers to ward off possible military intervention by the US. (CPJ)

A decree issued on 2 August warned that local media carrying 'alarmist and tendentious news' face seizure by the military. This follows the foreign minister's criticism of local journalists in July for not reporting all the regime's communiques. He also accused foreign journalists of carrying out a systematic campaign of disinformation with regard to human rights abuses committed by the military. A further decree, issued on 13 August, forbids local news media from publishing information obtained from foreign embassies or international groups. (CPJ, *Haiti Info*)

A three-member crew from the US programme *MacNeil/Lehrer NewsHour* was deported on 4 August after attempting to film

near the country's international airport. Their Haitian driver and interpreter have reportedly not been released. (CPJ)

On 8 August the radio station Arc En Ciel went off the air after three armed civilians threatened staff members. The station carried mainly Creole-language programmes from the Voice of America. (CPJ)

Members of General Cédras's personal security unit warned two radio directors not to criticise the regime, it was reported on 15 August. The directors have asked not to be named for their own protection. (CPJ)

Recent publication: *Rape in Haiti — A Weapon of Terror* (Human Rights Watch/National Coalition for Haitian Refugees, July 1994, 28pp)

## HONG KONG

On 17 June China attacked measures announced by the Hong Kong government to allow the public limited access to official information. The Xinhua press agency quoted a Foreign Ministry spokesperson as saying the measures 'violated provisions of the Sino-British Joint Declaration' and would involve major changes detrimental to Hong Kong's smooth transition. (*International Herald Tribune*)

On 1 July, one day after the Constitutional Reform Bill was passed by the Legislative Council, the Hong Kong government rejected a proposal, endorsed by the parliamentary

Foreign Affairs Committee, to set up an independent commission on human rights. Human rights activists and others accuse the government of seeking to appease China. (*Guardian, International Herald Tribune*)

In August Hong Kong publisher and retailer Jimmy Lai lost control of his retailing chain, Giordano, after publishing an article attacking Chinese prime minister Li Peng in his magazine *Next*. He was forced off the board by his partners and the Giordano store in Beijing has been closed by the authorities who say it has not met the necessary licensing requirements. (*International Herald Tribune*)

Recent publication: *Freedom of Expression in Hong Kong 1994* (Article 19/Hong Kong Journalists' Association, June 1994, 32pp)

## HUNGARY

From mid-September some 15,000 MPs, high ranking public officials, media editors and university rectors will be screened under the III/3 law passed by the outgoing Parliament (*Index* 3/1994). A parliamentary committee with access to former III/3 secret police files will investigate suspected former agents and members of paramilitary units set up in 1956. Those found to have collaborated will be under pressure to resign or have their names and activities published. (Reuter)

In June Istvan Palfy, state television news director, was dismissed and accused of propagating programmes favouring the previous government. Acting radio and television presidents Laszlo Csucs and Gabor Nahlik were dismissed on 8 July also for favouring the interests of the previous governments in their broadcasting policies.( RFE/RL, SWB)

On 22 July the television programme *Hirado* (Newsreel) was cancelled and Istvan Stefka, the programme's chief editor, was sacked and his staff told that they would be recalled when needed. *Hirado* was extremely critical of the Socialist Party and had been accused of favouring the former conservative coalition government. {SWB, Reuter)

On 23 July state radio president Janos Sziranyi pledged to reinstate the 129 radio reporters and journalists dismissed or sent into early retirement by former President Laszlo Csucs in March (*Index* 1&2/1994). (SWB)

Francisco Miranda Branco, Gregorio da Cunha Saldanha, Jacinto das Neves Raimundo Alves, Juvencio de Jesus Martins and Saturnino da Costa Belo, who were sentenced to between five years and life imprisonment in 1992 for their non-violent activities in support of East Timorese independence, were reported on 13 June to have disappeared after being removed from prison in Dili, East Timor. (AI)

In late June Semsar Siahaan, an artist and senior official of the

Yayasan Pijar pro-democracy movement, was imprisoned for his part in a demonstration against the banning on 21 June of the weekly magazines *Tempo, Editor* and *Detik*. The Information Ministry said the publications were banned because of their 'ignorance of press ethics'. *Tempo*, the country's largest circulation magazine, was also accused of threatening national security by covering a controversial deal involving the purchase of warships from the former East German navy. On 7 August a new organisation, the Alliance of Independent Journalists (AGI), was founded to protest the bannings. (*Jawa Post*, Reuter)

Prison terms imposed on 21 students for demonstrating against human rights violation under President Suharto (*Index* 1&2/1994) were increased in July by the High Court of Jakarta. The students had been found guilty in May of 'publicly insulting the head of state'. (AI)

Students clashed with Indonesian authorities in East Timor on 14 July. Several hundred students and demonstrators carried banners demanding religious freedom in East Timor, where there is tension between the Catholic Timorese and the mainly Muslim occupying army. (*Independent, Guardian*)

The English-language *Jakarta Post*, the magazine *Sinar* and the legal journal *Forum Keadilan* were officially warned at the end of July over their reporting of unrest in East

Timor. Other publications placed 'under watch' include the magazine *Indonesia Business Weekly* and the dailies *Kompas* and *Sinar Pagi*. (*Business Times*)

In late July the governments of Indonesia and Singapore announced their intention to work together to combat 'superficial' coverage of their countries by foreign media. (IFJ)

A sermon given by senior cleric Ayatollah Ali Akbar Meshkini in late June has offered hope that the *fatwa* condemning Salman Rushdie is not irrevocable. Meshkini announced that it was within the power of the country's spiritual leader, Ayatollah Khamenei, to overrule any preceding religious decree, apparently contradicting the stance until now taken by the country's leadership. (*Guardian*)

Two prominent Christians were found murdered near

Tehran in early July. The body of Presbyterian preacher Tateos Michaelian was discovered on 2 July and that of translator Mehdi Dibaj (*Index* 1&2/1994, 3/1994) on 5 July. The two had been missing since 29 June and 24 June respectively. A member of the outlawed Iraq-based organisation Mujahidin Khalq was arrested by Iranian police in connection with the killings. The Mujahidin Khalq in turn have blamed the government for the deaths. (AI, PEN, *Times*)

On 29 July Ayatollah Jannati said a possible ban on satellite dishes was justified on the grounds that they 'provoke lust and extravagance' and on 5 August senior politicians called for action to 'confront' foreign satellite broadcasts. (SWB)

**ISRAEL AND OCCUPIED TERRITORIES**

Nine students from Bir Zeit University were detained by Israeli security forces on 29 June and reportedly ill-treated while in detention. They are believed to have been interrogated about their involvement with the Islamic Bloc, a legal student group. Eight of the students are still in prison. (*Jerusalem Times*)

A television station in Beit Jala, Muhatat A-Rua' (Shepherd's Station), was forced to close on 27 July after Israeli security forces raided its premises and seized equipment. The station has a licence to operate and, according to station supervisor Walid Qumsiyah, no explanation was given for the raid. Tulkarem Peace television sta-

tion, broadcasting in and around Nablus, was also ordered to close by Israeli authorities in July with no reason given. (*Jerusalem Times*)

On 14 August the Jerusalem district commissioner revoked the licence of the paper Al-Bayan because of its alleged links with the Hamas movement. (B'Tselem)

Recent publication: *Collaborators in the Occupied Territories: Human Rights Abuses and Violations* (B'Tselem: The Israeli Information Center for Human Rights in the Occupied Territories, January 1994, 239pp); *Torture and Ill-Treatment: Israel's Interrogation of Palestinians from the Occupied Territories* (Human Rights Watch/Middle East, June 1994, 316pp)

**ITALY**

On 1 July the board of the state-owned RAI broadcasting corporation resigned after the Berlusconi cabinet issued a decree stripping the directors of their powers because the government disapproved of a restructuring plan they had presented for the loss-making corporation. (*Times*)

On 8 August RAI announced that it was suspending the advertising campaign bought by the prime minister, Silvio Berlusconi, promoting his government's achievements. (*Guardian*)

**JAPAN**

The brother of the late Emperor Hirohito said on 6

July that military leaders suppressed copies of a speech he made in 1944, denouncing Japanese atrocities in China. (*International Herald Tribune*)

**KAZAKHSTAN**

Journalist Boris Suprunyuk (*Index* 3/1994), arrested in April for his work on a Russian-language newspaper, has subsequently been released. Suprunyuk, a Kazakh citizen of Russian descent, is now living in Moscow. (PEN)

**KENYA**

Bedan Mbugua and David Makali of *The People*, imprisoned on contempt charges (*Index* 3/1994), were transferred to Manyani Maximum Security Prison on 16 June. It appears that no transfer warrant was issued, in contravention of the Prison Act. Manyani Prison has a reputation for harsh conditions and torture, and the transfer may be a deliberate attempt to further punish the pair. The paper's lawyer was not imprisoned, as stated in *Index* 3/1994. (CPJ)

Charges of subversion against Ngumo wa Kuria, Peter Rianga Makori, Kamau Kanyanga and John Nyaosi of *The Standard* (*Index* 3/1994) were dropped and replaced with more serious sedition charges on 23 June. The increased charges carry a maximum 10-year jail sentence. No date has been set for a trial. (AI)

John Lawrence, an Australian journalist and training editor

with the *Daily Nation*, was deported on 11 July. He was taken from the newspaper's office to the Immigration Department for questioning and put on a flight to Johannesburg that evening. No reason was given for the deportation, but the order stated that 'his continued stay in Kenya was contrary to national interest'. The *Daily Nation* is considering suing the government over the matter. (CPJ, MISA)

Geoffrey Kuria Kariuki, the cousin of Koigi wa Wamwere (*Index* 3/1994), John Kinyanjui, of the Release Political Prisoners campaign group, Michael Kung'u, also a relative of Koigi wa Wamwere, and Oliver Ngugi Gachamba were charged on 19 July with robbery with violence and possession of firearms. All were arrested on the weekend of 9 and 10 July and are reported to have been tortured while in custody. There is concern that the charges against Geoffrey Kuria Kariuki and some, if not all, of the others have been fabricated and that their arrests are connected to Koigi wa Wamwere's case. (AI)

Recent publication: *Multipartyism Betrayed in Kenya: Continuing Rural Violence and Restrictions on Freedom of Speech and Assembly* (Human Rights Watch/Africa, July 1994, 33pp)

### KYRGYZSTAN

On 13 July President Akayev called for a 'fundamentally new law' on the media, saying that a number of papers systematically make 'shameless and imperti-

nent' attacks on the leaders of foreign states. He singled out the parliamentary paper *Svobodnoye Gory* for particular criticism and threatened to close it down. (SWB)

### LEBANON

The 5 July edition of the London-based weekly *al-Wassat* was banned from distribution and thousands of copies were seized. The magazine carried an interview with a former Christian militia security chief, Ghassan Touman, in which he criticised the government. (RSF)

Restrictions on the broadcasting of news by private radio and television stations, which had been imposed in March, were lifted on 28 July. The measure is believed to be a temporary one, until the government brings in a new media bill to regulate private broadcasters. In the meantime, television and radio stations have been warned not to broadcast political programmes which could incite religious conflict. (Télé-Liban, Reuter)

### LESOTHO

Rabuka Chalatsi of the private weekly *MoAfrika* was shot and injured by security forces on 17 August while covering a demonstration outside the royal palace in Maseru to protest King Letsie's sudden dissolution of Parliament. Soldiers were also reported to have occupied the studios of the state-owned Radio Lesotho, apparently to ensure the continued rebroadcast of King Letsie's announcement of

the dissolution. (MISA)

### MALAWI

Recently inaugurated President Muluzi has lifted bans on television in Malawi and on the use of the main Thumbuka language, which was outlawed by his predecessor, Hastings Banda. Following his inauguration, President Muluzi also ordered the release of all political prisoners and the closure of prisons associated with detention without trial. (*Times, Guardian*)

Following a government-imposed court ruling banning the distribution of the 20 July issue of *The Malawian* newspaper, for printing a picture of President Muluzi taken after his conviction for theft in the 1960s, the President rescinded the banning order. The court made use of an act which criminalises the publication of anything liable to 'insult, ridicule or show disrespect' to the President. Muluzi has committed himself to repealing 'those laws that make it difficult for the media to operate'. (Article 19)

### MALAYSIA

Foreign minister Abdullah Ahmad Badawi said in late June that the government will not sanction conferences on East Timor because they strain relations with Indonesia. He was commenting on a proposal by the Malaysian Action Front, an umbrella organisation of human rights, political and environmental groups, to hold a forum on human rights violations in East Timor. (*International Herald Tribune*)

Malaysia outlawed the radical Islamic sect al-Arqam in August. A decree issued by the National Fatwa Council forbids it to run its businesses and schools or spread its teachings. Prime Minister Mahathir promised to break up its communes if the sect continues to teach its 'deviationist' brand of Islam. (*International Herald Tribune*)

## MALI

On 29 May two journalists and a technician working at the station Radio Kayira were detained. Siaka Konate, a technician, and Adama Kon and Adama Konate, programme hosts, have been accused of not respecting a closure order against the radio station dating from 6 May when Radio Kayira and Radio Jamana were closed by administrative order for 'disturbing the peace' and 'lack of authorisation to broadcast'. Apart from one station in Segou, the entire Radio Kayira network has now been closed for broadcasting recordings made during the trial of students arrested during demonstrations. (RSF)

On 13 June Belco Tamboura and Moussa Fofana, publisher and editor-in-chief respectively of the independent weekly *L'Observateur*, were summoned to the office of the deputy police chief in Bamako. They were interrogated for more than two hours about the sources for an article published that day, which cited a confidential document from the

national police directorate proposing the establishment of a 'security force for urban security operations'. (RSF)

## MAURITANIA

The 25 July edition of weekly *L'Eveil Hebdo* was seized under Article 11 of the media law, which forbids criticism of the state or of Islam. This follows recent seizures of other publications, *Le Calame* and *al Bayane*, for publishing information that displeased the government (*Index* 3/1994). (CPJ, RSF)

## MEXICO

Enrique Peralta Torres of the Cuernavaca daily paper *La Unión de Morelos* was murdered on 6 July. The body of another journalist with the same paper, José Luis Rojas, was found on 13 July, apparently after being strangled to death. In the weeks before the murders, the paper had published extremely critical articles about the state government. (CPJ, IAPA)

Amado Avendano, journalist and opposition Democratic Revolutionary Party (PRD) candidate, was seriously injured in a car crash in Chiapas on 26 July. It is believed the incident was an attempt to kill Avendano, who owns and edits the San Cristóbal de las Casas daily *Tiempo*. Avedano became nationally known for his paper's independent coverage of the Zapatista uprising early this year. (*Independent*)

The Zapatista National

Liberation Army (EZLN) banned several news media from attending its national convention held between 6 and 9 August in Chiapas. Those banned were reportedly all reporters connected with the television network Televisa, as well as those from media considered critical of the EZLN. (CPJ)

Recent publications: *Democracy Within Reason: Technocratic Revolution in Mexico* (Miguel Angel Centeno, 1994, 256pp); *Becoming a Scientist in Mexixo: The Challenge of Creating a Scientific Community in an Underdeveloped Countrry* (Jacqueline Fortes & Larissa Adler Lomnitz, 1994, 236pp)

## MOLDOVA

Parliament began a second reading of the new Constitution on 21 July. Article 13, concerning the adoption of an official state language, has proved to be controversial. The Parliamentary Commission probably has an overall majority in favour of Moldovan, but the Peasants and Intellectuals Bloc argue that to exclude Romanian from the discussions would severely insult a large minority. (Reuter)

## MONGOLIA

On 24 June it was announced that Tsahiagiyn Elbegdorj, leader of the opposition Democratic Union (MDU), is to be tried for 'disclosing a state secret' in speeches he made in April during a protest fast by MDU members and other opposition activists. (SWB)

Lodoisamjugiyn Sanjaasuren, the former head of counter-intelligence in the State Security Directorate, was sentenced to 18 months in a corrective labour colony in July after a closed trial found him guilty of disclosing state secrets. The charge arose from allegations of corruption he made against senior officials, including the prime minister and the parliamentary chairman. (AI)

### MOROCCO

Customs officials at Casablanca airport seized 3,000 copies of the magazine *Jeune Afrique*, published in Paris, on 8 June. A distribution quota of 3,000 copies has apparently been imposed on the magazine by the authorities. (RSF)

Ahmed Belaichi, a satirical cartoonist and member of the Moroccan Association for Human Rights (AMDH) jailed in 1992 for insulting the military, was among 424 prisoners released in an amnesty granted by King Hassan on 21 July. Others released include students, trade unionists, and Islamic and Marxist activists. The amnesty came after lists of names were drawn up by the Consultative Council for Human Rights (CCDH), appointed by the King four years ago. However, no-one who disputes Morocco's claim to Western Sahara was amnestied. (AMDH, Reuter)

From August, satellite dishes are to be subject to a 5,000 dirham tax. Opposition parties have denounced the levy, saying that it will cut off a major source of news from abroad for those on low incomes. (Radio France Internationale)

### NAGORNO-KARABAKH

Authorities issued a decree on 30 July, increasing penalties for unlawful religious activity. According to a Supreme Council spokesman, a number of unregistered sects are active in the enclave and are 'contributing to a split in society'. (SWB)

### NEPAL

On 23 July four journalists, Shakti Lamshal, Karna Bahadur Karki, Bihod Pahadi and Ashok Man Shrestha, were questioned at their homes and subsequently detained. The government has justified the detention of the four men by saying that it is trying to re-establish peace in Katmandu, the scene of several large demonstrations since the beginning of July. (RSF)

### NETHERLANDS

In late July the government launched an appeal against the Groningen Court's June decision to acquit author Graa Boomsma and journalist Eddy Schaafsma, who had been charged with defamation (*Index* 3/1994). Groningen High Court is expected to hear the appeal in the autumn. (PEN)

### NIGERIA

On 11 June the State Security Service (SSS) closed the Concord newspaper group, which publishes the country's most widely read independent publications, including the *National Concord*. The closure came hours after Concord's publisher, Moshood Abiola, the widely recognised victor in the annulled 1993 elections, declared himself president and demanded General Abacha's resignation. Abiola was arrested on 23 June and is awaiting trial on charges of treason. Also on 11 June police raided the offices of the magazine *Punch* and sealed off the building. The magazine's editor Bola Bolawole was held under office arrest until June 15. The government accused both *Punch* and Concord staff of stockpiling arms. The Federal High Court in Lagos, however, held that the occupation of the Concord offices was illegal and ordered security forces to evacuate the premises. In the wake of the crackdown on Concord, the Nigerian Union of Journalists has appealed to the government to stop 'the absurd act' of printing and circulating fake editions of popular magazines. This relates to the appearance on the streets of false copies of magazines carrying stories in disagreement with their stated editorial policies. (CPJ, RSF, *West Africa*, AI)

On 20 June Mary Ellen Ezakiel, publisher of the weekly paper *Weekend Classique*, was arrested following the publication in the 12 June issue of an article which reported that junior officers in the Nigerian army are 'angry' at General Abacha. (CPJ)

Shehu Kura, a journalist with

the Voice of America's Hausa-language service, and a number of other reporters covering demonstrations outside the Abuja courthouse where Abiola is on trial, were beaten by police on 27 July. Police also reportedly attempted to bribe Kura into stopping his reporting of alleged corruption among the delegates to the Constitutional Conference, called by General Abacha as part of his proposed restoration of democracy. (CPJ)

Armed police closed the offices of the *Guardian* newspaper chain in Lagos on 14 August. The evening before the closure, the *Guardian* had run a front-page article on a power struggle within the military government over the present political crisis. (RSF)

Recent publication: *Terror in Ogoni: Massacre, Rape, Extortion, Refugees* (Civil Liberties Organisation, 24 Mbonu Ojike St, Surulere, Lagos, Nigeria, August 1994, 17pp)

## PAKISTAN

Recent publication: *Use and Abuse of the Blasphemy Laws* (Amnesty International, July 1994, 29pp)

## PAPUA NEW GUINEA

Sir Pita Lus, the oldest serving member of Parliament, called for tougher sentences on graffiti writers and vandals in August, including amputating their arms. His demand was triggered by the desecration of a church he is building at Port Moresby. (SWB)

## PALESTINE (GAZA-JERICHO)

*An-Nahar* daily newspaper, based in East Jerusalem, has suspended publication until further notice after it was banned from sale and distribution in the self-rule areas by the Palestinian National Authority (PNA) on 29 July. The PNA also allegedly warned a director of *An-Nahar* not to distribute the newspaper in the West Bank. According to a PNA statement, the paper's political coverage is 'harmful to Palestinian interests'. (CPJ, RSF, *Independent*)

## PERU

Pedro Salazar Angulo, director of the daily *El Oriente*, and Santiago Gonzales Coronado, correspondent for the Lima paper *La República*, were both accused of contempt in early July. The accusation was provoked by articles and reports on the unexpected release from prison of an alleged cocaine trafficker. The prosecutor who laid the contempt charge has been criticised several times by police and journalists for freeing suspected drug traffickers. (FIP)

Journalist Jávier Tuanama Valera was transferred to prison in Chiclayo on 7 July, where he will face his third trial on charges of joining the Tupac Amaru Revolutionary Movement in December 1990, even though he has been in continuous detention since October 1990. Two previous acquittals of the charges have been successfully appealed by

the prosecution. No date has been set for the new trial. (FIP)

On 15 July Dario Macedo, journalist and director of the radio news programme *Hora Cero*, was assaulted on air by José Ponte, public relations officer for the municipality of Padre Abad. The programme was broadcasting reports criticising the mayor of Padre Abad and describing him as an autocrat. (Instituto Prensa y Sociedad)

The Congressional Constitution Committee voted to amend the controversial Habeas Data law (*Index* 1&2/1994, 3/1994) on 15 July so as to prevent its use in cases of corrections to information presented in the media. The amendment also requires approval from a plenary session of Congress. (FIP)

Oscar Tercero Cárdenas Bartra, director of the regional weekly *Selva*, was detained by police while waiting to board a flight at Lima airport on 17 July. The arrest order accused Bartra of 'contempt'. He is currently being held in Lima prison and is said to be fearful for his safety because of his vehement public criticism of official corruption. (FIP)

## POLAND

The prime minister, Waldemar Pawlak, dismissed Polish Press Agency (PAP) chief Ignacy Rutkiewicz on 19 July and appointed a computer science professor, Wlodzimierz Gogolek, in his place. Since Rutkiewicz's appointment in 1990, PAP has functioned as an impartial wire service, despite being government-owned. Pawlak's decision came a few weeks after the opposition party Freedom Union submitted draft legislation to privatise PAP, protecting the agency against possible government interference. (RFE/RL)

## ROMANIA

On 2 June Parliament endorsed article 8 of the Education Bill (*Index* 7/1993) which stipulates that education in all grades will be in Romanian and that all citizens must learn Romanian as the country's official language. Deputies also voted to guarantee the rights of ethnic minorities to study their own languages. On 12 July the Hungarian Democratic Union of Romania (HDUR) called for a boycott by Hungarian students. The HDUR objects to the compulsory teaching of history, geography and civics in Romanian. (SWB, RFE/RL)

On 7 June the registration of a new Communist party was declared illegal by the Supreme Court, acting under a law which bans groups that support totalitarianism, extremism, fascism or Communism. (RFE/RL)

The Constitutional Court ruled in July that homosexuals can be prosecuted for 'causing a public scandal'. Although the ruling moderates Article 200 of the Penal Code, which prohibits homosexual activity, gay rights groups continue to press for the full repeal of Romania's anti-gay legislation. (Reuter)

Armed police with dogs closed down a gay cultural event in Bucharest on 16 July on orders from the city's mayor. Police reportedly told those attending: 'There will be no gay celebrations in Bucharest' while checking identity cards and noting names. (International Lesbian and Gay Human Rights Commission)

On 17 July the Romanian Intelligence Service issued a report exonerating the former Securitate from causing bloodshed during the 1989 revolution, blaming deaths on badly co-ordinated action by the Romanian army and Russian agents. The report acknowledges the role of popular discontent in overthrowing the Ceaucescu regime, but alleges that KGB intelligence and diversionary teams were active throughout the uprising. (Reuter, RFE/RL)

On 11 August opposition MPs accused the government of trying to control all cultural activity through orders and decrees. All dissident anti-Communist theatre directors and cultural leaders who held prominent positions after 1989 have reportedly been replaced by members of the nomenklatura. (Reuter)

Recent publication: *Restrictions on the Freedom of the Press in Romania* (Human Rights Watch/Helsinki, June 1994, 15pp)

## RUSSIAN FEDERATION

Russia: The draft media law (Index 3/1994) was adopted by the State Duma on 14 July as the Law on Coverage of Activities of the Bodies of State Power by the State Media. The controversial statute compels state-owned media to inform the public of the activities of the president, government and Parliament within 24 hours of any noteworthy event. Journalists are required to assist the authorities in addressing the nation via the state-owned media and to refrain from making any commentary in the broadcasts. The law also provides for a separate broadcast of parliamentary debates on television during prime time. State institutions are now forbidden to own any media independently, except for purely informative bulletins. Accordingly, the Cabinet of Ministers must divest itself of two major newspapers, *Rossiisskaya Gazeta* and *Rossisskaya Vesti*. (RFE/RL)

On 15 July Orel region introduced a new tax on foreign trade names to 'protect the purity of the Russian language'. Russian enterprises wishing to advertise their names using non-Cyrillic characters will have to pay R10 million per year. (SWB)

Despite a 1992 agreement with France, Russia has frozen the return of French military and police archives seized by the Soviet Army at the end of World War II, French officials said on 20 July. The State Duma is reportedly examining a draft law which, if adopted, would prevent repatriation of archives and other cultural items seized all over Europe by the Soviet army at the end of World War II. (Reuter)

It was reported in August that chemist Vil Mirzayanov (*Index* 1&2/1994), who was prosecuted over his allegations about Russia's ongoing research into chemical warfare and subsequently released, was refused a visa to travel to two scientific meetings in Germany on the grounds that he is 'a holder of state secrets'. (AAASHRAN)

The Maritime Territory banned the open sale of printed matter displaying naked bodies on 7 August. Such material cannot be sold at all in the vicinity of schools or in sport and leisure areas. (SWB)

Chechnia: President Dudayev formed a committee on 28 July to look at ways of halting Russian television broadcasts to Chechnia. Russian stations are accused of 'attempting to provoke civil war in the Caucasus'. (SWB)

## RWANDA

At least six Rwandan journalists are known to have been killed in the violence which has engulfed the country this year. Anastase Seruvumba of the newspaper *Imbaga*; Jeanne d'Arc Mukamusoni, director of *Le Soleil*; André Kameya, editor-in-chief of *Rwanda Rushya*; and Vincent Rwabukwizi, former director of *Kanguka*, which is considered close to the Rwandan Patriotic Front, were probably all killed by the Rwandan Armed Forces (FAR). Ignace Ruhatana, editor-in-chief of the human rights journal *Kanyarwanda*, was killed by an FAR soldier.

Venant Ntawucikayenda, camera operator for TV Rwanda, was killed on 10 May by a bomb blast at the station. (RSF)

Two French journalists, Isabelle Staes of the television station France 2 and José Nicolas, a photographer with the news agency SIPA, were injured when they were fired on by Rwandan Patriotic Front (FPR) troops on 4 July as they crossed the combat line between Kigali and Butare. (RSF)

RSF initiated a civil suit in Paris on 8 August against four 'founders, financiers and organizers' of Radio-Télévision Libre des Milles Collines (RTLM) (*Index* 3/1994). The four, Agathe Habyarimana, Seraphin Rwabukumba, Protais Zigiranyirazo and Ferdinand Nakimana, are currently in France. RSF alleges that they are responsible for genocide, violations of humanitarian law, crimes against humanity, torture, and the vindication of war crimes and crimes against humanity. RSF is also requesting the UN Security Council to adopt a resolution obliging all countries present in the region to immediately halt all broadcasts from RTLM. (RSF)

## SAUDI ARABIA

Mohammed al-Khilewi, a diplomat at Saudi Arabia's mission to the United Nations, sought political asylum in June after accusing the government of human rights violations. (*Guardian, International Herald Tribune*)

A ban on the use of satellite dishes came into effect at the end of July. Foreign satellite broadcasts will now be vetted by the Information Ministry before being retransmitted to ensure that the material does not conflict with the kingdom's religious and social values. (Information Ministry)

## SENEGAL

A one-year ban on the distribution of the Paris-based weekly *Jeune Afrique* was overturned in August and charges of defamation against its director, Bechir Ben Yahmed (*Index* 3/1994), were dropped. (RSF, CPJ)

## SERBIA-MONTENEGRO

Serbia: The Belgrade television station NTV Studio-B, the only real opposition channel in the republic, has been denied permission to expand its operations despite a decision last year by the Ministry of Traffic and Communications to allow it to do so. The authorities apparently wish to prevent the station reaching a wider audience outside the Serbian capital. (International Press Institute)

In early August the IFJ and FIEJ called on the UN to reconsider the policy of sanctions against media in Serbia and Montenegro. The organisations say that independent media in Serbia — 'the only alternative voices' — suffer greatly from the adverse effects of the international economic and cultural sanctions. (IFJ)

Kosovo: Nebih Zogaj, chairman of the local branch of the Democratic League of Kosovo, has been summoned to Belanica police station on more than 10 occasions since the beginning of June. No charges have been brought against him and on each occasion he has been severely beaten. (AI)

Serbian authorities are tightening their control on the education system in Kosovo, according to a report by the International Helsinki Federation for Human Rights (IHF) released in July. The report says teachers and students belonging to the Albanian majority are being increasingly harassed through illegal detention and confiscation of educational material. (IHF)

## SIERRA LEONE

Ibrahim Seaga Shaw, editor-in-chief of the Freetown daily *Afro Times*, was arrested on 8 August after a lawyer in Bo, with government assistance, launched a defamation suit over an article which alleged his involvement in a major fraud case. Both Shaw and his assistant, Abdul Abass Dumbuya, are currently detained in Bo, awaiting a court appearance. (RSF)

## SINGAPORE

A bill was introduced to privatise the Singapore Broadcasting Corporation in July. A new broadcasting authority will have the power to set guidelines on censorship and programming, as well as to censure, fine or withdraw broadcasters' licences. If passed, the

bill will also give ministers the power to ban foreign broadcast services. (*Business Times*)

## SLOVAKIA

On 7 July Parliament passed a bill allowing the use of bilingual road signs in towns and villages where ethnic minorities make up more than 20 per cent of the total populaton.

The electoral coalition Democratic Party-Party of Entrepreneurs has announced that it will screen all its candidates, according to the 'lustration' (screening law), in the October general elections in order to prohibit those with previous secret police contacts from entering Parliament. (RFE/RL)

Recent publication: *Restrictions on Press Freedom in the Slovak Republic* (Human Rights Watch/Helsinki, June 1994, 24pp)

## SOUTH AFRICA

The appointment of former ANC publicity officer Solly Kotane as head of the Bophuthatswana Broadcasting Corporation on 21 July has angered freedom of expression activists who say it violates the national unity government's commitment to the independence of public broadcast media. (*Southern Africa Report*)

An application in late July by the *Weekly Mail and Guardian* to access state security files on the newspaper under section 23 of the new Bill of Rights, has been frustrated by the Ministry of Security and Safety.

Despite being the subject of dozens of police investigations during the 1980s, the minister says that he has only one incomplete and inaccurate file on the newspaper. (MISA)

The South African Broadcasting Corporation (SABC) released an early draft of its new language policy on 3 August. It says the use of Afrikaans will be decided 'by the whole board' and not by individuals. White supremacist leader Eugene Terreblanche has threatened a campaign of violence if Afrikaans is removed from SABC's TV1. (SWB)

## SOUTH KOREA

The information minister said on 13 July that it is not yet time to allow South Korean media to listen to broadcasts from the North. Reaction to Kim Il-Sung's death, he said, showed that the media do not 'correctly grasp the intention of North Korea and screen it properly'. (SWB)

Fifty-five students were arrested for putting up posters praising Kim Il-Sung and planning memorial ceremonies in his honour, it was reported on 15 July. Student demonstators later attacked police stations where the detained students were said to be held. The Seoul government also barred its citizens from visiting the North for Kim's funeral. (*International Herald Tribune*, *Times*)

Nine university professors — Chang Sang-hwan, Cho Tae-ryong, Paek Choi-hum, Lee

Hyu-suk, Lee Chang-ho, Song Ki-ho, Kim Chun-hyong, Kim Ui-dong and Chong Chin-sang — were charged in August under the National Security Law for a book they co-wrote entitled *Understanding Korean Society*, which has been used as a university textbook since 1990. The book allegedly contains material 'instigating class struggle and revolution'. The contents of lectures given by the professors, as well as other publications they have written, are also under investigation. (SWB, PEN)

## SRI LANKA

The sale of threatened Bangladeshi author Taslima Nasrin's novel *Shame* was banned on 19 July after the deputy minister for Muslim religious and cultural affairs said Nasrin's writings were 'blasphemous and have injured the religious sensibilities of Muslims the world over.' (Reuter)

At least 15 people, mostly members or supporters of opposition parties, were murdered in the run-up to the 16 August general elections. Chandrika Kumaratunga, the leader of the Sri Lanka Freedom Party, also received anonymous death threats. (RSF)

## SUDAN

Mohammed Abd al-Seed, a journalist with *al-Khartoum* newspaper, was detained at the paper's office on 23 June by the security forces. They accused Abd al-Seed of involvement in a plot, along with the former prime minister, Sadiq al-Mahdi, to kill the leader of the National Islamic Front. Mohammed Abd al-Seed had recently interviewed al-Mahdi, who was himself arrested earlier the same week. Al-Mahdi was released on 3 July, but Mohammed Abd al-Seed's whereabouts remain unknown. (CPJ/AI)

Recent publication: *Civilian Devastation: Abuses by All Parties in the War in Southern Sudan* (Human Rights Watch/Africa, June 1994, 279pp)

## SURINAME

Ludwig van Mulier, a Dutch journalist and editor of the monthly *De Ware Surinaamse Tijd*, was detained on 24 May, after allegations were made in the first issue of his publication about Vice-President Ajodhia's involvement in large scale drug-trafficking. Van Mulier was released on 4 July and expelled from the country for allegedly being 'a danger to the state'. (Journalists' Safety Service)

## SWAZILAND

A proposed amendment to the Sedition and Subversive Activities Act, published in late June, would make it an offence to publish 'false or derogatory' statements about the King, his mother or their immediate successors, punishable by between 10 and 20 years in prison. It is feared that the amendment would severely affect criticism of the government because the King is head of government and some

his immediate successors are ministers. (MISA)

## SYRIA

Journalist Ahmed Hasso (*Index* 1&2/1994) was reportedly released in May. Previously with the Lebanese paper *al-Safir*, he was imprisoned in 1992 for membership of the banned Committee for the Defence of Democratic Freedoms and Human Rights (CDF). (RSF)

## TAIWAN

Three Taiwanese journalists were injured on 1 August by demonstrators protesting a government crackdown on unlicensed radio stations. Lo Tsung-Ping and Fei Kuo-Yang, cameramen for Chinese Television, and Chao Chun-Hsiung, a photographer for the *Taiwan Daily News*, were attacked by demonstrators armed with clubs, torches and other weapons. Fourteen illegal stations have been closed in six cities in recent weeks after police raids to confiscate equipment. (RSF, *Far Eastern Economic Review*)

## TAJIKISTAN

Davlatali Rakhmonaliev, programming director at the state television station, was shot dead outside his home in Dushanbe on 18 August. The motive for the murder is unclear. (RSF)

## TANZANIA

On 30 June police raided the premises of Business Printers in Dar-es-Salaam and

RSF

Three distributors for the paper *Özgür Ulke* have disappeared while in detention. Ismail Agaya, Mehmet Deniz Bayram and Mansur Daslik have not been seen since June. *Özgür Ulke*, which began publishing in April, is the successor paper to *Özgür Gündem*. (AI)

On 14 June the trial of 13 former *Özgür Gündem* journalists began. Gurbettelli Erzoz, editor-in-chief, Ali Riza Halis, Istanbul bureau chief, Pahri Cetin, production director, Gulten Kisanak, information director and Yurdesev Ozsokmenier, reporter, are charged with being members of the Kurdish Workers' Party (PKK). Five other journalists are accused of supporting the PKK. They have been in prison since 10 December 1993. (RSF)

demanded to see articles about to be published in the weekly newspaper *Wasaa*. A rumour had circulated in Parliament that the paper was running a story alleging that the prime minister had accepted bribes. In fact, the paper had no such story and the police took no action. (MISA)

The Christian Awakening Society of Tanzania was banned on 31 July because of 'shortcomings in its behaviour and activities'. (SWB)

## THAILAND

Authorities prevented a seminar on human rights in East Timor taking place at Chulalongkon University on 15 July. Foreigners wishing to attend the seminar were denied visas. (SWB)

## TIBET

Unofficial sources report that Phuntsog Yangkyi, a Tibetan nun, died in a police hospital in Lhasa on 4 June, apparently as a

result of ill-treatment after prison guards beat her and several other nuns for singing nationalist songs on 11 February (*Index* 1&2/1994). (AI)

State television announced in early August that five Tibetan secessionists had been sentenced to prison terms of up to 15 years for putting up pro-independence posters 'with the aim of splitting the motherland', and for defacing a plaque on a Communist Party building. (*Far Eastern Economic Review*)

## TURKEY

Six Democracy Party (DEP) deputies have fled the country since the Constitutional Court outlawed the party on 6 June. Seven other former DEP deputies are in prison, charged with endangering Turkey's territorial integrity over their support for the Kurdish minority. The prosecutor is reportedly seeking the death sentence. (AAASHRAN)

Eleven Kurds, including Recep Marasli (*Index* 1&2/1994), publishing director of Komal Publishing House, were detained by police on 8 July. Marasli had beeen in hiding since September 1993, when he pleaded in a televised interview for a peaceful solution to the Kurdish problem. On 21 July Marasli was charged with being a leader of the outlawed Kurdish organisation Rizgari. (PEN, AI)

On 20 July Cem Ozen, editor-in-chief of the left-wing weekly *Emegin Bayragi*, was charged with publishing separatist propaganda. Two former editors of the magazine are currently in detention on the same charge. (RSF)

Mihriban Artiklar, a journalist with *Özgür Ulke*, was detained by police who blindfolded and beat her on 29 July after she went to the security force headquarters in Istanbul to apply for a passport. Another *Özgür Ulke* reporter, Bahattin Ozen, was summoned to the security headquarters in Mardin in late July and interrogated about his sources for several articles about military activity in the area. He was also threatened with death. And, on 30 July, security force officials ordered the paper's correspondent in Samsun, Servet Yazar, to stop all reporting and to leave the area immediately. (*Özgür Ulke*)

Anti-terror police raided *Özgür Ulke*'s Van and Agri offices on 10 August, removed documents and detained four correspondents, Newzat Bulut, Mustafa Aladag, Sayfettin Tepe and Berivan Kutlay. Tepe and Kutlay were released several days later. The raid is thought to be connected with the arrest on 1 August of the paper's representative in Van, Bulent Ciftci, for possession of a secret government document on the Kurdish problem. A further raid on the paper's Mardin office on 13 August led to the detention of correspondents Emine Igdi, Husnu Akgul, Husniye Tekin and Sukru Kaplan. (*Özgür Ulke*)

Recent publications: *1993 Turkey Human Rights Report* (Human Rights Foundation of Turkey, June 1994, 336pp); *Suffocation: A Report on the State of Press Freedom in Turkey* (Reporters Sans Frontières, June 1994, 48pp)

## UKRAINE

On 18 July parliamentary chairman Oleksandr Moroz called for the media to create an 'appropriate image' of Parliament and warned of possible restrictions to the accreditation of journalists who write 'untruthfully, subjectively and in a one-sided manner' about the legislature. (SWB)

Numerous newspapers and other media outlets, including *Holos Ukrayiny*, *Izvestiya*, the BBC and Radio Liberty, were barred from attending a press conference given by Crimean president Yuriy Meshkov in Simferopol on 20 July. Press secretary Vyacheslav Lebedev said that 'only those who do not criticise the president will take part in the conference.' (SWB)

## UNITED NATIONS

In recent months four journalists have lost their United Nations accreditation because they work for Taiwanese government-owed media. On 15 June the UN's Department of Public Information (UNDPI) reiterated its refusal to accredit David Wang and Lisa Chen of the China Television Company (CTV). In late July it was reported that the UN had not renewed the press passes of Ming Young of the China Television System (CTS) and Chiou Yueh of the Taiwan Television Enterprise (TTV). UNDPI officials justified the decision by saying Taiwanese government-owned media are ineligible for accreditation under a 1972 ruling.

Observers suspect that the UN has revoked the credentials in response to pressure from the Chinese government. (CPJ)

## USA

The new Freedom of Access to Clinic Entrances Act had its first challenge on 6 June, when it was invoked against six anti-abortion demonstrators in Milwaukee, Wisconsin. On 30 June the Supreme Court ruled that the speech of anti-abortion demonstrators may be limited by law. The Court determined that a state judge did not violate the First Amendment rights of protesters whom he ordered to stay at least 36 feet from a clinic in Florida. The ruling could affect more than 40 abortion clinics nationally (*Index* 3/1994). (national press)

On 9 June a federal appeals court reaffirmed the 1991 obscenity conviction of Stephen Knox for receiving three videotapes in the mail. The videos focused on the genitals of under-age girls who were clothed, but posed provocatively. The Justice Department argued last autumn that the videos did not meet the legal definition of obscenity and the Supreme Court sent the case back to the lower court. In March 234 members of Congress asked that the Justice Department's request for a new trial be denied. This latest ruling reinstates the stricter standard. (national press)

The owner, manager and clerk of the Pink Pyramid, a gay and lesbian bookstore in

Cincinnati, were charged with obscenity in late June for renting a video of Pier Paolo Pasolini's film *Sal, 120 Days of Sodom* to an undercover police officer. (National Coalition Against Censorship)

In July the Senate approved a bill to cut funding to the National Endowment for the Arts by five per cent and earmarked specific programmes for deeper cuts after a performance piece by Ron Athey provoked outrage from the religious right and conservative politicians. The piece was portrayed inaccurately in the press as including HIV-positive-blood-soaked towels hung over the audience's head. The bill will now go to conference to be reconciled with a more moderate House bill. (People for the American Way, Boston Coalition for Freedom of Expression, national press)

In a significant ruling on 28 July, Robert and Carleen Thomas were convicted of transmitting obscene material over interstate telephone lines via their electronic bulletin board and the InterNet. The bulletin board originated in California, but charges were brought after a user in Tennessee objected. The ruling has caused concern over how the 1973 Miller v California standard, which allows local definition of obscenity, will be applied to the borderless universe of computers (*Index* 2/1993). (Associated Press)

The computer games and video games industries unveiled their new rating symbols and criteria at a Senate hearing at the end of July (*Index* 1&2/1994). The ratings, which are voluntary, describe age appropriateness and the extent of sex, violence and bad language in each game. (Associated Press)

An education bill approved by the Senate in August includes an amendment denying federal funding to school districts that portray homosexuality as acceptable. This would include instructional material, counselling services and referrals to gay organisations. (Associated Press, National Gay & Lesbian Task Force).

Anti-gay activists gathered enough signatures to place initiatives limiting the civil rights of homosexuals on the ballot in Idaho and Oregon this autumn. The initiatives are based on Colorado's Amendment 2, which banned local statutes that protect gays from discrimination and which was ruled unconstitutional last December. A similar measure in Cincinnati, Ohio was ruled in violation of the First Amendment by a federal judge on 10 August. Colorado and Cincinnati are appealing the decisions. (Associated Press, Cable News Network)

Recent publication: *Silenced — The Unsolved Murders of Immigrant Journalists in the United States* (Committee to Protect Journalists, September 1994)

Two activists of the outlawed Erk opposition party were abducted on 17 June from their home in the Kazakh capital Alma Ata. Murad Dzhuraev and Erkin Asurov are believed to be held in Interior Ministry remand cells in Tashkent, although the authorities have not acknowledged their detention. The two men are believed to have links with a newspaper clandestinely produced and distributed by Erk. (AI, PEN)

Authorities cancelled an international journalists' seminar organised by the German Adenauer Foundation and the Institute for International Communication and Co-operation, to be held in Ho Chi Minh City in June. In March a seminar for Vietnamese journalists sponsored by the US-based Freedom Forum was also cancelled. (*Far Eastern Economic Review*)

Pierre Kabeya, a journalist with the weekly *Kin-Matin*, was found dead on the night of 8 July after he had delivered an article for publication on the 1990 massacre of protesting students at Lubumbashi University. His body bore signs of severe torture. (RSF)

*Compiled by: Natalie Benlolo, Laura Bruni, Juliet Dryden, Anna Feldman, Jason Garner, Oren Gruenbaum, Colin Isham, Robin Jones, Annie Knibb, Nan Levinson, George McDonald, Robert Maharajh, Philippa Nugent, Vera Rich, Jason Stephens, Han Shih Toh and Nathalie Vartanpour-Naalbandian.*

# CONTRIBUTORS

**ABDULLAHI AN-NA'IM** is executive director of Human Rights Watch/Africa. His most recent book is *Towards an Islamic Reformation* (1994).

**ERIC BARENDT** is Goodman Professor of Media Law, University College, London.

**JULIAN BARNES** has written seven novels including *Flaubert's Parrot, Staring at the Sun* and *A History of the World in 10 1/2 Chapters*. His work has been translated into more than 20 languages.

**LEO BOGART** is the author of *Commercial Culture: The Media System and the Public Interest*, soon to be published by Oxford University Press.

**BOGDAN BOGDANOVIC**, an award-winning architect, taught at Belgrade University before retirement, and was mayor of Belgrade from 1982-6. His books include *Small Urbanism* (1958), *The Futile Trowel* (1963), and *Urbs and Logos* (1976).

**A S BYATT** won the Booker Prize and the Irish Times/Aer Lingus International Fiction Prize in 1990 for *Possession*. Her other fiction includes *The Shadow of the Sun, The Game, The Virgin in the Garden, Still Life* and *Sugar and Other Stories*

**IVES MARIE CHANEL** is a journalist with Reporters sans Frontières.

**PETER CLARKE** is staff cartoonist at the *Guardian* newspaper, London.

**LINDSEY COLLEN** was born in South Africa. Her first novel, *There is a Tide,* was published in 1990.

**BORA COSIC** is a well known writer from Belgrade, currently living in Croatia.

**SAÏD ESSOULAMI** is programme co-ordinator for the Middle East and North Africa at Article 19, London.

**TOM FAWTHROP** is a freelance correspondent based in South East Asia for the *Irish Times* and other publications. He produced and directed 'Dreams & Nightmares', on Pol Pot's Cambodia, for UK Channel 4 TV in 1989.

**ZORAN FILIPOVIC** was born in Bosnia and has written widely about the Balkan war. His photographs have appeared in *Life* magazine, *Die Zeit, Le Figaro* and the *Times*, among others. He currently lives in Zagreb.

**GIL GONZALEZ-FOERSTER** is a journalist with Reporters sans Frontières.

**SAFA HAERI** is a freelance journalist based in Paris. He reports on Iran for *L'Expresse* in Paris and the *Independent* in London.

**MOHAMMED HARBI** is senior lecturer in the department of political sciences at the University of Paris- (VIII).

**JUDITH ADLER HELLMAN** is Professor of Social and Political Science at York University, Toronto, and the author of *Mexico in Crisis* and *Journeys Among Women: Feminism in Five Italian Cities.*

**CHRISTOPHER HIRD** is an independent television producer specialising in making factual programmes. His book *Murdoch, the Great Escape,* was published by Warner in 1991.

**MATTHEW HOFFMAN** is on the staff of the *Independent* newspaper in London, where, among other matters, he writes about freedom of speech issues and computers.

**CLIVE HOLLICK** is managing director of MAI plc, the owner of Meridian Broadcasting and Anglia Television, UK.

**IRFAN HOROZOVIC** is a writer from Bosnia, currently living in Zagreb, Croatia. His most recent collection of short stories, *The Refugee City,* was published this year.

**ANTHONY HYMAN** is a journalist and academic specialising in Afghanistan and Central Asia.

**IVES JAUMAIN** is a journalist with Reporters sans Frontières.

**GEOFFREY KEELING** trained as a draughtsman and painter in Bristol.

He has crewed long distance sailing boats, and now works as a full time painter and etcher.

**BERNARDO KUCINSKI** teaches journalism at the School of Communications and Arts at São Paulo University, Brazil.

**RADHA KUMAR** is liaison officer of the Sarajevo office of the Helsinki Citizens Assembly.

**JULIA LATYNINA** has been widely published in Moscow newspapers and journals, and is the author of two novels.

**AÏCHA LEMSINE** is an Algerian novelist. *Beneath a Sky of Porphyry* (1990) and *The Chrysalis* (1993) are published by Quartet Books, UK.

**CLAUDIO MAGRIS** teaches in the Faculty of Literature and Philosophy at the University of Trieste. He is the author of *Danube,* published in every major European language.

**FRANÇOIS MISSER** is a journalist with Reporters sans Frontières.

**CAROLINE MOOREHEAD** is a writer and film-maker specialising in human rights. Her latest book is *Bertrand Russell: a Life* (Sinclair Stevenson, 1992).

**STEPHEN MULVEY** works for the BBC Russian Service.

**TASLIMA NASRIN** is a doctor and writer from Bangladesh and author of the novel *Lajja* (Shame).

**JULIAN PETLEY** is head of Communication and Information studies at Brunel University, UK.

**HUGH ROBERTS** is at the Centre for Boundary Research at the University of London.

**TED TURNER** is Chairman of the Board and President of Turner Broadcasting.

**ILONKA VERDURMEN** is co-ordinator of the Scheherazade 2001 pro-

ject based in Amsterdam.

**DAVID WALTER** is presenter of BBC Radio 4's *Europhile*, for which he reports regularly on Italian affairs.

**SARA WHYATT** is co-ordinator at the London-based Writers in Prison Committee of International PEN.

**ABDELKRIM ZEROUALI** is editor of the newsletter *Echoes of Truth*.

**LYES SI ZOUBIR** is an Algerian journalist and special correspondent for *Le Monde Diplomatique*.

# Thank you very much:

Index on Censorship *and Writers and Scholars Educational Trust would like to thank all those who have given us their support since our relaunch, including:*

Andreas Harboe Foundation
Drue Heinz Foundation
Mr J Joffe
Open Society Institute

Pearson plc
Reuter Foundation
Time Inc
Virgin Communications Ltd

# Forthcoming:

CUBA: TO STAY OR GO
RADIO IN AFRICA Adewale Maja-Pearce & Richard Carver
INTERVENTION AFTER THE COLD WAR Somalia, Haiti, Rwanda, Bosnia
COUNTRY FILE Poland
BLASPHEMY LAWS
DEMOCRACY IN AFRICA Claude Ake
MARIO VARGAS LLOSA in Peru
INTERVIEW with Ryszard Kapuscinski